Pitt Latin American Series

Agrarian Structure & Political Power

Landlord & Peasant in the Making of Latin America

Evelyne Huber and
Frank Safford, Editors

UNIVERSITY OF PITTSBURGH PRESS
Pittsburgh and London

Published by the University of Pittsburgh Press, Pittsburgh, Pa. 15260
Copyright © 1995, University of Pittsburgh Press
Eurospan, London
Manufactured in the United States of America
Printed on acid-free paper

———

Library of Congress Cataloging-in-Publication Data

Agrarian structure and political power : landlord and peasant in the
making of Latin America / edited by Evelyne Huber and Frank Safford.
        p.   cm.—(Pitt Latin American series)
Includes bibliographical references and index.
ISBN 0-8229-3880-4 (cl).—ISBN 0-8229-5564-4 (pb)
1. Landowners—Latin America—History—Congresses.   2. Peasantry
—Latin America—History—Congresses.   3. Agriculture—Economic
aspects—Latin America—Congresses.   I. Huber, Evelyne, 1950–
        II. Safford, Frank, 1935–   .   III. Series.
                HD1331.L29A39   1995
        333.33'554'098—dc20   95-16082   CIP

———

A CIP catalogue record for this book
is available from the British Library.

Contents

Preface and Acknowledgments

The intellectual origins of this book lie in an interdisciplinary seminar on Latin America and the Caribbean for faculty and graduate students that ran over several years at Northwestern University. The seminar sessions were alternately devoted to presentation of the research of participants or to discussion of common readings. The four core members of the seminar were Josef Barton and three of the contributors to this volume, Frank Safford, John Stephens, and Evelyne Huber. Early on we decided to focus our reading on the relationship between agrarian structures and social and political structures and processes in the nineteenth and twentieth centuries, as this focus accommodated our various research interests.

The interdisciplinary nature of the seminar gave rise to an interesting and productive division of labor. The two social scientists, Huber and Stephens, were always in search of patterns and generalizations and became the presenters of theses and fourfold tables, whereas the two historians, Barton and Safford, assumed the role of skeptics and defended the diversity of historical experiences from being put into the straitjackets of general models. One of these debates, inspired by Barrington Moore's *Social Origins of Dictatorship and Democracy*, centered around the importance of large landowners engaged in labor-intensive agriculture for the problems of democracy in Latin America. Huber and Stephens pressed the relevance and substantial validity of applying to Latin America much of Moore's analysis of the relationship of agrarian structures to forms of political power. Barton and Safford were more skeptical, believing that the categories employed by Moore (landlords, bourgeoisie, labor-repressive agrarian systems) were likely to dissolve, or at least become fuzzy, under the close inspection of cases. They also believed that agrarian systems were likely to be quite varied, within a given country, and that the relationships between agrarian systems and the state were also likely to be quite variable among and within the various countries. Thus, we decided to extend the dialogue by inviting other scholars, particularly historians, to present conference papers in which they would examine the applicability of elements of Moore's analysis to Spanish American countries in which they had performed historical research.

The idea was to bring together experts on agrarian structures and political developments in the late nineteenth and twentieth centuries in a number of Latin American countries, and ask them to address a number of specific questions on the topic, in the hope that, if there were any patterns to be found, they would be revealed in a set of comparable studies of a variety of country experiences. The conference took place on April 28, 1990, and this volume is the result. Again, the historians explored the specific ways in which agrarian structures influenced political structures and processes in the countries they know so well, and the social scientists attempted to tease out of their essays those aspects that fit into systematic patterns of relationships. As expected, some, though not all, of the historians tended in various ways to question (or at least to complicate) the application of Moore's analysis to Spanish America. Nonetheless, as the introduction and conclusion indicate, the social scientists responded to these challenges with modifications, resilience, and firmness. No doubt, the discipline-specific preferences among the contributors will be reflected to some extent in the reactions of the readers. However, we hope that the readers will share our experience and find the tension between the two approaches to be fruitful.

In the course of organizing this conference, we benefited from the support of many people and institutions. Generous financial support was provided by the Alumnae of Northwestern University and by the Fulcher Fund of the Department of Political Science, administered by Ben Page, Fulcher Professor, and Jay Casper, former chair of the department. The History Department hosted the conference. Theresa Parker of the Department of Political Science provided invaluable logistical support.

In addition to the authors of the essays in this volume, several commentators made important contributions to the conference. Josef Barton, John Coatsworth, Paul Gootenberg, Mark Szuchman, and J. Samuel Valenzuela engaged all of the participants in interesting discussions and forced us to sharpen our arguments. We wish to express our gratitude to all of these people and institutions. Last but not least, the editors want to thank the contributors for being patient about the inevitable delays in bringing an edited volume to publication.

Agrarian Structure
& Political Power

Introduction

Evelyne Huber

The troubled history of democracy in Latin America has been the subject of much academic commentary. Social scientists and historians have attempted to explain the infrequency of periods of democratic forms of rule with universalistic as well as particularistic theories. Modernization theorists have argued that the level of economic development has been inadequate to sustain democracy. Analysts proposing a political culture approach have pointed to the corporatist elements in the Iberian heritage as inimical to the establishment of democracy. Scholars using the bureaucratic-authoritarian model have argued that the phasing and the bottlenecks in the process of industrialization in Latin America were responsible for the breakdown of democratic regimes. As demonstrated below, the first two of these explanations are inadequate, and the third is only applicable to the second half of the twentieth century; thus, we need a better understanding of the historical roots of the weakness of democracy in Latin America. The studies in our volume break new ground in that they systematically explore the linkages between the historical legacy of large landholding patterns, agrarian class relations, and political regime forms. These studies are inspired by the insights offered in Barrington Moore's *Social Origins of Dictatorship and Democracy*.[1] At an intuitive level, Moore's insights clearly appear relevant to Latin America, but they have never been systematically investigated through a comparison of a significant number of Latin American countries.

This introduction first discusses the weaknesses in the explanations mentioned above to build the case for the need for an alternative perspective on Latin American democracy. Then it outlines the attractiveness of Moore's perspective as well as the limitations of attempts to transfer this perspective wholesale to Latin America. The introduction proposes a new way of posing the question of the relationship between agrarian class relations and democracy. Finally, it offers a brief preview of the approaches and major findings of the individual essays in this volume.

Conventional Theories on Latin American Democracy

Modernization theorists have seen the low level of economic development as the chief impediment to democratization in the Third World, including

3

Latin America.[2] Economic growth would lead to democracy by bringing increases in urbanization, industrialization, communication, and education and would foster a larger middle class with an inherently democratic orientation. Furthermore, it would bring greater affluence for all and a decrease in socioeconomic inequality, and thus more room for compromise and political moderation on the part of the lower classes. A large number of crossnational quantitative studies have found positive correlations between economic development and democracy, and they, by and large, interpreted their results in a general modernization framework.[3] Other authors have argued that such universalistic theories are of little use for understanding Latin America. Instead, they have proposed that Latin America needs to be understood on its own terms, in the framework of the corporatist tradition that is the crucial characteristic of the Iberian heritage. The hierarchical and authoritarian nature of the colonial heritage shaped political institutions and the political culture in ways inimical to the establishment of democracy. Economic development could not be expected fundamentally to alter these institutions and practices; rather, new social forces would be integrated into these institutions and new elements grafted onto old political institutions.[4]

Whereas both of these sets of explanations contain some valid elements, they are wrong in a number of their assumptions and they fall short of providing satisfactory answers to a number of important questions. The modernization view overestimated not only the beneficial socioeconomic effects of economic growth for the lower and middle classes but also the solidity of the democratic leanings of the middle classes. The support offered by the middle classes first to the coups that installed bureaucratic-authoritarian regimes and then to these regimes in their initial phases starkly demonstrated the conditionality of middle-class commitment to democracy. The Iberian heritage view underplays the profound institutional discontinuities in many Latin American societies brought on by the independence wars and by later violent upheavals. Moreover, both views fail to explain the long history of experiments with democratic or protodemocratic forms of rule and the strength of pressures for democratization, which in turn led to repeated heavy repression, particularly in the more economically advanced countries of Latin America. To understand the political outcomes it is essential to look at the social setting, the class structure, and class relations, in which economic growth as well as the cultural and institutional heritage are embedded, and to look also at the structure of the state and its relationship to social classes.

Dependency theorists like Cardoso and Faletto have used such a theoretical framework, but they have concerned themselves more with broader developmental outcomes than with the question of democracy per se.[5] O'Donnell proposed a powerful analytical model based on class and class-state relations for understanding the replacement of more open and inclusive political systems by bureaucratic-authoritarian regimes at advanced stages of Latin American import substitution industrialization.[6] However, his model is designed to analyze the strains on democracy in the second half of the twentieth century rather than the historic sources of the weakness of democratic forces or, conversely, the sources of the strength of antidemocratic forces in Latin America. If one adopts such a long historical view and searches for a general theoretical approach to analyze the emergence of different regime forms, the argument of Barrington Moore's *Social Origins of Dictatorship and Democracy* stands out. In this work Moore develops an influential theoretical framework for studying the role of class relations and class-state coalitions in shaping political outcomes in the transition to the modern world.

Moore's Social Origins of Dictatorship and Democracy: Lord and Peasant in the Making of the Modern World

As the subtitle indicates, Moore focuses in particular on the political consequences of agrarian class relations. One of his central arguments is that those European countries that suffered a breakdown of democracy into authoritarianism were characterized by patterns of large landholdings and the survival of a powerful class of large landowners into the period of modernization. Furthermore, these landlords had historically been engaged in labor-repressive agriculture; that is, they had used political coercion to secure themselves a cheap labor force. Given the prevalence of large landholding patterns and the frequency of coercive practices in rural labor relations in Latin America, Moore's framework suggests itself strongly for a systematic exploration of the sources of democracy's troubled history in the region.

Moore develops his framework in analyzing England, France, the United States, China, Japan, India, and (though he does not devote entire chapters to them) Germany and Russia. His work has inspired many attempts to analyze other cases with hypotheses derived from this framework, such as additional European cases,[7] the South of the United States,[8] the Middle East,[9] Japan,[10] South Africa,[11] and a comparison between South Africa and the United States.[12] Despite the strong intellectual impact of Moore's work and its saliency for Latin America, as we establish below, there are few attempts to apply his framework to a study of Latin American cases, one of them by Coatsworth[13] and another one by this author.[14] The present volume provides a number of Latin American case and comparative studies that allow us to investigate more systematically the class and class-state relations that Moore has identified as crucial historical sources of authoritarian and democratic forms of rule.

Moore focuses on "the varied political roles played by the landed upper classes and the peasantry in the transformation from agrarian societies (defined simply as states where a large majority of the population lives off the land) to modern industrial ones."[15] He distinguishes three main historical routes from the preindustrial to the modern world: bourgeois revolution leading to Western parliamentary democracy, revolution from above leading to capitalist authoritarianism, and peasant revolution leading to communism. In a highly schematic and oversimplifying way one can sketch the three routes as follows. The democratic route, or better democratic routes (since they differ significantly from each other) are characterized by the emergence of "a group in society with an independent economic base, which attacks obstacles to a democratic version of capitalism that have been inherited from the past."[16] These attacks take violent forms and the ensuing upheavals eliminate or significantly reduce the power of traditional dominant classes. Among the traditional dominant classes, large landholders engaged in what Moore calls labor-repressive agriculture play the crucial role in the development of modern capitalist authoritarianism. The survival into the modern age of large landowners who rely on "strong political methods to extract the surplus, keep the labor force in its place, and in general make the system work,"[17] rather than relying on the labor market, is one feature of the reactionary capitalist route to modern authoritarianism. The other is the formation of an alliance between these landlords, the state, and a dependent bourgeoisie of intermediate strength. The route to communism is characterized by the same type of landlords, a weak bourgeoisie, and a structure of peasant society that creates ties of solidarity and thus a high peasant revolutionary potential. Under this constellation of conditions, the attempts of labor-repressive landlords to intensify the extraction of surplus in the process of the commercialization of agriculture lead to peasant revolution and the subsequent installation of a communist regime.

Moore's theoretical framework offers important insights into broad dynamics of economic and political change, but the way in which it can be applied to the study of Latin American political development is not self-evident. Certainly, the focus on large landlords and their relationship to rural labor and the state is crucial; indeed, it can be expected to yield powerful results. However, a wholesale transfer of the rest of the model is problematic. Rather, several modifications of the model and a new specification of the approach are necessary.

First of all, Moore himself warns against looking for the same dynamics in smaller countries because, as he argues "the fact that the smaller countries depend economically and politically on big and powerful ones means that the decisive causes of their politics lie outside their own boundaries."[18] Certainly, most Latin Americanists would agree that external forces have been very important in shaping Latin American economies and polities. Nevertheless, one can focus on agrarian class relations and the development of relations between the state and social classes, taking into account very systematically the way in which external forces have shaped the class structure, class relations, and the state itself.

Second, as several authors have pointed out, the conceptualization of the strength and role of the bourgeoisie is problematic in Moore's work.[19] Certainly, if the point of comparison is the core countries, one could not speak of a strong bourgeoisie in any Latin American country. But how is one to assess, independent of the political outcome, whether the bourgeoisie is weak or of intermediate strength? Can one assume that foreign capital reinforces the strength of the bourgeoisie by reinforcing the capitalist impulse, or weakens it through competition? Moreover, even in core countries the bourgeoisie was hardly the democratic force that Moore assumed it to be. Whereas it often did support representative and responsible government, it usually opposed the political inclusion of the lower classes.

A further point that is problematic not only for the transfer of Moore's framework, but also in his own analysis, is the question of the endpoint of political development. On the one hand, democracies have broken down into authoritarian regimes not only after short periods of unstable democracy, as in Moore's authoritarian path, but also after long phases of apparently well-consolidated democratic rule. On the other hand, Moore's own fascist cases ended up as parliamentary democracies.[20] Moreover, authoritarianism has in general been an unstable form of rule in modern capitalist societies, and it has collapsed in most modern communist societies as well. Rather than attempting to explain a political outcome defined by a specific regime and time period, then, it makes sense to define the explanandum as democratic or authoritarian trajectories, that is, a predominance of democratic or authoritarian rule in the twentieth century.

Even if we accept a simple formalistic definition of democracy, as a political system with responsible government and high levels of institutionalized contestation and political inclusion,[21] and do not ask any questions about the reality of participation in political power by the masses, it is clear that there are very few countries in Latin America with a democratic trajectory. Only Costa Rica and Uruguay qualify unambiguously. Chile, as Bauer's essay makes clear, is more problematic; only the periods between 1932 and 1973 and since 1990 can be classified as democratic. Before this period, the restrictions on political inclusion were such that the system has to be classified as a constitutional oligarchy.[22] Colombia has had a mixed trajectory; formal democracy has repeatedly been disrupted by uncontrollable violence and was interrupted by an authoritarian period. Venezuela embarked on a democratic trajectory only in 1958. Only in one case was a communist regime established in Latin America, in Cuba, and that outcome was very heavily shaped by foreign powers. All the remainder of the Latin

American countries have followed predominantly authoritarian trajectories. Therefore, the most fruitful strategy appears to be to approach the question of the weakness of democracy in Latin America primarily by identifying the central dynamics of the authoritarian trajectories and investigating which elements of the authoritarian trajectories are weak or missing in the countries with democratic trajectories, and secondarily by identifying the groups that exert pressures for democratization in the democratic trajectories but are absent or weak in the authoritarian trajectories.

In Moore's framework, the central role in the authoritarian trajectories is played by a reactionary alliance between landlords, the state, and a dependent bourgeoisie of intermediate strength. The landlords were historically engaged in labor-repressive agriculture, which led them to ally themselves closely with the state in search of political support. At a later stage in the process of modernization this alliance is joined by an emerging commercial and industrial bourgeoisie, which, even if it is weak, "must be strong enough . . . to be a worthwhile political ally."[23] If the bourgeoisie and thus the authoritarian alliance is too weak, then a peasant revolution may intervene and the result may be communist dictatorship. In Moore's cases,[24] this alliance modernizes the country through a revolution from above, but this revolution is not a necessary feature of the authoritarian path, as, for instance, the Italian and Spanish cases demonstrate. Even where a revolution from above is carried out, the important characteristic of this process is that modernization is attempted while preserving as much of the original social structure as possible. The authoritarian coalitions eventually give way to the establishment of unstable democracies, in which, however, the landlords retain a significant share of power. The door to fascism (or capitalist authoritarianism) is opened by the failure of these democracies to deal adequately with economic and social problems and bring about reforms.

To Latin Americanists most elements of this trajectory sound all too familiar: the importance of large landowners, the nonmarket coercion of rural labor, relatively weak and dependent bourgeoisies, unstable democracies, and breakdowns into authoritarianism after a democratic period. There is much research on these individual elements, and on the relationships between some of them, but few attempts that seek to systematically relate them to broad patterns of economic, social, and political change. Huber's attempt, inspired by Moore, to integrate the structure of the export economy, the power base and labor needs of large landowners, the pattern of industrialization, the role of the state, and the emergence of middle and working classes and their political articulation into an explanation of democratic and authoritarian trajectories in South America remains at the macro level, as does Coatsworth's essay on the origins of modern authoritarianism in Mexico.[25] In particular, both essays omit an investigation of the links between the micromechanisms of labor control, the political posture of large landowners, and system-level political outcomes. Moore's framework suggests itself very strongly as a guide to research into these micro-macro linkages in the authoritarian trajectories. For the reasons stated above, then, we are not proposing a test of Moore's model, but rather an investigation of hypotheses derived from Moore's framework that concern the political consequences of agrarian class relations.

Landlord and Laborer in Latin America

The questions posed to the authors in our volume center around the following major issues. What was the economic importance of large land-holders among the dominant classes curing the first significant push of modernization, the period of export expansion, starting roughly in the last quarter of the nineteenth century? What were the labor needs of the most important type of agricultural production? What were the methods used to ensure a sufficient supply of cheap labor for the large landlords? What role did a variety of forms of legal coercion play in ensuring this labor supply? Legal coercion includes much more than restrictions on labor mobility; of perhaps greatest importance was the legally backed closing off of alternatives to estate labor for the rural population, such as barring access to land and water and thus subsistence agriculture. This means that coercion was not restricted to the resident labor force on the large estates but also extended to the population of independent peasant villages. To what extent was the resort to the legal coercion of labor related to landlord attempts to control the state apparatus at local and national levels? What sort of state apparatus did exist; that is, how centralized was it, how interventionist, how strong its repressive capacity? How successful were landlords where they attempted to control the local and national state apparatus? Were other sectors of the dominant classes in competition with landowners for control of the state apparatus, or did the state have significant autonomy from the dominant classes? Did the dominant classes have to contend with other strong groups with independent economic bases? What were the implications of the relations between the dominant classes and the state for the political outcome in terms of institutionalized contestation and political inclusion, in other words, for authoritarianism or democracy?

To investigate these questions and arrive at some well-grounded theoretical generalizations about the political consequences of agrarian class relations, we chose a number of cases with contrasting political histories. Mexico and Peru are two cases with clearly authoritarian trajectories, punctuated by revolution and repeated challenges and intense pressures for the establishment of democratic procedures. Argentina is a case with a comparatively early breakthrough to democracy and then a breakdown into authoritarianism without a sustained recovery. Chile is a case that was apparently on a democratic trajectory since the 1930s but then underwent a profound reversal from 1973 to 1990. Colombia has had an ambiguous trajectory in the sense that formal democracy broke down into uncontrolled violence and authoritarianism from 1948 to 1958, and in the 1980s the rule of law, which is central to a democracy, was eroded again. Costa Rica, finally, is the only case with a consistently democratic trajectory. What we expect to find across these cases is systematic variation in the answers to the questions outlined above. Most importantly, we expect variation in the strength of large landlords, their labor needs and practices to satisfy these needs, and their relationship to the state.

The contributions to our volume approach these questions from somewhat different angles, focusing on different aspects of landlord-peasant and landlord-state relationships and on different time periods, but they all, directly or indirectly, confirm the importance of the labor needs of large landlords and of legal mechanisms to satisfy them as important influences on political outcomes. We preview these contributions and draw out the major common themes below.

Mexico and Peru

Florencia Mallon's essay focuses mainly on the period before the big push of export expansion but traces the implications of the political struggles of this period into the twentieth century. She looks at landlord-peasant and landlord-state relationships in two regions: Morelos, Mexico, and Cajamarca, Peru; and discusses how regional dynamics interacted with state-building at the national level. Her central argument and critique of Moore's framework is that the strength of subordinate classes has to be incorporated more systematically into our attempts to explain political outcomes. It was the difference between the presence of a strong popular movement resting on a strong traditional peasant community in Morelos, and the absence of such a communal tradition and autonomous popular movement in Cajamarca, that made the state an important ally of landlords in backing up the repression of the popular movement in Morelos but not in Cajamarca. Accordingly, the construction of a centralized, repressive, authoritarian state in Mexico, supported by Liberal as well as Conservative landlords, had roots reaching back into the period before the Porfiriato. In contrast, the state in Peru mainly backed and respected what one could call privatized authoritarianism; that is, local landlord power based on a combination of a monopoly on economic resources and the maintenance of private repressive forces on their estates. The strength of the popular movement and a centralizing authoritarian response reemerged in Mexico in the twentieth century, whereas the Peruvian state remained relatively weak and fragmented, though predominantly authoritarian, until the second half of the twentieth century.

Despite Mallon's explicit and important critique of Moore's focus on elites and the state, which will be taken up in our concluding essay, her analysis confirms essential hypotheses derived from Moore's framework. In both cases, landlords supported an authoritarian option; what differed was only the form of authoritarianism. Though landlords fought each other and sometimes the state over resources and aligned in factional fights at the national level, often driven by regional rivalries, their primary objective was control over land and labor. When challenged by resistance from below, they closed ranks to preserve and extend that control, and they attempted to enlist state support in their endeavor. Though direct coercion of labor through restrictions on labor mobility did not figure as an issue in either case, the totality of landlord treatment of the peasantry was obviously coercive and backed by at least local state authorities. In Morelos, local authorities supported hacienda encroachment on land and water, which had the effect of greatly curtailing the peasantry's alternatives to estate labor. They did this even during the short periods, such as the Regency, when those in control of the central state attempted to enlist peasant support through legislation protecting labor and village lands. In Cajamarca the landlords already held a near monopoly on land and ensured the availability of estate labor through a combination of clientelistic and estate-based strong-arm tactics. During the Chilean occupation, the state became a competitor for resources and manpower, and some landowners took up arms in resistance and formed cross-class movements in opposition to the central state. However, after the occupation these movements collapsed and, faced with social disorder, landlords appealed for and received (after 1895) state support in rebuilding privatized, decentralized authoritarianism.

Argentina

Tulio Halperín's essay takes a sweeping view, tracing the economic and political position of large landowners in Argentina's Littoral from 1820 to 1930. He focuses mainly on the relationship between landowners and the state; the relationship between landowners and rural labor enters into the discussion of the landowners' inability to achieve a socially hegemonic position and elicit deference from the rural population. The thrust of his argument is somewhat paradoxical. On the one hand, he argues that the relationship between the landed class and the state was antagonistic, particularly between 1820 and 1880, because of periodic competition for financial resources and for manpower. He paints a picture of state elites pursuing state aggrandizement and war, contrary to the interests of the landed class, and ruthlessly enforcing policies through centrally appointed local officials. On the other hand, he argues that the landed class did not

need to hold state power to effect economic policies that guaranteed they
would reap the major share of the benefits. The agrarian export model
remained unchallenged because it brought such significant growth.

   In the period after 1880 state-landlord relations improved as the need
for soldiers decreased and general prosperity made taxation less of an
issue. Still, Halperín argues, landowners as a class lacked both the class
consciousness and the rural social structure to become a socially and
politically hegemonic force. Rural labor relations were characterized by high
instability; there was much use of temporary wage labor and of tenancy
arrangements with short duration. Landowners competed with each other,
going as far as buying cattle stolen from others. In their relations to the
state they preferred to rely on personal clientelistic ties rather than corporate
action and party representation, even though, as Halperín argues, political
leadership positions in the Conservative and Radical Parties were theirs
almost for the asking. With the assumption of power by the Radical Party,
tensions between the state and the landowners increased again over the
issues of the use of public funds. Still, given the hegemony of the export-
led growth model and the prosperity resulting from it, the landowners did
not have to fear any attacks on their properties or taxes that would hurt
their competitiveness. Accordingly, they could and did accommodate to the
democratic regime until they felt acutely threatened by the turmoil in the
international economic system in the aftermath of the 1929 crash.

   Several points in Halperín's essay are relevant for Moore's framework.
First, it is clear that, at least up into the 1880s, the Argentine landowners
favored legal coercion in the form of vagrancy laws to satisfy their labor
needs. Whatever the conflicts between the landed class and the state, the
former was certainly not pushing for a more open and inclusive political
system. Nevertheless, it was not a class of labor-repressive landlords in the
traditional sense, with a high need for large amounts of cheap labor and a
position of domination firmly rooted in the rural social structure. They were
not pressed nor did they seek actively, as a class, to diffuse authoritarian
values and control the state in order to use it for labor repression. Second,
with a growing world market demand for beef and wheat and the consequent increase in immigrant labor and the fencing of pastures, the issue of
labor control lost its saliency. Also, as made clear by Halperín, the hegemony of the agrarian export model remained unchallenged. Accordingly, the
landed class was secure enough in its economic position to tolerate the
installation of a democratic regime. However, when the depression endangered the traditional growth model, the question of control of the state
apparatus assumed renewed importance, and the landed class supported a
return to authoritarianism and a prominent role for the Conservative Party.
Again, though, the reason for seeking control of the state apparatus was

not control over rural labor but control over general economic, tax, and spending policies.

Chile

Arnold Bauer's essay covers the entire century from the extension of the franchise to all literate males in 1874 to the destruction of democracy in 1973. Noting the ambiguities in Chile's political trajectory, in particular the severe restrictions on participation before the 1950s and the Pinochet years, Bauer still opts for treating the case as an essentially democratic one. Thus, when he asks whether Moore's hypotheses have any relevance for the Chilean case, he arrives at a negative answer. Certainly, there was no bourgeois revolution setting the country on the democratic path. In fact, there was no significant bourgeoisie separate from and opposed to the landed class. Bauer emphasizes the fusion of landed, commercial, financial, and industrial segments into one unified oligarchy, most of whose members had holdings or at least family ties to class segments in multiple sectors. This fusion also means that landowners could not be singled out as a particularly repressive and authoritarian class at the political level. As Bauer points out, the repression suffered by striking nitrate and other urban workers far exceeded any direct, state-backed coercion imposed on the rural population, at least before the 1960s. Not that Chilean landlords were particularly enlightened socially and politically. On the contrary, in the decades after the 1870s even those landowners who were intent on boosting economic output opted for an expansion of the traditional system of labor relations with labor residing on the estates and performing services in exchange for a plot of land and rations. Still, the residents were not bound to the estate. The landlords simply did not need to resort to the direct coercion of labor because the availability of cheap labor was not a problem. The population to land ratio was kept highly favorable through legal measures and occasional coercion outside the estates, particularly the denial of access to land in the established agricultural regions and the last frontier region to members of the rural lower classes, and the eviction of squatters. In such cases, the landlords could invariably count on the support of the state apparatus. Moreover, there was no tradition of peasant communities that could have become the basis for challenging landlord prerogatives.

The position of Chile's large landlords toward democracy shows paradoxical but easily understandable characteristics. As Bauer argues, Conservative landowners supported the extension of the franchise in 1874 in order to compete in the electoral process with the executive. They proceeded to use the votes of the male population residing on their estates to achieve and maintain a very prominent and powerful political position. Very importantly, they used this position to keep the rural sector insulated from the organizational activities going on in the urban sector. In order to keep the rural sector quiescent and to ensure that "their" votes would continue to carry weight, they strenuously opposed any increase in political participation. Such an increase would necessarily have come from "uncontrolled" sectors and would have diluted landlord power. As a result, participation levels remained below 10 percent of the population until the 1950s. How important this was is underlined by Bauer's discussion of policy toward the rural sector under the Popular Front. Even under an ostensibly center-left government, the landlords were able to muster state support in repressing unionization and militancy.

It was only in the 1960s that Chilean landlords lost their ability to prevent rural unionization and mobilization and that, consequently, the countryside escaped their political control. Accordingly, it should not come as a surprise that they supported the replacement of the democratic with an authoritarian society. Whether they did this to a greater or lesser extent than the captains of industry and finance is a moot question, given the fusion of the different segments of the dominant class. One could detect here the nonstate side of Moore's authoritarian alliance. This alliance could tolerate restricted democracy as long as the urban and rural masses did not really enter the political scene. Once the masses did become effectively included and landlord and bourgeois interests were fundamentally threatened, the dominant class actively courted the coercive arm of the state to effect an undemocratic solution. The Chilean trajectory does not really fit Moore's authoritarian path any better than his democratic path, since the state and foreign capital played very different roles than in Moore's cases. Nevertheless, one could say that the oligarchy behaved in ways consistent with hypotheses derived from Moore's insistence on the antidemocratic leanings of large landlords carrying over traditional labor relations into the period of modernization and of a weak and dependent bourgeoisie.

Colombia
Frank Safford raises three fundamental questions about the applicability of Moore's framework to Colombia. First, he argues that geographic and economic fragmentation prevented the emergence of a national market and of a significant export thrust before the 1880s. This in turn meant that land ownership was not a source of rapid accumulation of capital, but rather that the dominant class had its economic base mainly in commerce. With the expansion of coffee, though, and the large-scale appropriation of public lands, land ownership per se became economically much more important. Many merchants became large coffee growers themselves and profited both from production on their own land and from local control over the coffee trade. Still, this process did not lead to the formation of a more or less cohesive class or class fraction of coffee growers-merchants at the national level for two main reasons. Geographical fragmentation remained an ob-

stacle and the deep historical enmities between Liberals and Conservatives continued to divide the landed class.

Second, Safford emphasizes the weakness of the central state, which lacked the capacity to penetrate large areas of the country, particularly before the 1880s. The coffee boom brought greater revenue for the state and improvements in transportation, but state control over many areas remained tenuous. In the 1920s and 1930s the central state did intervene in some rural conflicts involving collective action by the peasantry, in part repressively and in part in a mediating manner, but generally central state action had little impact on conditions at the local level. The system of domination came under challenge in this period, and at the national level some reform policies began to protect tenant farmers and agricultural labor, but local authorities by and large continued to side with large landowners and thus to facilitate labor repression.

The third point that Safford emphasizes is that labor relations in Colombian coffee production were very mixed, ranging from the traditional arrangements of labor in exchange for usufruct of a plot of land to share-cropping and wage labor. Again, control over land was the central means for ensuring an adequate supply of cheap labor. Given the large-scale availability of previously uncultivated land for coffee production, squatting was a widespread phenomenon and large landowners had much more difficulty in enforcing their control over land than their counterparts in Chile, for instance. Consequently, conflicts over land were widespread, intense, and violent. Though, as Safford points out, there is debate about the original intent of Law 200 of 1936, which regulated the appropriation of public lands, it is clear that large landowners in practice managed to turn its implementation to their advantage and to inflict heavy costs on tenants. Thus, Safford's essay implies that large landowners were a major obstacle to political order and to the move toward democratization. They obstructed democratization not by forging an authoritarian coalition with the state at the national level but by resorting to violence at the local level to enforce their control over land, by influencing the central state to protect their control over land, and by resisting if the central state made any attempts to enforce policies perceived as inimical to landlord interests. As a result, even the formally democratic and reformist period of the 1930s was a phenomenon confined to national politics and had little impact on the reality of authoritarianism at the local level.

Costa Rica
Lowell Gudmundson discusses the emergence of Costa Rican democracy between 1830 and the present. Pointing out that research on political structures and processes is scarce, he finds that research on economic and social conditions suggests that some hypotheses derived from Moore may

be applicable. The Costa Rican elite had its main economic base not in land but in commerce, and it took control of coffee processing and exporting, in addition to getting involved in the growing of coffee. Since the dominant class did not attempt to restrict popular migration and access to public lands when coffee production expanded, much of the coffee produced in Costa Rica came from smaller growers. Starting in the nineteenth and continuing into the twentieth century a process of differentiation took place among coffee growers, with a strong segment of medium and small farmers emerging, and other segments becoming semiproletarianized or fully prole-tarianized. At the same time, a significant urban artesanal petty bourgeoisie emerged. Thus, the constellation of social forces, with a predominantly commercial-bourgeois dominant class, a strong medium-farmer and urban middle class, and a small-farmer lower class, allowed democracy to emerge gradually. The 1948 civil war, then, was by no means a bourgeois revolution sweeping away quasifeudal institutions and classes; there were no such obstacles to overcome. Rather, the civil war followed at least two decades of elite-led populist reformism in an essentially formal democratic framework, which, however, came under threat from electoral fraud perpetrated by the incumbent party.

What Gudmundson can state with confidence about hypotheses de-rived from Moore, then, is that there was no Costa Rican class of labor-repressive landlords that would have constituted a crucial obstacle to democ-ratization. On a more speculative level, his discussion suggests that the urban and rural middle classes and the class of independent smallholders were important prodemocratic forces. These groups were further strength-ened through the post-1948 reforms, which supported the formation of cooperatives and the bypassing of the processor-exporter monopoly of the dominant class.

Another crucial reform for democratic stability in the post-1948 era in Costa Rica was the dismantling of the military. Here, Gudmundson offers a theoretically very interesting suggestion. He points out that recent work implies that the dismantling of the military was possible because it had been weakened earlier, through U.S. intimidation in forcing an end to the border war with Panama in 1923. This suggests that pressures from a powerful foreign power might substitute for popular insurrection in elimi-nating the obstacle to democracy posed by the potential of autonomous political action of the coercive apparatus of the state.

Gudmundson ends his essay with some interesting observations and questions coming out of a comparison between northern and southern Central America. Again, the available evidence does not allow for firm conclusions. The dominant classes in Nicaragua and Panama, as in Costa Rica, also had their economic base in commerce rather than land, and the subsistence-based peasantry was by and large not under their control.

When coffee production expanded in Nicaragua, most of it was done by smallholders who sold to processor-exporters, as in Costa Rica. Yet the political outcome, of course, was very different from that in Costa Rica, and the question of why remains open. One could safely suggest that U.S. intervention had an important impact on the political developments of Nicaragua and Panama. In Guatemala and El Salvador, in contrast, large landlords retained coercive forms of labor exploitation into the period of coffee expansion. The political outcome in both cases and the role of the landed oligarchy in bringing about these outcomes appear strongly to confirm our hypotheses inspired by Moore's views on the importance of large landlords dependent on a large labor force as obstacles to democratization.

Moore and Latin American Democracy

Three main points relevant to Moore and the question of democracy emerge out of these essays. First, the essays confirm what we, following Moore himself, argued in the beginning—that Moore's model cannot be applied to Latin America without significant modifications. In none of the cases was there a bourgeois revolution. Costa Rica and, to the extent that one looks at it as a democratic case, Chile demonstrate that there were other paths to democracy than via bourgeois revolution. In the authoritarian trajectories, the state played a very different role from the one it played in Moore's cases. State consolidation remained a problem into the period of modernization, and accordingly there were no strong states of the Prussian variety to form alliances with a landed class and an emerging bourgeoisie. In all cases, foreign actors, both foreign capital and foreign states, were important in shaping political outcomes, actors that Moore does not even include in his framework.

Second, Moore's theoretical framework pays insufficient attention to the role of the subordinate classes. In his cases, subordinate classes only seem to shape the political outcome on one path: peasant revolutions leading to communism. Mallon is very explicit and convincing in her criticism of this omission. She demonstrates how the variation in the strength of the Mexican and Peruvian peasant movements induced elites to support different forms of authoritarianism. The essays on Chile and Costa Rica suggest that the crucial prodemocratic forces in these two cases were the middle and lower classes.

Third, the hypotheses derived from Moore about the role of large landlords in forming authoritarian coalitions at the point of entry of the masses into politics are confirmed implicitly or explicitly in the essays. Whereas the use of legal coercion as opposed to a formally free labor market does not seem to matter for landlord behavior, dependence on large supplies of cheap labor does. Landlords dependent on cheap labor were crucial obstacles to democratization. In all cases, they used legal means to close off alternatives to estate labor for the rural population. The extent to which such means still had to be used in the periods under consideration depended on the historical monopoly of large owners on land and water, on the historical strength of peasant communities, and on the availability of labor markets in urban areas and mining centers.

Landlords in Chile were in a comparatively favorable position secured by a well-established monopoly on land and the absence of strong peasant communities. Thus, they enjoyed true hegemony in the rural areas and could use democratic institutions to maintain their political power. Nevertheless, they remained essentially authoritarian in the sense of strenuously opposing unrestricted political participation and any rights of organization for the rural sector. In Mexico large landowners, whether Liberals or Conservatives, promoted the building of a strong, centralized authoritarian state, as they were confronted with locally very strong popular movements based on historical community solidarity. In Peru landlords were firmly authoritarian as well, but they could rely for the most part on their own private coercive forces and on local state authorities to maintain their control over labor. The large landowners in Argentina who were engaged in stock raising had comparatively low labor needs. Furthermore, state policy worked in their favor insofar as it supported the agrarian export model. Accordingly, there was little need for them to act as a class and attempt to control the state or restrict popular participation in politics, until the beginning of the depression endangered the Argentine export model. In Costa Rica, control over the processing and export of coffee, not its production, was crucial for the economic position of the dominant class, though they were also landowners. Thus, labor availability and costs did not pose a serious problem and the dominant class did not attempt to close access to public lands. Similarly, they did not prevent the gradual political integration of the emerging classes of medium farmers and smallholders who, together with urban artisans and small merchants, became important supporters of reformist political forces.

These issues are taken up again in our concluding essay. The conclusion presents additional analyses of the political consequences of agrarian class relations in Latin America and in other areas of the world. Our comparison of the evidence from these other cases corroborates the three points emerging from the essays in this volume. In particular, it confirms the importance of the presence of large landlords dependent on a large supply of cheap labor for authoritarian political outcomes, as opposed to the democratizing impact of the presence of smallholding patterns.

NOTES

1. Barrington Moore, *Social Origins of Dictatorship and Democracy* (Boston: Beacon Press, 1966).

2. Seymour Martin Lipset, "Some Social Requisites of Democracy: Economic Development and Political Legitimacy," *American Political Science Review* 53, no. 1 (1959): 69–105; reprinted in Lipset, *Political Man* (Baltimore: Johns Hopkins University Press, 1980), exp. ed.; Karl W. Deutsch, "Social Mobilization and Political Development," *American Political Science Review* 55, no. 3 (1961): 493–514.

3. Philips Cutright, "National Political Development: Measurement and Analysis," *American Sociological Review* 28, no. 2 (1963): 25–64; Philips Cutright and James A. Wiley, "Modernization and Political Representation: 1927–1966," *Studies in Comparative International Development* 5, no. 23 (1969); Kenneth A. Bollen, "Political Democracy and the Timing of Development," *American Sociological Review* 44, no. 4 (1979): 572–87.

4. Howard Wiarda, ed., *Political and Social Change in Latin America: The Distinct Tradition* (Amherst: University of Massachusetts Press, 1982).

5. Fernando Henrique Cardoso and Enzo Faletto, *Dependency and Development in Latin America* (Berkeley: University of California Press, 1979).

6. Guillermo O'Donnell, *Modernization and Bureaucratic Authoritarianism: Studies in South American Politics* (Berkeley: Institute of International Studies, University of California, Berkeley, 1973); O'Donnell, "Reflections on the Patterns of Changeg in the Bureaucratic-Authoritarian State," *Latin American Research Review* 13, no. 1 (1978): 3–38.

7. Francis G. Castles, "Barrington Moore's Thesis and Swedish Political Development," *Government and Opposition* 8, no. 3 (1973): 313–52; Timothy Tilton, "The Social Origins of Liberal Democracy: The Swedish Case," *American Political Science Review* 68, no. 2 (1974): 561–86; Jonathan Tumin, "Pathways to Democracy: A Critical Revision of Barrington Moore's Theory of Democratic Emergence and an Application of the Revised Theory to the Case of Netherlands" (Ph.D. diss., Harvard University, 1978).

8. Jonathan M. Wiener, *Social Origins of the New South: Alabama, 1860–1885* (Baton Rouge: Louisiana State University Press, 1978).

9. Haim Gerber, *The Social Origins of the Modern Middle East* (Boulder, Colo.: Lynne Rienner, 1987).

10. Ronald P. Dore and Tsutomi Ouchi, "Rural Origins of Japanese Fascism," in *Dilemmas of Growth in Prewar Japan*, ed. J. Morley (Princeton: Princeton University Press, 1972).

11. Stanley Trapido, "South Africa in a Comparative Study of Industrialization," *Journal of Development Studies* 7, no. 3 (1971): 309–41.

12. Stanley Greenberg, *Race and State in Capitalist Development: Comparative Perspectives* (New Haven: Yale University Press, 1980). In addition, Moore's comparative historical approach has influenced an entire generation of scholars who study social change at the macro level, including Theda Skocpol, *States and Social Revolutions: A Comparative Analysis of France, Russia and China* (Cambridge and New York: Cambridge University Press, 1979); Robert J. Brenner, "Agrarian Class Structure and Economic Development in Pre-industrial Europe," *Past and Present* 70 (1976): 30–75; Jeffery M. Paige, *Agrarian Revolution* (New York: Free Press, 1975); Nora Hamilton, *The Limits of State Autonomy: Post-Revolutionary*

Mexico (Princeton: Princeton University Press, 1982); Nicos P. Mouzelis, *Politics in the Semi-Periphery* (New York: St. Martin's, 1986); and others. See Peter B. Evans and John D. Stephens, "Development and the World Economy," *Handbook of Sociology*, ed. Neil J. Smelser (Newbury Park: Sage, 1988), for a review of this literature.

13. John H. Coatsworth, "Los orígenes del autoritarismo moderno en México," *Foro Internacional* 16, no. 2 (1975), reprinted in Leopoldo Allub, ed., *Orígenes del autoritarismo en América Latina* (Mexico: Editorial Katun, 1983).

14. Evelyne Huber Stephens, "Capitalist Development and Democracy in South America," *Politics and Society* 17, no. 3 (1989): 281–352.

15. Moore, *Social Origins*, xi.

16. Ibid., xv.

17. Ibid., 434.

18. Ibid., xiii.

19. Theda Skocpol, "A Critical Review of Barrington Moore's *Social Origins of Dictatorship and Democracy*," *Politics and Society* 4, no. 1 (1973): 1–34; Dietrich Rueschemeyer, Evelyne Huber Stephens, and John D. Stephens, *Capitalist Development and Democracy* (London: Polity, and Chicago: University of Chicago Press, 1992).

20. Whereas one might argue that defeat in World War II was the reason for the democratic outcome in Germany, Italy, and Japan, this is clearly not the case for Spain.

21. See, e.g., Robert Dahl, *Polyarchy: Participation and Opposition* (New Haven: Yale University Press, 1971), for such a conceptualization of democracy or, in his terminology, polyarchy.

22. Due in large part to deliberate actions on the part of the dominant classes, political participation rose above 5 percent of the population in only one election before 1924. See the sources cited by Bauer in this volume.

23. Moore, *Social Origins*, 437.

24. Only Japan appears as a fully explored case, with an entire chapter devoted to it, but Germany enters into many of Moore's comparisons and general statements. He also puts Italy, Spain, Greece, Poland, Hungary, and Romania into this category; see Moore, *Social Origins*, 438.

25. Huber Stephens, "Capitalist Development"; Coatsworth, "Orígenes."

Landlord and Campesino in the Chilean Road to Democracy

Arnold J. Bauer

Barrington Moore's hypotheses present several difficulties for Chilean history. Not only are there formidable problems of definition—the Chilean "peasantry" or "bourgeoisie" are uncertain categories of analysis—but the historical road stretching into the past looks very different depending on the particular hillock one stands on. Were we now on the grassy knolls of Frei's Christian Democracy regime, we could follow a fairly serene long path back through the political free-for-all of the parliamentary republic and beyond to the precocious electoral reform that gave all adult literate males the vote in 1874. Through Moore's lens we might be able to detect here a rising bourgeoisie gradually pushing aside the landed aristocracy and eventually proletarianizing the peasantry to culminate in a full participatory democracy. That's how it looked in 1969. Were this 1972 and we higher up on the seismic ridge of the Popular Unity, waching below us rural militancy in Cautin and the armies of marching workers at the Plaza Italia—whose own tortuous path led back to Recabarren and the nitrate strikes—we might imagine that these were real peasants vanquishing the troglodytic landlords, pushing aside a weak and artificial bourgeoisie, while the country followed *la via Chilena al Socialismo*. Later, from the granitic peaks of the Pinochet years many people thought they could discern the autobahn of Chilean fascism created by the Moorean coalition of a dominant and repressive landed aristocracy and a weak native bourgeoisie, which regained control of the state to crush both workers and peasants.

But now democracy has returned to Chile and the historical road is all a jumble. Can we argue that the marxist and authoritarian years were really aberrant stops on a fundamentally democratic road? And if so, can we discern that this not wholly joyful route was characterized by "the early establishment of balance between the state and the landlords, the emergence of a strong bourgeoisie which replaced or absorbed the landowners as the economically and politically dominant class" together with the "removal of the peasants from the land in the process of commercialization of agriculture"? Along the way how do we account for change or persistence

21

in agrarian class relations, the key element in Moore's democratic track hypothesis?

I believe that Chile's main route has been the democratic one, that Barrington Moore's schemes hatched elsewhere are useful to focus the Chilean evidence, but that things here did not work out at all the way his hypotheses suggest. Let me first set out the main features of agrarian class relations as they emerged through the wrenching crisis of the Long Depression of the last third of the nineteenth century. Running parallel to change in the countryside was the extraordinary development of an export economy based first on nitrates and then copper. This gave rise to an ever more autonomous state, foreign-dominated mining and industrial sectors, a democratically minded but amorphous middle class, and a militant, marxist labor movement. For much of the last hundred years, then, the Chilean countryside and city have run on quite separate political tracks. The interplay of these rural and urban societies, mediated by a coalesced but conflictive oligarchy in which landowner interests remained long dominant, profoundly shaped the course of Chilean history and reveals once again the multiplicity of historical times present at once in regions peripheral to the capitalist core.

The Long Depression of the Late Nineteenth Century

In its agricultural manifestations the so-called Long Depression of the nineteenth century (approximately 1873–1896) drove down the prices of bulky food items throughout the Atlantic world economy. Behind this decline were much cheaper transportation costs, themselves the result of rail and steam, the tramp steamer, the Suez canal, and a better knowledge of ocean geography that cut travel time for sailing ships. All of this permitted producers of grain and livestock from the vast new or newly broken lands of Canada, the United States, Argentina, Australia, and the Ukraine to enter the world market with dramatic effect on local economies. The average annual world export of wheat, for example, increased nearly sixfold, from 130 million bushels in 1873–1874 to nearly 750 million in 1924–1929. In central Chile, where the effect was felt a bit later than elsewhere, wheat prices of 3.38 pesos per *fanega* in the 1870s plummeted in subsequent five-year periods to 2.62, 2.49, and 1.85 (in sterling equivalent pesos).

Local reaction varied but one can discern two main trends: in the newly settled lands, especially the U.S. Midwest, western Canada, and Australia but also in the older areas such as East Anglia (U.K.), the individual household of family farms or tenant farmers became the main unit of production and family members provided (often unpaid) labor.[1] Kinship, it turned out, was a more effective device of exploitation than capital. In other cases, falling agricultural prices drove smaller European producers and traditional peasants off the land. Thus the same steamships carrying tons of cheap American grain east to Europe returned with their holds filled with dispossessed peasants who, soon to be resettled in the new lands on larger and mechanized farms, furthered the original process. So one response, then, to the conjuncture of the later nineteenth century was specialized grain production in household units where wives, daughters, and sons provided the labor. This process, as everyone knows, V. I. Lenin called the "farmer road" to agrarian capitalism.[2]

The second broad response to the late nineteenth century crisis was a transition to wage labor. In many regions of older, established estate agriculture, landowners rationalized production by expelling their resident workers and hiring wage laborers. This process has drawn the attention of several scholars, among them Max Weber, who shows how the Junkers of East Elbia in Prussia replaced their service tenants, who had worked the estates in exchange for rights to a cottage and parcels of land, with seasonal Polish migrant workers at low wages. Professor Jan Bazant describes the same tendency: Porfirian *hacendados* in north-central Mexico reduced the number of their *peones acasillados* and hired wage workers from the local communities where population increases combined with reduced resources to drive people into the labor market. In more recent years one can detect this pattern in El Salvador, Colombia, Peru before 1968 and, in fact, Chile itself in the 1950s and early 1960s. Drawing on a case close at hand, Lenin called this the "Prussian road" to agrarian capitalism.

The Chilean Anomaly

On the eve of the nineteenth-century agricultural crisis, Chile's rural structure, described in the classic work of Claudio Gay, resembled and yet was substantially different from other agrarian systems in Spanish America and Western Europe. As in Mexico, Ecuador, Peru, and Bolivia, large estates dominated the landscape and on them lived large numbers of service tenants, in Chile called *inquilinos* and elsewhere *peones acasillados, huasipungueros, yanacones, colonos,* or *concertados.* But unlike those countries or continental Europe, in Chile there was no independent peasant counterpart in the form of peasant communities or villages. In the absence of a deeply rooted, sedentary, native farming community, the Spanish Crown attempted to form peasant villages *a la Europea* all through the central valley in the eighteenth century, as respectable havens for the thousands of already landless rural people. These came in time to be the towns of Chillán, Talca, Curicó, Los Andes, and so on, but they were never recognizable as peasant villages.[3]

From the eighteenth century on, the seasonal workers required to supplement the stable populations residing on central valley *fundos* and haciendas were drawn from the increasingly large floating populations that migrated the length of the central valley. They struck shallow roots in the straggling towns—the *pueblos de calle larga*—that crowded into the interstices of an estate-dominated countryside, and they rattled the hacienda gates in search of work. So, although both *inquilinos* and *peones* were campesinos, neither made up a peasantry in the sense that Moore uses the term.

As prices for wheat began their inexorable drop during the years of the nineteenth-century Long Depression, Chilean landowners and the state had some choices to consider. It seems as unlikely now as it did then that land in the central valley could have been parcelled out to family farmers, that any pressure might have been generated from below that would have led to a nineteenth-century land reform, or that the agrarian might have undertaken schemes of colonization. In fact, in circumstances where this was feasible, on the Araucanian frontier opened to settlement in the 1880s, the large estate once again came to dominate.[4] So if that road, taken as we have seen by many societies in those years, was not a realistic option, what about the possibility of a reform in the system of *inquilinaje* or even a transition to wage labor, that is, a transition to full-scale agrarian capitalism?

In the 1870s and 1880s, in the depth of the crisis, *inquilinaje* became the target of vociferous criticism, mostly from the capital city of Santiago where the application of the new revenues from mining and agriculture to urban amenities had recently widened the social gulf between city and country-side. Urban critics deplored the always present but now newly discovered serf-like conditions, the squalor, misery, and ignorance of the service tenantry. A bit later, *El Mercurio*, the country's venerable daily, called the system of rural labor "simply monstrous . . . unworthy of a civilized country and an affront to landowners."[5] But at the same time the landowners undertook not the abolition but the expansion of *inquilinaje*; moreover, the expansion of this archaic institution was pushed not just by conservative *hacendados* but by the progressive landowner sector as well. "What would agriculture be without this element of vital importance?" a writer for the National Society of Agriculture's *Boletín* asked in 1887. Without *inquilinos*, he wrote, modern agriculture would be impossible. Julio Menandier, the astute editor of the *Boletín* and a spokesman for the dynamic segment of *agricultores progresistas*, wrote that "inquilinaje is an institution sui generis and far from combatting it, landowners and legislators should make an effort to develop it on a larger scale."[6]

And so they did. During the subsequent decades, thousands of additional families were settled on the estates to augment the stable and conservative core of service tenants or *inquilinos*. Since it is difficult to isolate the various categories of rural inhabitants in nineteenth- and early twentieth-century statistics, four recent and valuable books on the subject have somewhat different interpretations. Gabriel Salazar, whose marvelous *Labradores, peones y proletarios* (1985) has rescued and brought to light those who lived in the shadow of Chilean history, rightfully points out the importance of workers other than *inquilinos* in Chilean agriculture. He is inclined to see the settlement of new workers on the estates not as an extension of *inquilinaje* but as "stable peonage." Thus, for example, when Menandier praises the owner of Viluco (a huge estate just south of Santiago) for extending *inquilinaje* by settling an additional two hundred people on individual house and garden plots of three-fourths of a hectare on the estate, Salazar calls this the "abandonment of inquilinaje" and a turn toward a system of "stable peonage."[7] Newly recruited service tenants were allotted less land, less pasturage, and fewer sharecropping rights, while the work required of them was stepped up. Roberto Santana's closely reasoned *Paysans dominés*, written five years earlier, stresses the "new form of inquilinaje" that appeared in the 1870s and then argues that a two-track development occurred: on one side a minority of original *inquilinos* as relatively well-off sharecroppers and petty entrepreneurs, and on the other, a growing number of "semi-proletarianized" tenants for whom a money wage increasingly replaced the traditional perquisites or *regalias*.[8] José Bengoa, the author of two recent and useful books on rural Chile, interprets the same census data available to Salazar and Santana but concludes (rightly, I believe) that in the last years of the nineteenth century, *inquilinaje* was increasing in central Chile—he uses the term *reinquilinización*—while proletarianization was essentially limited to such operations as dairies near Santiago and medium-sized *fundos* in the region of San Felipe and Los Andes.[9] This idea is supported by the more systematic and somewhat more reliable twentieth-century statistics. In 1935, some 30 percent of all rural workers in Chile were described in the Censo de Agricultura as *inquilinos* but another 33 percent were *peones* or *gañanes* who were members of *inquilino* households. Only 28 percent were described as *afuerinos*, or seasonal day laborers.[10] George McBride, writing at about this time, had no doubt about the central importance of *inquilinos* who, he thought, outnumbered wage workers two to one.[11]

There is no doubt that *inquilinaje* changed over the century before 1965, and few would hold now that the term *inquilino* describes a single type of service tenant. But whether one calls the various mutations stable *peones* or semiproletarians, their economic and social relations with landowners remained essentially intact: they still exchanged labor service for precarious rights to land and rations, and they remained beyond the reach of urban politics and culture. Thus it appears that under the impact of falling world grain prices during the Long Depression, Chilean landowners and workers took neither the "farmer road" of smaller, capitalist farms nor the "Prussian road" of reduced resident workers and wage labor. Rather, there was *reinquilinización* in a form somewhat different from the original, and the consequent reinforcement of a manorial economy and landlord dominance in the countryside.

Counterfactual Hypotheses

How can the persistence, indeed the extension, of *inquilinaje* be explained? And what were its political consequences? In order to understand more clearly the implications for Chilean history of what did happen in the countryside, let us imagine for a moment history in the subjunctive mood: what would have happened had political and peasant gone a different route in the 1870s? As mentioned above, it seems foolish to imagine a "farmer road," that is, a precocious agrarian reform in property or a massive redistribution of land, in the nineteenth century. The large estates were firmly entrenched and their owners hardly prepared to entertain schemes of internal colonization, even had the political pressure for such a movement been present. Even in the frontier region of Arauco, where one might imagine a kind of Homestead Act, the "farmer road" was not taken. But among the alternatives open in the 1870s, it is possible to imagine the "Prussian road" or at least a Chilean variant of it. It is especially easy to imagine this since, in fact, that road was taken some eighty or ninety years later in the 1950s and early 1960s.

So our question is, what would have been the most likely effect on Chilean historical development had the "Prussian road" been taken earlier? Let us imagine that instead of *inquilinización,* the landowners had expelled their service tenants and made a transition to wage labor. Or suppose that the *inquilinos* themselves had endeavored to abandon the *fundo* en masse to seek employment elsewhere. In examining the obstacles to such policies and their implications had they been successful, we may understand more fully the importance of the countryside in Chilean politics.

Economic Considerations
Assuming for the moment their ability and willingness to make a purely economic decision, we may ask, under what conditions might landowners have expelled their tenants or the tenants have abandoned the estate? There are, it seems to me, two main conditions a landowner would have had to consider: 1) Had the value of the land and perquisites let to *inquilinos* risen above the value of their labor services? and 2) Would the replacement cost in cash paid to wage earners be less than the package of land and perquisites extended to *inquilinos*? As for the *inquilinos* themselves, they would have to ask whether higher income was possible elsewhere. Had landowners expelled their *inquilinos* and changed to a full-fledged wage system they would have had to compete with wages paid in industry, mining, and construction

or risk losing their workers. Put another way, to retain the labor services of an expelled *inquilino*, the landowner would have had to pay him a cash wage equal to the total benefits he had received as a service tenant—or pay local *peones* a sufficient wage to guarantee their presence at crucial moments in the agricultural year. Had either expulsion or abandonment driven wages up in the labor market, landowners would have been forced to invest their earnings not on luxury imports and Santiago mansions but on mechanical reapers and threshers; in other words, to modernize agriculture. On the other hand, the expulsion and proletarianization of *inquilinos* may have added to the supply of rural workers and driven wages, or at least total labor costs, down. This, of course, is the guiding logic in the "Prussian road."

We cannot know what effect the "Prussian road" might have had on wages but we do have some notion of how the landowners perceived the problem of labor supply. They were acutely aware of the threat of a free labor market, or put more accurately (because *inquilinos* were formally free to leave the estate), landowners were aware of the threat that alternatives might pose to the retention of their workers in a world without the restraints of custom and paternalism. As railroad construction and the nitrate fields offered wages sufficient to tempt workers from agriculture in the 1870s (and some thirty thousand actually left), landowners over and over expressed the need to root (*arraigar*) their workers to the estate through the offer of land and perquisites. And their broad strategy was successful. Because a handful of large landowners had already gained control of most of the agricultural land in Chile, any tenant family seeking an independent rural existence faced bleak possibilities. In the typical agricultural department of Caupolican, for example, twenty-six landowners with an average of 5,600 hectares each controlled some 80 percent of all arable land and nearly all irrigated land.[12] Local constables and the courts could be counted on to expel squatters and define boundaries. Frontier lands in the far south at midcentury and in Arauco after 1880 were made available not to the rural poor but to German immigrants in the first case and to victorious army officials and entrepreneurs in the second.

It is in this sense, in the control of alternatives and in the application of a measured paternalism, rather than through debt peonage or violence, that the rural elite insured the discipline and loyalty of their workers. To be sure, force was available, just offstage, waiting in the wings; but before the cadres of the other political culture—of the gathering middle-class groups and organized workers—began to intrude into the countryside after World War I, overt, politically backed coercion was rarely necessary.

Inquilinización could not have been carried out, of course, without the cooperation of the *inquilinos* themselves. Rather than see them inevitably as acted upon we should remember that in this story they too were actors, and we should attempt to put ourselves in their sandals. This is admittedly difficult, since the humble leave few written records and motive must usually be inferred from action. But in the remarkable oral histories being put together by Ximena Valdés and her coworkers, we are occasionally able to hear the voice of the historical actors themselves. Although these voices are, generally, women's, not men's and women's, and they apply to a later period—from the 1930s on—rural mentality in its fundamental sense still comes through.[13] Most people, even after radios and newspapers were common, lived with the conviction that nothing could be changed; many others believed that if things were bad, a change would only make them worse. Given the scant alternatives of the Chilean countryside, rural people sought positions as *inquilinos* on the estate rather than casting their lot with the desperate and insecure wage earners beyond the gates. They were free, in the liberal sense, to move onto the estate, and no statute or extralegal device bound them to stay, but they had no defense in the face of expulsion; indeed, the threat of being cast out into the subproletariat of migratory workers was the most powerful weapon at the landowner's disposal. Most *inquilino* families undoubtedly judged their welfare on the estate superior to life outside or in the nitrate fields of the northern desert. (Most of the thirty thousand who left the estates, mentioned above, were single men, seasonal workers.)

All of these justifications for *inquilinaje* can be expressed in economic terms. Few landowners, however, made such explicit calculations; as long as letting land seemed cheap relative to wages, and above all, required no cash outlay, they were understandably reluctant to change. Wage labor accompanied by mechanization and modernization might have been economically beneficial but it was not so perceived in the 1870s (whereas it was in the 1950s). Moreover, and most importantly, *inquilinaje* was not, either for the landowner or the *inquilino*, merely an economic system.

Social and Cultural Considerations

There are important but elusive cultural explanations for the persistence of Chile's peculiar institution. The interviews and surveys gathered at the beginning of the 1967 agrarian reform, Brian Loveman's research in the records of the Labor Office, and the testimonials of *mujeres del campo* published by Ximena Valdés and others, provide the beginnings of a potentially rich source of information for the reconstruction of the ideas and values not only of the humble folk but of landowners as well.[14] In these records one begins to glimpse the ties of affection and fear, of hate and even love that bound *hacendado* and *inquilino* together in a long-lasting community of oppression. Looking at all this from the landowner's point of view, I believe the idea of personal service is important. Although I have never enjoyed the personal service of dozens of servants, people who saddle one's horse, wordlessly open the gates and close them behind you, attend to guests, and offer, in public at least, deferential respect—and all without cash wages—I can at least imagine its attraction. And I have no doubt that the rather intangible pleasures Chilean landowners derived from giving orders and being obeyed and being waited on, were heavily, if not very explicitly, weighed in any calculation about the advantages of modernization and proletarianization.

The satisfactions of personal service for those who received them are as difficult to quantify as many other vital elements in historical explanation, but they seem to me a powerful feature in the long persistence of *inquilinaje*. Personal service derived from and conditioned a system of power and subordination in the countryside that had its roots in the sixteenth-century *encomienda* and continues today. The underside of personal service is personal punishment, or the assumed right and practice of landlords or their agents to fine or punish "their" workers outside the law. There is, to my knowledge, no systematic research on this melancholy subject in Chile, but I have the impression that the degree of personal service and personal punishment still present in the Chilean countryside as late as the 1940s had disappeared at least a century earlier in France, certainly by the time of Bismarck in Prussia, and with the 1910 Revolution in Mexico.[15]

Landlord and Campesino in the Politics of Modern Chile

Inquilinaje as a Political Base

The landowners' political power in the countryside derived from control of land and people; but in the course of the nineteenth century, as Chile's formal democracy emerged, landowners had to compete in an electoral game with an ever more autonomous state. This meant that in order to use the state to coerce their workers, they had first to extract from their workers the votes necessary to compete in a restricted but nevertheless formally democratic political system.

In the first half-century of independence from Spain, the state rested on a society of notables in which central valley landowners were the dominant element. Armed revolts from the somewhat more democratically minded periphery—primarily the mining north and the flour-milling south—were put down in 1851 and 1859.[16] As increased public revenue from agricultural and mining exports made possible a larger and increasingly autonomous state, the executive insisted that its list of congressional and municipal candidates be placed on the ballot and then mobilized National Guard members and lower-level public employees to vote them into office. By the 1860s, the executive controlled some twelve thousand voters or over half of the total electorate in those years.[17] A decade later, the *aristocratic fronde*, dominated by the great landowners, saw the need to combat presidential maneuvers with their own manipulation, and in 1874 they helped push through a Law of Electoral Reform that permitted universal literate male suffrage, an apparent democratic precociousness effectively present at the time only in France, the United States, and Switzerland. Chilean landowners supported the reform not because of an enlightened faith in the civic qualities of the lower classes but as a measured way of counteracting the executive's disconcerting autonomy in a democratic political system they supported in principle, used when possible, and tenaciously endeavored to restrict and control.[18]

From the 1870s on, landowners were able to enfranchise their workers, fraudulently or not, and then encourage or, if necessary, purchase enough of their votes to compete. Here, then, is a powerful motive for the retention of a loyal and generally obedient service tenantry. No one, for example, visiting the great hacienda of San Jose del Carmen, "El Huique," home to a resident population of over a thousand people (and two Chilean presidents), can fail to sense the social and political base it once represented.[19] The political advantages of *inquilinaje* were obvious to landowners and they undoubtedly saw that expulsion and proletarianization would have dealt a blow to their electoral chances. This was not a concern that weighed heavily in the calculations of nineteenth-century Junkers or Porfirian *hacendados*, neither of whom had to worry about peasant votes.

Returning to our counterfactual hypothesis for one brief moment, we can see that the proletarianization of service tenants would have led to other and most unsettling ramifications. Even had landowners somehow retained a measure of political power for a few more years, it is difficult to imagine a rural proletariat politically quiescent in the turmoil of the 1930s. Out from under the paternalistic domination of their masters we would more likely have seen unionized and even rebellious rural workers who, far from supporting the landowners, would have sought political alliances with urban parties—just as in fact occurred thirty years later. Had landowners taken the "Prussian road" earlier, they might have modernized agriculture but, in the process, weakened their own political base; had *inquilinos* pushed for, or acquiesced in, proletarianization, one can imagine them with less security but somewhat more independent political power.

The change in politics after passage of the 1874 law and the electoral importance for the landowners of a cooperative *inquilinaje* can be seen in table 1, in J. Samuel Valenzuela's figures, where the electorate in the landowner-dominated province of Rancagua is broken down into occupational groups.

The exceptionally large increase in agriculturalists (*agricultores*), a census term that excludes *peones* but includes *inquilinos*, can only point to the inclusion of several thousand service tenants, qualified practically overnight, to vote more or less as they were told.

TABLE 1—Registered Voters by Occupational Groups (Rancagua, 1872 and 1878)

Occupation	1872	1878
Proprietors and capitalists	142	11
Professionals, merchants, and other middle strata	167	625
Public and private employees	111	151
Agriculturalists (inc. *inquilinos*)	780	5,223
Artisans and other specialized workers	266	1,573
Miners	14	115
Workers and others low strata	0	24
Total	**1,480**	**7,722**

Source: J. Samuel Valenzuela, *Democratizión via reforma* (Buenos Aires: Ediciones IDES, 1985): 119.

Landowners in a Coalesced Oligarchy

Chilean *hacendados* subsequently maintained a disproportionate weight in national politics well into the twentieth century. But they did this not as a discrete class, as an abstract landed aristocracy, but as the important and often dominant sector of an economically and socially mixed oligarchy.[20] The road to Chilean democracy, thus, at least until the 1960s, involved neither the assault of an insurgent bourgeoisie on a backward landed aristocracy nor the presence of a fully commercialized and proletarianized agriculture, because until then, none of these things existed. Let us see why this was true.

From the 1870s on, Chile entered a rapidly expanding phase of mineral exports and industrial growth. Nitrates and then copper generated a torrent of wealth for private investors and the state, while the industrial sector employed, by 1914, some 16 percent of the active population. But 60 percent of nitrate mining was in foreign hands, and a 1914 analysis of industry classified according to the nationality of owners reveals that 56 percent of all industries (those employing more than five workers) were also foreign owned.[21] This meant that the extraordinary economic growth in those sectors did not elevate to political power corresponding representatives of miners and industrialists. As elsewhere, capitalism in this region peripheral to Western Europe and the United States provided scant opportunity for the development of an autonomous bourgeoisie. Instead, the landowner faction of the elite absorbed those Chileans who had prospered in mining and industry and, as foreigners came to settle in Chile, incorporated them as well. That is to say, in economic terms, landowners invested in banks, business, and industry while the newly rich of those sectors bought and improved languishing rural estates to make money and also "decorated themselves with a fundo" to ease their entry into the social elite.[22] In 1882, the *Mercurio* of Valparaíso published a list of fifty-nine "millionaires" to demonstrate the possibilities available "through order and effort in a free country." Some writers have used this list to show the relative insignificance of agriculture as a generator of individual wealth, since only twenty are described as landowners. But the more interesting point is that the remaining thirty-nine—shown as miners, bankers, and "capitalists"—all subsequently invested their earning in rural estates.[23]

Chilean history, then, on its trajectory of limited democracy, reveals not a conflict between an industrial or mining bourgeoisie and a landed class but, rather, coalescence. This does not mean, of course, that no intraclass differences arose among specific interest groups within the elite; in 1891 those even erupted into civil war. But it does mean that agrarian interests within the elite remained disproportionately prominent well into the twentieth century, and landowners themselves managed to exploit the votes of their subordinate workers while at the same time pressuring the state to keep political "agitators" and union organizers out of the countryside.[24] The landowners thus lacked authoritarian power; they had to compete politically in Chile's precocious but limited democracy. Paradoxically, their need for captive votes helps explain their retention of an archaic and subservient labor force.

It should also be made clear that if landowners used the votes of a handful of their service tenants, they and their oligarchical colleagues stoutly opposed broad political participation. Although the 1874 law made all literate males over twenty-five eligible to vote, "only a small proportion exercised this right." Whereas the proportion of the population voting in Britain, France, and the United States fluctuated between 10 and 25 percent in the first quarter of this century, in Chile the rate of electoral participation was typically around 5 percent. Even when the male literacy rate rose from 20 to 40 percent, as it did between 1915 and 1925, there was little change in participation. As Karen Remmer points out, as table 2 demonstrates, "until women began to vote in 1950, liberal democratic institutions in Chile were based on the electoral participation of less than 10 percent of the population."[25]

The persistence of landowner interests and their effective control of the rural vote can be measured in the composition of the national congress. In

TABLE 2—Expansion of the Chilean Electorate, 1873–1949

	Registered Voters		Votes Cast	
Year	Thousands	% of Total Population	Thousands	% of Total Population
1873	—	—	26	1.3
1876	—	—	80	3.9
1879	—	—	104	4.7
1882	—	—	97	4.2
1885	—	—	79	3.2
1888	—	—	90	3.5
1912	598	17.6	295	8.7
1915	185	5.3	150	4.3
1918	342	9.4	183	5.0
1921	383	10.2	197	5.3
1925	302	7.7	256	6.6
1945	641	12.0	450	8.4
1949	592	10.4	470	8.3

Source: Karen Remmer, Party Competition in Argentina and Chile (Lincoln: University of Nebraska, 1984), 84.

Note: In 1915, a new system of permanent registration, renewable every nine years, was introduced to cut down on fraudulent registrations.

1874, twenty-one of the thirty senators (70 percent) and forty-two of the ninety-six diputados (44 percent) had, as part (at least) of their economic holdings, a large rural estate. A quarter century later, in 1902, this was true of 73 percent of all senators and 52 percent of all diputados. Even in 1918, with the economy fully integrated into the Atlantic economy through nitrate exports, banks, and burgeoning industry, two-thirds (67 percent) of all Chilean senators and 40 percent of all diputados were owners of a large estate.[26] Likewise, few if any of the dozen or so presidents between the first Errazuriz (1871–1875) and the years of the Popular Front (1938–1942) failed to enjoy and profit from the ownership of a fundo.

For most of those years, until 1919 at least, the rural landscape I sketched above inhibited workers' movements or any peasant revolt. In the absence of a village or cultural base for political action, the large estate, with its hierarchy of overseers and foremen often drawn from among the most reliable *inquilinos*, was generally able to placate, coopt, and control the rural work force through a paternalism at best benign and occasionally tyrannical. From the later eighteenth century onward, a steady population growth accustomed landowners to a man-land ratio favorable to themselves; so much so that any slight shortage of workers during harvest—or any timorous request for better pay—led inevitably to complaints of *escasez de brazos,* or lack of hands. For all of these reasons, landowners required little direct political coercion from state or local officials in those years. The countryside remained essentially tranquil, yielding up its annual quota of work and votes for a rural elite usually resident in distant Santiago.

The Challenge from Below

By the 1920s, the other Chile, a society of militant workers, impatient bureaucrats, and urban middle groups, began to intrude into the countryside. In fact, the first development was a bill introduced in Congress in 1919 to regulate *inquilino* housing. But more was to come as unemployed nitrate workers and urban political leaders began to unionize rural workers close to Santiago and to organize local strikes. In 1924, under unexpected political pressure in part caused by the collapse of the nitrate industry and the wide recognition of a severe "social question," Congress enacted a series of social and labor laws, later codified as the Labor Code in 1931. The still-powerful landowner faction now bent every effort to keep the provisions of this legislation from being applied in the countryside.[27]

A key moment in rural-urban conflict came in the early years of the Popular Front (1938–1942) when the interests of mine workers, the urban proletariat, and the new industrialists coincided in the need for cheap bread. At the same time militants in the Socialist and Communist Parties pressed for the politicization of the countryside and renewed their efforts at rural unionization. The resulting conflict, as Thomas Wright puts it, transcended the direct economic interests of landowners and agricultural workers: "The larger question was the potential effect of agricultural unionization on national politics." Unions might provide the organizational basis for wresting the rural vote away from landowners and "thus undermine the bastion of rightist electoral power . . . unless a new restraining order were forthcoming."[28]

The president of the Popular Front coalition was Pedro Aguirre Cerda, from the conservative wing of the middle-class Radical Party and himself, in fact, a wealthy landowner. Fearful that union penetration into the countryside would indeed tilt the electorate irretrievably to the Left, and respectful of the still formidable landowner power—Aguirre Cerda had won only by a whisker in 1938, as the rural districts had gone overwhelmingly for the right-wing candidate—the president bent to landowner pressure energetically presented by the National Society of Agriculture. He expressed his concern for "social harmony rather than conflict," formed a study group, and suspended further unionization. At the same time he unleashed his minister of the interior, who later described his own methods of dealing with rural militancy:

> A group of carabineros would arrive at a farm (a fundo) accompanied by a convoy of trucks. When the inquilinos were assembled in the area, the carabinero officer would order those who wished to continue the strike to stand on his left. The officer would then order that the strikers gather their families, cats, dogs, chickens and belongings and get in the trucks to be evicted. . . . I did not have to use this (system) many times.[29]

Such tactics, and even more violent ones in 1934, when the police massacred some one hundred smallholders protesting their eviction, kept the countryside isolated from the mainstream of Chilean politics. The economic payoff for landowners came in the form of lower labor costs: according to Brian Loveman, "real wages for rural workers fell by approximately 18 percent between 1940 and 1952 and by another 38 percent between 1953 and 1960."[30]

By the early 1960s, landowner interests in the Chilean political system had become untenable, and with the Christian Democratic victory in 1964 the floodgates of urban pressure were opened onto the countryside. Political activity, concientization, and union organization quickly followed as Left, Right, and Center scrambled to add a rural constituency to their urban parties. The large estates were at the same time rapidly modernizing production through capital investment and proletarianization, while their owners, more fearful of the gathering forces on the Left, reluctantly and bitterly acquiesced in an urban middle-class-led agrarian reform. By this time the political incorporation of women (1949), improved literacy rates (75 percent in 1960), the legality of all political parties, and the free and even licentious flow of information meant that Chile was an increasingly participatory, as opposed to a merely representative, democracy. It was during this fleeting moment that Barrington Moore's model for the democratic road might seem to have had some relevance to the Chilean case. At the time few people could see that complete disaster lay just ahead.

Conclusion

I have tried to explain both the internal logic for landlord-peasant relations in Chile and why Barrington Moore's hypotheses have little relevance to the Chilean case. To begin with, work in rural Chile was governed by a labor market. Both service tenants (*inquilinos*) and seasonal workers were free, a

least in principle, to negotiate their remuneration. There was no requirement for compulsory labor; no statute or peonage bound them to the estate.
As railroad construction or mining offered better wages, some rural people
chose to migrate and landowners had to compete with consequent changes
in the wage level. Remuneration in the form of access to land or rations
rather than cash, however detrimental to the development of an internal
market for local products, does not alter the market function. Landowners
did not, by and large, employ extra-economic measures to obtain their labor
force because they had no need to do so. They had a favorable man-
land ratio, and when that was threatened they developed, consciously or
unconsciously, a broad strategy that included the complex of practices
conveniently called paternalism as well as the assistance of a rural clergy
that could be counted on to inveigh against sloth and disloyalty from the
hacienda's own pulpit. Few people today would call this a just world, nor
was it a smoothly working or fully integrated labor market, but it was a
"free" world in the liberal economic sense of the term.

After 1919 and especially during the precariously balanced Popular
Front years, when the landowners' very existence was threatened by
marxist-led urban parties, the still powerful landowners prevailed upon the
state to forbid rural unionization. They blunted the instrument of their
destruction while at the same time, on their terms, enabled themselves to
maintain a market wage. Thirty years later and threatened again by a
marxist challenge to their very existence, landowners and their middle-class
allies—the Chilean bourgeoisie—acquiesced in the military's destruction of
what appeared to them to be a democracy run amok.

Did landowners in the later nineteenth and early twentieth century
favor authoritarian national politics or restrain the development of a fuller
democracy? The record shows that landowners pushed for the Electoral
Law that precociously enfranchised adult literate males in 1874 and thereafter used these votes, over which they exercised a great deal of control, to
compete in a limited, formal, fraudulent, but hotly contested democracy.
The sharp limits to participation (before 1920 less than 5 percent of all
Chileans voted) were not imposed any more by the landowners than by
other factions of the elite. Indeed, rather than push for authoritarian
measures to coerce rural labor, Chilean landowners used their workers'
votes to gain access to state power. In all of this, it's hard to argue that
landowners were more authoritarian or repressive than miners, industrialists, or the state. Nothing occurred in the countryside to equal the violence
called down upon the heads of striking nitrate workers in 1907 or the urban
proletariat in 1905. The Chilean bourgeoisie, far from playing a decisive role
in the development of full parliamentary democracy, fought tooth and nail
to restrict political participation at least up to 1950.[31]

But then, perhaps a bourgeoisie never existed until 1950. Because foreign investors controlled more than half of all Chilean industry and mining, the impressive growth in the export sector did not create a strong, self-conscious class of native industrialists, bankers, and miners. Rather, politically fragmented groups from these sectors came to blows in the 1891 Civil War and squabbled interminably throughout the Parliamentary Republic (1891–1925). Rather than absorb or push aside the landed aristocrats, they were themselves absorbed into an oligarchy where landowner elements were dominant. Perhaps, as Jeffery Paige puts it, the concept of a "bourgeois revolution" leading automatically to parliamentary democracy may "finally be ready for a decent burial by Marxists and non-Marxists alike."[32] In the end, or at least up to now, and for good or evil, it was the mass of Chilean people who came to participate fully in politics and create, with all its twists and turns and idiosyncrasies, the Chilean road to democracy.

NOTES

All quotes in this essay from Barrington Moore are from his *Social Origins of Dictatorship and Democracy* (Boston: Beacon Press, 1966): 413–32.

1. Harriet Friedmann, "World Market, State, Family Farm: Social Basis of Household Production in the Era of Wage Labor," *Comparative Studies in Society and History* 20, no. 4 (1978): 545–86.

2. For a recent exposition and Latin American applications of the "farmer" and "Prussian" roads, see Alain de Janvry, *The Agrarian Question and Reformism in Latin America* (Baltimore: Johns Hopkins University Press, 1981), especially pp. 106–09. For thoughtful comparisons of the Chilean case, see Cristóbal Kay, "Comparative Development of the European Manorial System and the Latin American Hacienda System," *Journal of Peasant Studies* 2, no. 1 (Oct. 1984): 69–98; and "Political Economy, Class Alliances and Agrarian Change in Chile," *Journal of Peasant Studies* 8, no. 4 (July 1981): 485–513.

3. Gabriel Salazar, *Labradores, peones y proletarios* (Santiago: Ediciones Sur, 1985), 45–56.

4. José Bengoa, *Historia del pueblo mapuche*, 2d ed. (Santiago: Ediciones Sur, 1987), 345–53.

5. Quoted in Thomas Wright, *Landowners and Reform in Chile* (Urbana, Ill.: University of Illinois Press, 1982), 146.

6. Jullio Menandier, *Boletín* (Sociedad Nacional de Agricultura), vol. 1 (Santiago, 1870–1875), 147.

7. Salazar, *Labradores*, 45–56.

8. Roberto Santana, *Paysans dominés: Lutte sociale dans las campagnes chilienne 1920–1970* (Paris, 1980), 84–91.

9. José Bengoa, *El poder y la subordinación* (Santiago: Ediciones Sur, 1988), 267–68; and *Haciendas and Campesinos* (Santiago: Ediciones Sur, 1990).

10. Arnold J. Bauer, *Chilean Rural Society from the Spanish Conquest to 1930* (Cambridge: Cambridge University Press, 1975), 169.

11. George McBride, *Chile: Land and Society* (New York: American Geographical Society, 1936), 164.

12. Bauer, *Chilean Rural Society*, 127.

13. Ximena Valdés et al., *Historias testimoniales de mujeres del campo* (Santiago, 1983).

14. Brian Loveman, *Struggle in the Countryside: Politics and Rural Labor in Chile, 1919–1973* (Bloomington, Ind.: University of Indiana Press, 1976), and *Chile: The Legacy of Hispanic Capitalism*, 2d ed. (New York: Oxford University Press, 1988), 229–69.

15. *Congreso Nacional*. Camara de Diputados, Sesiones extraordinarias, Dec. 1939 to July 1940.

16. Maurice Zeitlin, *The Civil Wars in Chile (or the Bourgeois Revolutions that Never Were)* (Princeton: Princeton University Press, 1984), chap. 2.

17. Arturo Valenzuela, *Political Brokers in Chile: Local Government in a Centralized Polity* (Durham, N.C.: Duke University Press, 1977), 185.

18. J. Samuel Valenzuela, *Democratización via reforma: La expansion del sufragio en Chile* (Buenos Aires: Ediciones IDES, 1985), 12–19, 106–21.

19. Arnold J. Bauer, "La hacienda el Huique in the Agrarian Structure of Nineteenth Century Chile," *Agricultural History* 46, no. 1 (Oct. 1972): 78–98.

20. Maurice Zeitlin and R. E. Ratcliff, *Landlords and Capitalists: the Dominant Class of Chile* (Princeton: Princeton University Press, 1988), 201–14; see also Henry Kirsch, *Industrial Development in a Traditional Society* (Gainesville: University of Florida Press, 1977), 64–95.

21. José Gabriel Palma, "Chile 1914–1935: De economia exportadora a sustitutiva de importaciones," *Nueva Historia* 2, no. 7 (1983): 165–92; Carlos Hurtado Ruíz-Tagle, "La economía chilena entre 1830 y 1930: Sus limitaciones y sus herencias," *Collección Estudios Cieplan*, no. 12 (1984): 56.

22. Gonzalo Vial, *Historia de Chile (1891–1973)*, 4th ed., vol. 1, 2d tome (Santiago: Editorial Santillana, 1987), 642–51.

23. *El Mercurio* (Valparaíso), vol. 4, no. 1647 (26 April 1882); Alberto Edwards Vives, *La fronda aristocrática*, 6th ed. (Santiago: Editorial del Pacifico, 1966), 166–79.

24. Loveman, *Chile*, chap. 8; Sergio Aranda and Alberto Martínez, "Estructura económica: Algunas caracteristics fundamentales," in Anibal Pinto et al., *Chile Hoy* (Santiago: Siglo XXI, 1970), 134.

25. Karen Remmer, *Party Competition in Argentina and Chile* (Lincoln: University of Nebraska Press, 1984), 83.

26. Bauer, *Chilean Rural Society*, 215–16; Remmer, *Party Competition*, 112–20.

27. Wright, *Landowners and Reform*, 148.

28. Ibid., 157.

29. Loveman, *Chile*, 249. His chapter 8 is the best discussion available on this subject.

30. Ibid., 235.

31. Sofía Correa S., "La derecha en Chile contemporaneo: La perdida del control estatal," *Revista de Ciencia Política* 11, no. 1 (1989): 11–12.

32. Jeffery Paige, "The Social Origins of Dictatorship and Democracy and Social Revolution in Central America" (paper given at the American Sociological Association, San Francisco, Calif., August 1990).

The Buenos Aires Landed Class and the Shape of Argentine Politics (1820–1930)

Tulio Halperín Donghi

The rise of one of the most successful primary export economies in what had been until the late eighteenth century a very unpromising colonial backwater offers the central theme for the history of modern Argentina. This stunning transformation, which started in earnest around 1820, was substantially completed by 1910. But the rise in exports still continued—albeit more haltingly—in the unsettled economic climate of the first interwar decade. It was in 1928, on the very eve of the catastrophe that destroyed the world economic system in which the country had prospered, that Argentine exports, by reaching one billion dollars, doubled the highest levels achieved before 1914, after having grown more than five hundred times since the start of the independent era.

Buenos Aires, the largest province in the Littorine and Pampas regions, to which this massive growth was confined, offered the main territorial base for one of the most affluent landed classes in the world. In *belle époque* Paris the wealth of Argentines was legendary, and the legend had a solid base in reality. The yearly income of some *estanciero* families was by then higher than the total budget of a middle-rank federal ministry.[1] As the Canadian historian H. S. Ferns showed decades ago by a very simple calculation, the larger landowners were the main beneficiaries of the opening of Argentina to the world economy. Not only did they quite predictably outdistance less affluent participants in agropastoral production, from minor landowners to farmers to rural labor, but—more surprisingly—they also did considerably better than the foreign investors and entrepreneurs who helped to introduce Argentina to the railway age.[2]

Even before their rise to unmatched affluence, the landed classes came to be recognized as the first estate in the realm; common opinion saw them as the very core of the *oligarquía*, the sociopolitical establishment that until 1916 had total control of the political institutions and even later continued to impose its own severe norms on all aspects of national life. While the landowners' all-pervasive influence was widely resented, it was also universally accepted as an unmodifiable fact of life.

Considering all this, the notion of using the Argentine example as a benchmark for the hypotheses Barrington Moore developed in his influential *Social Origins of Democracy and Dictatorship* would appear extraordinarily promising. And indeed the conventional wisdom of Argentines had anticipated Moore in recognizing the *estancia* as the crucible in which a political order had been forged; as late as the 1940s and 1950s, the *órdenes generales* that General and President Perón broadcast to his followers on the eve of every general election started with instructions on how to respond to the *estanciero's* attempt to influence their vote ("if he tries to stop you from voting by closing the *estancia's* gate, cut the wire fences to reach the voting places; if he offers transportation, thankfully accept, but don't vote for his candidates").[3] Perón's readiness to devote so much time and eloquence to an occupational group (the *peones de estancia*) that by then formed a minuscule fraction of the electorate, supported as it was by the implicit recognition of the landed classes' influence on the rural areas as the main source of their political clout, was so clearly irrelevant to the circumstances of mid-twentieth-century Argentina that it could only be understood as testimony to the unacknowledged influence such received wisdom retained even on that exquisitely pragmatic political leader.

It is argued here that this view of Argentina was worse than an anachronism, and that the received wisdom that still survived in Perón's electoral messages proposed an image of Argentine historical development far too simple to do full justice to the peculiarities of the national experience.

The sociopolitical order that presided over the expansion of Pampean agriculture was from the start less Moorean than Argentines were ready to believe. That discovery shouldn't be surprising. The subtitle of Moore's book reads *Lord and Peasant in the Making of the Modern World,* and in the Argentine pampas of the formative period, while the presence of the lords couldn't be more conspicuous, the peasants were nowhere to be found.

It was instead in the Interior, a region of steppes, mountains, and irrigated valleys only minimally touched by the vast transformations that created modern Argentina, that a peasantry could be found. Not that the Interior presented a totally homogeneous social landscape; only in the northernmost provinces of Salta and Jujuy did truly large properties appear predominant in nonpastoral areas. And—no less important—in the Interior, as in many other archaic regions of Spanish America, the economic position of landlords was made less dominant by the importance of other instruments besides control over land for the appropriation of agricultural surplus. While members of the clergy and civil authorities made up for their insufficient or nonexistent salaries with a legally established or customary access to that surplus, trade and credit relations proved an even more effective means of siphoning it.

Admittedly, the social patterns created by this complex past, in which steep economic inequalities were legitimized by a hierarchic view of society that *ex hypothesi* burdened the lower socioeconomic groups with an inferior ethnic affiliation, still weigh heavily on today's Argentina. The social views ripened in the Interior were to achieve a nationwide impact during the formative years of the national state, when the oligarchic regime that kept power until 1916 laid the basis for a modernized national society. Under the oligarchic republic, the impecunious Interior elites crowded federal political, administrative, and military offices. Their commonsense views on social and political issues colored (and not only for themselves) the ideological certainties they shared with the rest of the political elites and influenced how ideology was translated into policy.

But these elites' rise to (mostly indirect) influence doesn't lend itself to a Moorean treatment; the Interior had been only minimally affected by the process that incorporated the Pampean lowlands into the "modern world," and its elites had an equally limited participation in the expanding export sector or its rising profits. When we turn to these lowlands, the reasons why, in Argentina, export expansion left no place for a peasantry become even more evident. Admittedly the recent studies on the Platine regions on the eve of that expansion are too fragmentary to justify any definitive conclusions. But the contributions of Samuel Amaral, Juan Carlos Garavaglia, and Jorge Gelman[4] draw a composite first sketch of a rural society not too different from that of the Chilean central valley, as reflected in M. Góngora's classic essay on the origins of the *inquilinos*.[5]

On both sides of the Andes the large landowners appeared equally interested in gaining access to the temporary labor of the petty agriculturalists they allowed to settle in their estates as service tenants or even squatters, and of other squatters established in neighboring public lands. Of course, the fact that these large landowners were stock raisers rather than agriculturalists did create a difference with Chile. But it didn't make the few comparatively large market-oriented exploitations and a larger number of petty agriculturalists necessarily in conflict over labor. The very fact that the seasonal demand for labor was not the same for grain agriculture as for stock raising may well have achieved the opposite effect.

The conditions under which these arrangements had matured didn't survive the end of the colonial regime. While in viceregal times stock raising for export was already on the rise, as J. C. Garavaglia has shown,[6] the figures from tithe revenue suggest that grain agriculture still contributed more than stock raising to the total value of rural production.

While in Chile the quickening pace of foreign trade during the nineteenth century was to increase the pressure applied by landowners on petty agriculturalists, with the purpose of exacting a higher price in services for a more restricted access to land, nothing similar could be found in the River Plate after the opening to non-Spanish overseas trade decreed by the last viceroy of the River Plate in 1809. Instead, direct foreign trade joined its effects with those of revolution and civil war to introduce radical changes in the economic map of the Littoral and the Pampas, the effect of which was to loosen the links between petty agriculture and stock raising.

The very expansion of stock raising made such loosening unavoidable. Agriculture couldn't follow the progress of the pastoral frontier, since high transportation costs made grain production unprofitable except in close proximity to the small urban consumer markets or on the narrow strips with easy access to river navigation. But the circumstances of revolution and war deeply affected the subregional impact of this development. Until 1810 the most dynamic stock-raising areas in the Platine lands had developed in the future Republic of Uruguay and the province of Entre Rios. The abundance of public land, the favorable relief of the soil (with numerous creeks necessary to water and corner *rodeo* cattle), the absence of a serious Indian threat, and in Uruguay the availability of an avid Brazilian market that encouraged the massive smuggling of cattle and mules, were reasons enough for the stock raisers' preference for the lands beyond the Paraná and the River Plate. Meanwhile, in the Buenos Aires countryside some observers feared that the temporary closure of the overseas markets to pastoral produce, as a consequence of the French Revolution, might bring about a definitive phasing-out of stock raising to the advantage of grain agriculture.[7]

After 1810 the pastoral economy of these transriverine areas was almost permanently disrupted by chronic military conflicts, from which they were to emerge only decades later (Entre Rios in the 1840s, and Uruguay, after several recoveries aborted by the return of war, only in the second half of the nineteenth century). A welcome opportunity was thus opened for the Buenos Aires Creole elite to create a new rural base for itself in its own *campaña*, which soon emerged as the dominant pastoral district in the River Plate. The new rural vocation of the exquisitely urban *porteño* elite owed, however, less to the prospects of future aggrandizement offered by stock raising than to the disappointments brought to it by the revolution of independence.

The installation of the (mostly British) agents of the new economic metropolis in the upper reaches of the import-export trade had denied the Creole elite the spoils of its vicarious victory over the mostly peninsular agents and associates of the Cadix merchants who dominated imperial trade under the old regime. And the rise of a new political power more zealous in the defense of its own supremacy than the Crown had been, and frequently insolvent to boot, made the conquest of the administrative, ecclesiastic, and judiciary apparatus a much less rewarding prize than expected. Settling cattle *estancias* was to elite *porteños* a more attractive alternative or complement to urban activities than in the past.

Even this necessarily simplified sketch suggests to what extent the metamorphoses of the Buenos Aires elite were influenced by those of a state apparatus that during the same decades underwent even more radical transformations. The provincial—and then national—state with which the Buenos Aires elite was to establish an intimate, if deeply ambivalent, relationship emerged in the aftermath of the wars for Independence as the end result of two successive waves of institutional innovation. The first was launched by the Spanish Crown to oppose the Portuguese southward expansion on the Atlantic coast of South America. With the creation in 1776–1777 of the viceroyalty of the River Plate, carved from Peru's territory, Buenos Aires suddenly rose to the position of a primary bureaucratic and military center in the Spanish empire, while the reform of colonial trade made it the mercantile as well as administrative metropolis of southern Spanish America. Since the Platine region's financial resources were insufficient to sustain the new viceregal administration, Upper Peru, still the wealthiest mining district in Spanish South America, was included in the new viceroyalty in order to enlarge its tax base. Thus the imperial deus ex machina installed a vast and affluent state apparatus in a still comparatively undeveloped area; revealingly, in the last colonial decade the yearly expenditure of the Caja (treasury) of Buenos Aires was more than double the value of total exports from the Platine lowlands.

The second wave of institutional innovation was unleashed by the final crisis of the colonial regime. In 1806 a miniscule British expedition conquered Buenos Aires by surprise, easily surmounting the pathetically inadequate resistance of the significantly larger royal army garrison. The liberation of the city by local militias and in 1807 its successful defense against a much larger British expedition by locally recruited voluntary regiments transferred military power from that army to local forces under the influence of the Creole elite. The consequences were momentous. Buenos Aires, the only Spanish American revolutionary capital never to be reconquered by the Royalists in the course of the wars of Independence, was also the only one where, even before the start of the 1810 Revolution, the Creole elite could count on the support of a politically as well as militarily mobilized popular base. This development was made possible by the availability of the comparatively large financial resources accumulated in the new viceregal capital.

The 1810 Revolution brought about the hasty consolidation of a political-military establishment, recruited from the ranks of the Creole elite, which turned the administrative despotism inherited from the old regime into an instrument of revolutionary dictatorship, and which, by refashioning the voluntary regiments on the model of the regular army, concentrated their political influence in the hands of their officers. Amid these political shifts, the trend toward a more developed and costly political-military apparatus, opened by the creation of the viceroyalty and accelerated since the British invasions, further intensified. After 1810 public expenditure didn't fall from the impossibly high levels of 1806–1810, while the negative financial consequences of the revolutionary regime's inability to win firm control of Upper Peru were gradually made up for by the rise in customs revenue brought about by the expansion of overseas trade.

When the revolutionary regime broke down in 1815, it had already degenerated into the administrative-military dictatorship of a narrow coterie, whose claim to legitimacy as the agent of the revolutionary will of the people had been irretrievably compromised by the universal rejection of revolutionary ideologies in the aftermath of the defeat of revolutionary and imperial France. The political reconstruction that followed recognized a very different inspiration. It proclaimed an end to revolution, redefined the war as an unideological struggle for survival made necessary by the bloodthirsty stubbornness of the restored Spanish king, and strove to find new roots in society, not now as the instrument of the egalitarian ambitions of the masses but as the political expression of the respectable classes.

As long as the war for Independence retained its first claim on the government's energies and resources, this new political orientation had very limited practical consequences. Supreme Director Pueyrredón's decree of July 22, 1817, reflects very clearly the dilemmas his regime faced. Ever anxious to find areas of understanding with the elite of his own capital, Pueyrredón reminded it of the opportunities for economic recovery it could find in settling with cattle *estancias* the Indian territory to the south of the Salado River. Unfortunately, he couldn't go much beyond wishing the best to those ready to follow his advice.

By then both the revolutionary state and the *porteño* elite appeared on the brink of final ruin. A few years later the situation would appear completely changed, thanks to the massive pastoral expansion prophetically proposed in the 1817 decree. While for those who lived through that dizzying transition it appeared to have changed everything, retrospectively it is clear that the basic features of the post-1820 developments only become intelligible when proper attention is paid to the legacy of the revolutionary years.

In particular, the position of the emerging landed classes both in relation to the state and in rural society can only be understood against that background. Two specific aspects of the revolutionary legacy are here particularly relevant. One was the precocious consolidation of a comparatively well-developed state, already in place when those classes came into their own; the other was the universally accepted commitment to the export economy, to which both the state and the elite owed their very survival. The consolidation of the state can best be followed through its changing impact on the tortuous curse of first *porteño* and then Argentine political history, and we discuss it throughout the pages that follow. The commitment to the export economy lends itself better to a briefer, global consideration.

The Argentine lowlands were among the very few Spanish American regions for which the full incorporation to the Atlantic economy through the liberalization and intensification of trade unarguably offered enormous advantages with very few drawbacks. Here the promise of a constant rise in prosperity under the benevolent influence of Adam Smith's Invisible Hand, so cruelly disappointed in so many Spanish American lands, was to be instead fully honored. It was not only that a productive economy that had found little opportunity to prosper under the colonial compact left exceptionally large room for improvement; equally important, already in colonial times its specialization in pastoral products had forced it to import even basic consumer goods from other colonial areas. The damage done to local producers by the competition of foreign imports might now be felt in the Interior and what was left of the Upper Paraná missions, and even more in Upper Peru. But in the Littoral its main consequence, besides the stimulant it offered to the rise in exports, was a more generous access to the necessities—and even the amenities—of life. And the beneficiaries of the new commercial order were not limited to the elite: by midcentury the River Plate provinces' per capita imports of British cheap cotton cloth had reached forty yards a year.

It is then not surprising that the commitment to an export economy in a framework of free trade not only enjoyed the universal and active support of the propertied classes but also could count on the more passive but equally firm consensus of most nonelite *porteños*. Nothing like the intense conflicts on trade policies that brought new complications to the Peruvian and Mexican political panorama, or those reflected in the division of New Granadan liberalism, could be found here. Instead, the same powers that in the Far East had to impose the opening to foreign trade by military force, in the River Plate used the forced interruption of trade through a blockade as their most formidable weapon, and Rosas proudly recognized in the *porteños'* resignation to the sacrifices it imposed the proof of the steely temper their patriotism had acquired under his leadership.

While few indeed were excluded from the general advantages of the turn toward the export economy, its main beneficiaries were of course the state and the propertied classes. The massive consequences that this turn achieved for both can be measured by two figures: in 1825 the per capita exports of the roughly one hundred fifty thousand *porteños* reached 4.94 pounds sterling (those of the United Kingdom were slightly above one pound), and the per capita expenditure of the new provincial state, excluding service of the public debt, was 3.17 pounds sterling (1.23 in the United Kingdom). After saving both the state and the propertied classes from imminent ruin, the new economic course ensured them both an exceptionally large share in the provincial economy.[8]

The advantages the new course offered the state were obvious. The export boom saved the Buenos Aires administrations from the financial penury that struck most new republics, not only by ensuring them high revenues from taxes on foreign trade (especially imports), but by sustaining the economic expansion that underlay the success of the notorious *moneda de Buenos Aires*, the Buenos Aires paper money that from the midtwenties to the early sixties provided a last-resort financial instrument in times of crisis. Thanks to the rising demand for circulating money on the part of the quickly expanding internal market, this unconvertible currency, unprotected though it was by any metallic guarantee, showed a resiliency that made of it a political asset the adversaries of the province soon learned to fear.

The advantages of the export economy to the landed elite were even more clear. The universally shared commitment to the export economy brought about an equally universal recognition of its new position at the core of the propertied classes. This circumstance influenced in more ways than one the insertion of the export economy into both rural society and the sociopolitical power game in the province and later the nation. Thus, for more than a century the universal support for the dominant economic course eliminated even the possibility of the conflicts on policy issues that in other latitudes encouraged social groups to establish a corporate presence in the sociopolitical arena and celebrate alliances with other interests to support mutually beneficial policies (such as the "steel-rye" alliance to which many assign a momentous negative influence on the political course of the Second Reich).

The tardy development of a corporate presence on the part of the landed elite was, however, not exclusively due to its unchallenged position as the first beneficiary of an equally unchallenged policy. At least equally important was that elite's only gradual emergence as a specific social group detached from the magma of the propertied classes. It can be argued that the landed elite was to a considerable extent a creation, and not just a beneficiary, of the expansion of the export economy, and that it had risen in the framework of a *porteño* rural society so completely reshaped in the course of that expansion that it should also be seen as a new creation.

The ambivalent partner the landed classes had found in the state appeared considerably more mature; its significant headstart is reflected in the very fact that the new rural society with a more powerful landed elite at its core matured most quickly in the new lands the state was conquering from the Indian nations. The precocious maturity of the state strengthened the importance it was to retain in the history of the landed elite.

The initial moment in that history can safely be set in 1820, when the defeat of the national army by the provincial *caudillos* of the riverine provinces of Santa Fe and Entre Rios brought about the dissolution of the revolutionary state that in 1810 had inherited its power from the Spanish viceroys. This defeat ended Argentine participation in the wars of Spanish-American Independence. The province of Buenos Aires, which inherited what had survived of the revolutionary government's military and administrative apparatus, was then born as a child of defeat and was forced to accept a humiliating unequal alliance with the victors. But only a few months later the new province more than doubled its territory by pushing the Indian frontier from the line of the Salado River, reached in the 1780s, to the *sierras* of Tandil.

In 1823, after a new military campaign, the Indian nations confirmed their recognition of the new frontier. Finally, in the aftermath of yet another campaign led by Rosas in 1833, Indian resistance was successfully countered by the alliance with subsidized *indios amigos* who served as a barrier against the incursions of the only nominally pacified semisedentary populations of the rest of the Pampas. These policies carried obvious long-term dangers. (Califucurá, who by midcentury was to emerge as the most formidable and defiant Indian leader, had slowly built his base of support within the framework of this system of subsidized alliances.) But during the first stages of pastoral expansion these policies served the purpose remarkably well.

Indian resistance had been stiffened by the unexpectedly speedy occupation of the new territories, in the course of a pastoral boom that—as mentioned above—transformed the Buenos Aires *campaña* into the most important source of River Plate pastoral exports. By the mid 1820s a rough estimate was that two-thirds of Platine exports originated in the new province, and up to midcentury its share was to remain consistently higher than half these exports. Such expansion went hand in hand with the massive private appropriation of public land, first in emphyteusis (long-term rentals at a very low fixed payment), and then from the thirties through sales and more conventional rental arrangements. The barriers established by law against excessive land concentration, systematically ignored from the start, were eventually eliminated, together with emphyteusis.

A new group of much larger and more affluent landowners than in the colonial past was thus being created. Only some of its members belonged to colonial landowning families; most were recruited from the ranks of the Buenos Aires urban political and economic elite, the latter including by then the foreign-born beneficiaries of free trade.

These new actors in the rural scene didn't allow their urban roots to wither; even large-scale stock raising found a natural complement in mercantile, transportation, and financial activities best managed from the city. (Revealingly, even in the 1840s Felipe Senillosa, whom we would describe as a landowner, chose instead to describe himself as a merchant.) This circumstance—and the extremely primitive conditions in the pastoral frontier—made for a landowning class whose most affluent members were absentee owners, although few of them went as far as the richest of them all, Nicolás Anchorena, who according to legend boasted of never having set foot in his vast territorial empire (including the largest *estancia* in the whole province, with 410 dwellers in 1838).

The consolidation of this new class was much favored by the new political order emerging in Buenos Aires after the breakdown of the revolutionary central state in 1820. Conflicts lasting from February to October of that year were resolved by a victory of rural army and militia forces against the factions brought to the fore by popular urban agitation.

In 1821, while the homicidal rivalries among its victors allowed Buenos Aires to reconquer its hegemony in the Littoral, a new institutional framework was put in place in the new province. A set of basic laws (*leyes fundamentales*) created a legislature, elected yearly in polls open to practically all adult males; the legislature in turn elected a governor for a three-year period. With the abolition of the *cabildos* of Buenos Aires and Luján, the rural administrative, judiciary, and police authorities were also appointed by the legislature, for one-year terms that could be renewed indefinitely.

Within this institutional framework a short period of peace and prosperity was inaugurated, which would later be remembered with universal heartfelt nostalgia. From 1821 to 1824 a military reform pruned the bloated officers' corps inherited from the Independence wars; the province converted its vast floating debt into a regular public debt, which held its own surprisingly well in the market; and the pastoral boom sustained an expansion in trade that enhanced private prosperity and alleviated fiscal stringency, both reflected in public and private urban improvements.

The return to peace was followed by a cultural renaissance and a rebirth of the aspirations to a more polished society. Now political figures proudly proclaimed their roots in the socioeconomic elite. In contrast with the professional politicians of the revolutionary era who, "having nothing to lose," had aspired only to personal gain and aggrandizement, the first allegiance of the new political leaders went to the propertied classes. Their first commitment went to social normalization and economic improvements in which they had no less but also no more at stake than all other members of these classes.

The new rulers liked to be known as the Partido del Orden, and the order they were determined to enforce fully reflected their programmatic identification with the propertied classes. Thus in their attitude toward the popular masses, both when reinforcing old norms (such as those requiring rural non–property owners to carry an employment certificate, a *papeleta de conchabo*) and when introducing new ones (such as those forbidding most forms of mendicancy and strictly regulating the ones still tolerated), their main concern appears to have been to create a legal obligation for non–property owners to make themselves available in the labor market.

Even so, the relations between the state and the propertied classes were from the start more complex than these program statements suggest. Even after its successful financial normalization, the state absorbed a large fraction of the provincial resources. In the golden years 1821–1824, the level of government expenditures reached more than half the value of Buenos Aires exports. And, while the tax system spared property owners (the *contribución directa*, a new tax on assets, was universally recognized as a joke because of blatant underassessment), and taxes on exports were just a fraction of those on imports, more than half the revenue from the latter (which accounted by themselves for more than 80 percent of total tax revenue) fell on goods consumed by the social elite. Whatever its other virtues might be, the new provincial state didn't come cheap.

Moreover, its demands were not exclusively financial. The army, while reduced in numbers after the end of the Independence wars, was still a sizable body, and its personnel demands conflicted with those of a pastoral boom in chronic need of new hands. This area of potential conflict was also to become, however, an area of accommodation—by using the army as a penal institution to enforce the antivagrancy and antimendicancy laws. Accommodation required, however, for the state to restrain its demands within reasonable limits and, perhaps even more important, to be able convincingly to justify them in terms of its commitment to the goals of social tranquility and quick economic progress dear to the economic elite of the province. Thus, military demands were more easily accepted when geared toward the expansion and defense of the provincial territory along the Indian frontier. As long as this basic element in the compact between political and socioeconomic elites was respected, the former were allowed to entertain the most controversial innovations (from Lancasterian schools to a reform of convents and monasteries with the avowed intention of suppressing as many of them as possible).

While proclaiming its identity of origins and orientation with the propertied classes, the political elite zealously maintained control of its own power bases. On this point it was helped by an electoral system haphazardly developed during the first revolutionary decade, that left as its unintended legacy an almost universal male franchise. In the city this created an electoral body far too large to be manipulated by its social betters, and one that was sullenly, if passively, hostile to the new compact between the state and the propertied classes. The latter were happy to leave to the government the task of ensuring satisfactory electoral results by mobilizing the public employees and, when necessary, the army rank and file. In the countryside the lack of a previous politicization comparable to that of the urban masses ensured the undisputed electoral dominance of the forces of order. However, even here the influence of the landed classes was limited by an electoral system in which the whole *campaña* formed a single district, and in which only an improbable alliance of the largest landowners in most rural *partidos* (counties) would have stood a chance against the list of pro-government candidates to the legislature, zealously supported everywhere by the rural justices appointed by the legislature, who were in charge of the polls. While in the countryside the commitment to the collective interests of the propertied classes was a more stringent requirement to ensure the electoral victory of governmental candidates, and some of these candidates happened to have close links with some rural districts, even there their electoral roots in the landed elites or elsewhere in rural society were less decisive in ensuring their election than governmental favor.

From the beginning, then, the state was too affluent and the political elite too independent for both to abide for long the role of completely subservient political agents of the propertied classes. By the midtwenties, politics as conflict returned with a vengeance to Buenos Aires. The leaders of the Partido del Orden led an attempt to recreate the central state that precipitated a civil war and also welcomed a war with Brazil that brought about a return to the crushing military expenditures of the previous decade. When a Brazilian blockade closed Buenos Aires to overseas trade and deprived the treasury of its most important source of revenue, the resulting paper money inflation added to the misery caused by the paralysis of overseas trade.

At that critical moment a political leader rose from the ranks of the new landowning class: Juan Manuel de Rosas, who had made a fortune first as a cattle merchant and salting-plant owner and already by 1820 was acquiring land and settling cattle *estancias* in which, at least in this early formative period, he untypically retained a managerial role. Rosas shared his peers' deep distrust of the postrevolutionary political class, a distrust that the catastrophic blunders of the luminaries of the Party of Order turned into irreconcilable hostility. But he was also convinced that party politics were an ineliminable fact of life in the River Plate provinces, a polity that regrettably had been born democratic. In his opinion the only way to save the social order from the ravages of political democracy was for the political leadership to channel the masses' political passions in directions that, while flattering their uneducated instincts, would reorient their energies toward objectives compatible with those of the propertied classes. Thus a protective barrier would be raised against the potential consequences of the envy of the have-nots (*los que no tienen*) against their betters.[9]

The compact he thus proposed to the socioeconomic elite was more self-serving than it sounded. The socioeconomic elite was to receive protection against a social danger perhaps less pressing than it appeared to Rosas's truculent prophetic imagination. But the price was enormous: it included the total and permanent subordination of the landed elite to its savior. The compact was accepted, however, and with good reason: in 1829 Rosas appeared as indeed the only leader able to extricate the province, if not from the dangers of an unlikely social war, then from a return to the chaotic situation created by the foolish and self-serving policies of the previous political establishment. When the propertied classes discovered that their new savior was ruthlessly committed to a political agenda even costlier than the one that had brought ruin to the Partido del Orden, it also found out that it had already lost the ability to act on such a discovery. The rabid factional passions Rosas had carefully kindled allowed him to create a system of political control that imposed universal participation in public rituals of allegiance to the ruler's faction, under the vigilance of a remarkably efficient security apparatus that kept personal political records for tens of thousands of *porteños*.

Thus the propertied classes became captive supporters of policies that, in order to end factional strife and external war, imposed rabid factionalization and, since 1837, permanent war. But, while carrying on policies that eventually provoked two European blockades, Rosas strove tenaciously, and with remarkable success, to limit the damage these policies brought to the Buenos Aires economy. He systematically turned to inflation (from the consequences of which the stock raisers-exporters were of course protected) to limit public expenditure, notwithstanding the massive expansion of the province's police and military personnel. Thus the pastoral boom, while of course suffering from temporary interruptions, didn't lose its momentum. By 1850 the River Plate exported pastoral staples worth two million pounds (ten times the prerevolutionary figures), and between 1822 and 1854 the share of the *campaña* in the provincial population (itself risen from 118,646 to 267,937 inhabitants) rose from 53 percent to 63 percent.[10]

These impressive achievements fostered, however, the conviction (propagated in part by Rosas's exiled adversaries) that, were it not for his idiosyncratic policies, economic progress would have been even more rapid. Not surprisingly, the burdens from these policies were much resented in the countryside. In 1839 the French blockade was in part responsible for the rebellion of the Libres del Sur: militia gauchos by the thousands were led to battle by their officers, most of them second-rank *estancieros*, only to be crushed by the army garrisons of the Indian frontier. The episode offered several lessons to the propertied classes, the most important being that the state and its agents were too powerful to be defied even in these classes' rural fortresses. And the state's grip on the pastoral areas was further strengthened by the outcome of the ill-fated rebellion. Now its local agents, men of proven Rosista loyalty still selected on a yearly basis by the completely domesticated legislature, were feared not only by the landless majority but by the landowners themselves, who knew very well that one of their tasks was to keep the rolls of local friends and enemies of the regime properly updated. Such fear was intensified by another lesson from the episode: namely that, when pushed to the extreme, even a regime solemnly committed to protect the social standing and the property rights of the respectable classes couldn't be counted on to honor such a commitment. Not only did the repression include executions of members of those classes, but it was followed by massive confiscations of rebel properties, which became even more frequent with the recrudescence of civil war in the early forties.

Not surprisingly, until the fall of Rosas we hear very little about the complaints of the propertied classes. The reasons to complain were, however, very much there. Among the damaging consequences of the conflicts caused by Rosas's uncompromising attitude toward political dissidents and in his external conflicts, the intensified competition between the *estancia* and the army for the rurals who were to provide personnel for both was perhaps the most intensely resented. As mentioned above, from 1837 to the fall of the dictator in 1852, Buenos Aires waged continuous wars against Rosas's political enemies in other River Plate provinces and the new republic of Uruguay. The constant pressing of rurals into the army appeared more objectionable than in the past, because it now served Rosas's unfathomable political designs rather than the task of garrisoning the Indian frontier, which of course the landowners considered to be very much in the public interest.

After 1852, while it became again possible to discuss the aspirations of the landed classes in the open, the reasons for their discontent were not eliminated. The fall of Rosas was followed by an attempt to organize a Federalist constitutional regime under the leadership of General Urquiza, the former Rosista governor of Entre Rios who had won the decisive battle that sent the aged dictator to a British exile. Led by an alliance of anti-Rosista exiles and former Rosista worthies, Buenos Aires rebelled against Urquiza, whom it denounced as unworthy of leading the country in the new constitutional era because of his Rosista past.

For seven years Buenos Aires refused to enter the Argentine Confederation. After two civil wars, in 1859 and 1861, General Bartolomé Mitre, the ablest political leader in the ranks of the Buenos Aires dissidents, finally won the presidency of a unified Argentina. Urquiza accepted the outcome with comparative good grace, but his followers in the Interior launched two civil wars and could only be suppressed after new and costly campaigns. To make things worse, once again the conflict crossed state boundaries into Uruguay. In 1865—when Brazil's military campaign against the Blanco government of Montevideo, and Mitre's only nominally secret support for the Colorado General Flores's Cruzada Libertadora, brought about a Paraguayan attack against Brazil and eventually Argentina—an unexpectedly costly and bloody international war ensued, which ended only in 1870.

Not only did the draft remain as oppressive as under Rosas, but the defense of the Indian frontier was now comparatively neglected. In late 1852, when the frontier garrisons, after offering their support to the Buenos Aires dissidents, joined Urquiza's failed attempt to impose a friendly government on the province, they were replaced by a more loyal but less effective frontier force. To make things worse, the Indian foe was rendered more formidable by the new situation. The *indios amigos*, skillfully playing on the divisions among the Christians, routinely subjected the *campaña* to highly profitable raids now reaching even long-settled areas that had been free from such attacks for decades.

These raids were even more profitable because amid so many uncertainties the pace of the pastoral boom had further accelerated, with wool gradually replacing hides as the first staple in Platine exports. Buenos Aires had never known such prosperity. But at the same time the contradictions that Rosas's enemies, now in power, had so bitingly denounced before 1852 had only become more glaring and more abrupt. The chorus of complaints was now incessant, but the querulous or indignant words were followed by very little action. Certainly prosperity didn't favor outbursts of militant action on the part of the propertied classes. In addition, the grip of the state on the countryside was as strong as ever: the appointment of local authorities in the *campaña* continued in the time-honored way, and these authorities had added to their traditional functions that of getting electoral results agreeable to the faction in power in Buenos Aires (which was now less a matter of course than under Rosas, when nobody in his senses had dreamed of opposing the official candidates). Thus an additional reason had been created for the state to support the local authorities to the hilt as long as they delivered the vote by means as brutal as might be required.

The landowners were aware that, if pushed to a corner, the post-Rosista political leadership, while fully mastering the honeyed language of enlightened constitutionalism, was as ready as Rosas to defend its power with all the resources inherited from the ruthless and destructive traditions of factional war. While proclaiming its religious respect for the sacred character of property rights, the new regime presided over the confiscation of the fugitive dictator's estates (most of which he had acquired before reaching power). Even more disturbing, in 1858, when the tenant farmers in Chivilcoy, a grain-growing district in western Buenos Aires, refused to pay rents to their landlords, who had been beneficiaries of Rosas's grants of public land to reward political or military services, the grants were nullified and property transferred to the farmers. Amid a journalistic firestorm, Mitre, usually the voice of moderation in social matters, denounced large *estancias* as a shameful relic of colonial feudalism, and Sarmiento quoted in his incendiary articles the passages from the New Testament already favored by the 1848 Christian Socialists for their revolutionary propaganda. The reaction of the landed interests was then remarkably muted; only the conviction that the people in power, enmeshed as they were at that moment in a struggle for survival, were ready to respond very harshly to any interference in their plans, can explain this otherwise enigmatic silence.

Such reluctance to offer challenges liable to achieve potentially destabilizing political repercussions didn't extend to discussions dealing in loftier and more general terms with the negative role of the state in the *campaña*. The silent acquiescence of the Rosas era had been replaced by a combination of a careful avoidance of such challenges and an abstract audacity of political and ideological discourse that invites comparison with Porfirian (and not only Porfirian) Mexico.

In these circumstances, a small group of enlightened landowners took upon itself the twofold task of giving a voice to the aspirations of their peers and inviting them to engage in an ambitious transformation, or rather regeneration, that would allow the landed classes to conquer the leadership position that was rightfully theirs in *porteño* and Argentine society. Already ten years before the foundation of the *Sociedad Rural Argentina* in 1866, its first president, Eduardo Olivera, then a young man writing to his father from Europe, had sketched for his native Buenos Aires a new social profile modelled on that of Victorian England. In the home of the Industrial Revolution he had discovered a landowning class universally recognized as the first in society, both in the countryside (where the subordinate classes looked up to it for guidance and support in the defense of their legitimate aspirations) and in the nation at large, which it led in its strivings for technical improvement and economic progress.[11] For the *porteño* landowners to win such preeminence in their own province, Olivera believed, they needed to renounce their absenteeism, their routine-bound hostility to the introduction of technological improvements in the *estancia*, their lack of leadership in the promotion of social and cultural improvements in the *campaña*, their supine passivity in matters of public interest, and their reluctance to make their potentially overwhelming clout fully felt in public and political life.

The self-appointed guides of the landed elite even provided it with an ideology intended to lend legitimacy to the claim for a leading role it had been until then so reluctant to articulate. Its most important axiom proclaimed a total harmony of interests between the landowners and the rest of the rurals. The landowners' economic power, social respectability and influence, and intimate connections with the urban elites designated them as the most effective available representatives of the rural interests in the political arenas. They could be entrusted with such a role because they didn't need to fear the temptation of pushing an agenda better tailored to their specific sectorial interests than to those of the *campaña* as a whole. The total identity between the former and the latter ensured that in defending their self-interest they also engaged in a public-spirited defense of a much larger cause.

Obviously, there were some issues in connection with which such identity of interests did indeed exist, and it was these issues that offered the best opportunity to create a current of opinion able not only to mobilize the landowners as a group but—equally important—to persuade the landless rurals to accept the corporate organizations of the landed class as their natural advocates. This was easier when dealing with issues opposing the *campaña* as a whole to other interests or social sectors. Thus, the constant hammering of the *Anales de la Sociedad Rural Argentina* on the dearth of credit and outrageous rates of interest plaguing the rural economy would arouse no negative response in the countryside. But the most obvious outside actor to confront was, now as before, the state. The cooperation and rivalry between the state and the stock raisers for the control of the landless rurals, while maintaining the basic features established in the 1820s, was being modified in its impact on that landless population in ways that made the claim of solidarity between the state and the *estancieros* more credible than in the past. The growing numbers of immigrant rural workers exempt from the draft, added to the exceptional demands of civil and external wars, intensified the pressure on landless natives, to the point that certificates of employment didn't always offer sufficient protection. By the late sixties even petty tenant stock raisers and *estancia* workers who received a share in the product in lieu of wages were included among the independent entrepreneurs whom the law assumed to be affluent enough to pay for a *personero*, a salaried volunteer to replace themselves in the ranks.

From the seventies on, thanks to the end of the Paraguayan war, the issue progressively lost its urgency, until in 1879 the conquest of the Indian territory finally eliminated the last remnants of the system. While the role of the state as claimant for the human resources of the countryside lost salience, its role as the creator of the legal and institutional framework for the deep transformations Argentine society was undergoing became more significant. Thus, the debates around the projected codes of civil, commercial, and rural law demanded the active participation of the representatives of the rural interests, and more specifically, of the landed classes.

Should this corporate participation in public life have included a specifically political role for the rural elite? Some landowners linked to the Sociedad rural supported political reforms that would have facilitated such a role, on the lines of those insistently proposed in *El Rio de la Plata*, the newspaper published by Jose Hernandez in 1869–1870.[12] The creation of popularly elected municipalities, and the transformation of the justices of the peace, until then agents appointed by the provincial government, into equally elected local magistrates, would finally transfer local power to the true representatives of the populations under their authority. By making authorities more responsive to local needs and demands, by creating for the first time a democratic power base in the countryside, decentralization would allow the landowners to acquire the political clout they were entitled to exert, because the new democratic institutions would faithfully reflect the views of a society that spontaneously recognized these landowners as its legitimate political leaders.

When the provincial constitution of 1874 introduced elective municipalities and (only fleetingly) justices of the peace, the impact however was minimal, and it is not difficult to understand why: the former agents of the central administration had now an even more pressing interest in manipulating elections. For the results to be validated by the provincial authorities they had to be equally satisfactory to these authorities, and thus the unholy alliance between the corrupt petty tyrants of the countryside and a provincial authority indifferent to the aspirations of the rural classes was strengthened by the reforms introduced to eliminate the grip of provincial authority on the countryside. Once again, the *ruralistas* refused to accept this explanation, which in their opinion begged the question. The reform had offered an opportunity for the landowning class to challenge the power of the local agents of the provincial state, and the opportunity had been passed over. With a landowning class regenerated by the strenuous self-improvement preached by the *ruralistas*, the reaction would have been quite different.

When even affluent landowners in depressingly large numbers were apparently ready to act as fences for the rustlers who robbed their fellow landowners, it was difficult to avoid the conclusion that the landed classes hadn't as yet acquired the class consciousness required to perform the political role the enlightened *ruralistas* had assigned them. As the *ruralistas* liked to stress, this deficient class consciousness had other consequences. One was the landowners' reluctance to move to the countryside, and act there as catalysts for change. Another was their excessively individualistic approach to their relations with the state, which made them prefer the search for personal contacts with influential figures to corporate public action. Critics argued that these tendencies were even more directly responsible for the landed classes' inability to become the natural leaders of the rural populations at large.

While these criticisms had merit, they ignored what political activity was both more difficult and perhaps less necessary than they assumed. When tracing the profile of a regenerated rural society in the Pampas they didn't reproduce any specific existing model. In all of their implicit or explicit terms of reference a comparatively large sector of the rural population appeared solidly incorporated into a hierarchical order that, while created by a centuries-long process, appeared dynamic enough to have successfully adapted to the conditions of commercialized agriculture. Thus in England, but also in France, the enlightened landowners who led the battle for agricultural progress enjoyed a privileged position in what still was, for all its new cult of agricultural productivity, a deferential society. In those blessed regions the social cohesiveness built on such sturdy traditions survived in a radically new context because even those who occupied less privileged positions in the social hierarchy had a stake in it. No doubt, day laborers, who could be found everywhere, were confined to the margins, both in economic and in social terms, but their marginalization added to the homogeneity of the powerful rural block that willingly followed the lead of the largest landowners.

But the conditions in Buenos Aires were vastly different, so different indeed that it can be doubted whether these examples were truly relevant there. The *ruralistas* argued that they were relevant. While they were the first to stress the distance between these admirable models and the dismal local conditions, they attributed them to the universal rural backwardness and especially to the immaturity of the landowning class. Once these shortcomings were corrected, conditions comparable to those found in these privileged European corners would finally emerge on the shores of the River Plate. But could all the differences be imputed to the backwardness of the *campaña*? Let us for the moment ignore the very different historical background—though since the very inception of the Spanish American colonial societies the role of the state in shaping them to serve its own objectives had created different attitudes to public life and had lent these societies a radically different social configuration from what could be found in the Old World. This difference could hardly be ignored when prospecting possible and desirable changes in the relations between the political and the socioeconomic elites in Spanish America.

Leaving this retrospective consideration aside, the *ruralistas* were perhaps too hasty in ascribing to backwardness all the negative features they found in the present. Sometimes this imputation was plainly wrong. For example, Olivera linked the stagnation in grain production to the high rates of interest for short-term credit, and attributed these rates simply to the absence of a modern banking system in the countryside, which left the small farmers at the mercy of merchants doubling as moneylenders. But he conveniently ignored the fact that, while this could explain the difference between the rates forced on these farmers and those available in the city for favored borrowers, even the latter were much too high to sustain the desired expansion in grain agriculture. High interest rates prevailed not because of insufficiently modern attitudes but because the available capital couldn't easily accommodate the rising demand created by the sustained rural boom.

It was on the strength of such dubious assumptions that Olivera proposed the creation of a state-owned rural bank to provide cheaper credit. Once again he was disappointed in his efforts to recruit the support of his fellow landowners; while his peers were probably too unsophisticated to see where his argument went wrong, in this case their robust skepticism toward his calls for melioristic action was better justified than he liked to believe.[13]

An even more important implicit assumption of the *ruralistas* was that, as soon as the landed classes abandoned their passivity, they would gather the support of a rural population unanimously eager to march under their banners. This assumption was equally problematic. True, both apologists and critics of the *porteño* landowning class coincided in projecting an image of the countryside as a collection of cattle and sheep *estancias* whose *peones*, numerically predominant in the rural population, had been disciplined to acquiesce to a socioeconomic order ruled, if not by the landowners themselves, then at least by their agents acting on their behalf and for their benefit. The *ruralistas* had this social profile in mind when arguing that in order to win the political leadership of the countryside the landed classes needed only to extend into the political arena the undisputed authority they wielded in society.

Even had this image of rural society been valid, it didn't follow from it that *estancia* workers offered a readily available base for the political hegemony of the landowners in the countryside. Again, let us ignore historical background, although every testimony suggests that the Platine pastoral society, while abruptly unequal, was far from deferential. (Rosas was fond of reminiscing on the manifold occasions when, as a novel *estanciero* trying to impose his authority on his workers, he had been forced to withstand the attacks of threatening *peones* who brandished their daggers dangerously close to his throat; while the dictator was fond of embellishing his memories with the help of a truculent imagination, even these fantasies needed a base in reality.) Further, the role of a centrally controlled judiciary and police power in the disciplining of the landless rurals couldn't fail to weaken even further the claim to undivided social hegemony on the part of the landed classes.

The conditions under which the pastoral boom took place imposed forms of labor organization detrimental to the creation of a large and stable *estancia* population. The latter did not have the time and leisure required for the consolidation of the links on whose strength the landed classes would have been able to claim a leading political role. The sustained boom ensured that labor would always be scarce, and hence comparatively expensive; for both reasons it was as difficult as it was inadvisable to retain workers in the *estancia* for longer than strictly needed. From early on, in both the highest and the lowest fringe of pastoral labor, instability became the rule. At the top, specialized workers received daily wages several times higher than those of the permanent *peones* and took charge of taming, branding, or castrating cattle; since midcentury, less well-paid itinerants in much larger numbers roamed the wool districts to shear the sheep; even before the start of the pastoral boom, grain agriculture depended on temporary labor from the cities or from the Interior, and low-paid temporary workers had a large place even in stock raising. No doubt, at intermediate levels of the labor force more permanent *estancia* workers could be found: overseers and, in establishments too large to function as a single unit for most routine tasks, *puesteros* in charge of tasks in separate sections of the *estancia*. Their numbers were, however, too low for their presence to ensure the rise of a rural society comparable in stability and spontaneous acceptance of the hegemony of the landed class with the European examples the *ruralistas* held dear.

There was yet another obstacle for such a desired development: as the 1869 national census revealed, not all pastoral production was based on *estancias* functioning as centralized enterprises with a hierarchical-authoritarian organization. Much of it was in charge of tenants, some of them quite substantial stock raisers, others tending only a small number of animals; in other arrangements cowboys were put in charge of an equally reduced number of the landowner's cattle and were paid with a share in the offspring. In the wool districts, while arrangements whereby the landowners rented land to independent shepherds for a share in the clip were less common than they had been in the fifties, when such shepherds (immigrants from Ireland and the Basque regions of France and Spain) were scarcer, they were still relatively frequent. As a result, and notwithstanding the extreme concentration of land property, for the provincial population at large the census category of *estancieros y ganaderos por cuenta propia* (landowners and independent stock raisers) with 6.9 percent of the Argentine-born economically active males in the province, was only slightly less numerous than that of *peones rurales* (rural laborers), which reached 7.4 percent.[14]

Even more tellingly, the former category reached 19.4 percent of all Argentine-born males active in the primary economy; had they been a true social group and not just a census category, their weight would by itself have ensured the emergence of the social profile desired by the *ruralistas*. But they were nothing of the sort; the link between the landless entrepreneurs and the landowners with whom they contracted was a necessarily ambivalent one, and the boom, by creating a fluid market for such contracts, allowed the former to act according to this ambivalence; they didn't offer favorable material for the making of a deferential society.

A glimpse of the social profile reflected in the census figures can be obtained from *El gaucho Martín Fierro*, the gaucho poem published by José Hernández in 1872, soon to become the most successful bestseller for all of Spanish America in its time. Admittedly, what Hernández offers is not a neutral portrait of pastoral society, but a highly stylized presentation of the predicament of the gaucho. While his originality and poetic genius was to ensure him a towering place in Argentine literature rivalled only by Sarmiento, there was nothing original about his ideological inspiration; in *Martín Fierro* he offers as faithful an echo of the *ruralistas* as in his newspaper articles of 1869–1870. His ideological bias may explain his total concentration on the arbitrary recruitment practices and the corrupt and oppressive administrative ways of the state in the sorry life of the gauchos. That bias may also explain his refusal to consider the possibility that once the state's sinister influence was eliminated, the life of a landless *peone* might still be anything less than blissful. Hernández's focus on the exploitative role of the state tended, of course, to absolve landowners of responsibility. But what is intriguing is that, in Hernández's portrayal, landowners have no role at all; they are simply not there.

And why should they be? While Hernández, who stylizes his central character as the archetypal gaucho, doesn't dwell on his specific position in the pastoral economy, he describes it in passing but with total precision: Fierro, after buying cattle with money he made betting on and taking part with his own horse in *carreras cuadreras* (similar to quarterhorse races), settled as an independent minor stock raiser on rented land. There was no reason for a landowner to occupy a central place in his story.

Admittedly, the social profile reflected in the census figures and implicitly in Hernández's poem was soon to suffer significant changes. The seventies witnessed the massive wire fencing of the pastoral areas. The impact of fencing on both the organization of the *estancia* and its social relations was almost immediately felt: by the eighties it was already obvious that, in order to satisfy the more stringent technological and organizational standards necessary to produce higher quality cattle and sheep, *estancias* were moving closer to the model of centralized, unified enterprises. Simultaneously, with the end of the Indian wars, while the state abandoned its claim to the hands needed by the pastoral economy, the threat of the draft disappeared as an inducement for the landless rurals to take up jobs in *estancias*. Some concerned landowners proposed alternative antivagrancy legal measures, but the provincial rural code of 1864 (otherwise very favorable to the landed interest) didn't include any. Even in their absence the recruitment of *estancia* personnel apparently didn't pose problems as acute as in the past. All this suggests some underlying changes that favored the consolidation of the landowners' hegemony on rural society.

Other inveterate hindrances to such a consolidation now carried more weight than in the past. From the start of the pastoral expanion in frontier areas, *estancias* hadn't developed the ancillary activities that would have made them more self-contained, socially and economically, because both labor and women were scarce. Thus, the very few women in the *estancias* didn't have any spare time for the domestic weaving, for example, that still had a very significant place in the economy of the Interior. There were still other reasons to discourage diversification of productive activities; a more diversified production would have been less easily controllable by the landowner's agent. A more diversified production risked strengthening the rival trade networks manned by peddlers (the notorious *pulperías volantes*, illegal since colonial times but never completely eradicated) or even by the regular *pulperos*, managers of the rural general stores, who couldn't be trusted not to dabble in irregular (and even criminal) but lucrative deals. (They were frequently suspected of trading in hides of stolen cattle.)

Thus, when Rosas in his *Instrucciones a sus mayordomos de estancia* (first written in 1819 and expanded in 1825)[15] forbade the *peones* or their women-folk to raise chickens, he was being less unreasonable than his enlightened critics were to assume by the end of the century. While chickens could have provided a cheap source of food for *estancia* workers, they already had a market value (trade to the capital was so significant that the number of poultry entering its markets was included in official statistics together with those of livestock) and would have created dangerous temptations both for the *peones* and the agents of those rival networks.

But this concern didn't go far enough for the *estancieros* to take charge themselves of the functions of the *pulperias*; except for the larger *estancias*, even the staples customarily provided the workers as a complement to money wages were purchased in these local stores. There were of course good reasons for this. In most *estancias* the workers were too few to justify the creation of a separate supply system. But the consequences were obvious: a constant vigilance was needed for the *estanciero* to keep adequate economic control of his workers.

There were other, less conflictive ways in which this obsessive concentration on the raising of livestock limited the ability of *estancia* labor relations to influence social relations in the countryside at large. With transportation contracted out (except for cattle in the largest *estancias*), a large number of people (*arrieros*, carters, and such) active in the rural economy were outside the social structure of the *estancia*. While only a minority of these transportation workers were independent petty entrepreneurs, most of them worked instead for specialized enterprises, themselves usually rather small, but a few quite significant.

Both the transport workers and the *pulperos* controlled the links between the *estancia* workers and the world at large. While the first can be compared to the *colporteurs* who, in the wine districts of Restoration France, were feared as dangerous to the *ordre moral*, the *pulperos* were even more influential. The *pulpero* offered more than just the mercantile link with outside innovations; by necessity literate (albeit sometimes barely so), it was he who read aloud the news and editorials in the city papers to an avid public made up of *peones* in the several *estancias* of the area he served. Rosas knew this very well, and his awareness of the role of the *pulpero* in shaping rural public opinion is well reflected in the attention he dispensed them during his political tug-of-war with the dissident Federalists in 1832–1834.[16]

The economic progress that was gradually introducing a tighter centralization into the *estancia* also favored the expansion and diversification of the economic activities developing outside of it. Already in the forties the forts and trading posts of the Buenos Aires *campaña* were developing into tiny villages supplied with unexpected amenities by an array of specialized merchants, from bakers to cobblers. The creation of a secondary urban network in the *campaña* gathered speed in the second half of the century. Slightly later, agriculture started its dramatic expansion, and by 1914 Buenos Aires was the first producer of grain in the nation. Even within the rural production tenant farmers and sharecroppers enjoyed very little stability on the land. And they lacked any feeling of allegiance to their landowner, seeing the relationship with him as inherently conflictive. These tenant farmers were now more numerous than workers and managers active in stock raising. Only a small, and diminishing, fraction of the rural population was still integrated into the tightening social order of the modernized *estancia*.

The electoral consequences became evident when the electoral reform of 1912 introduced an honest count of the votes. In Buenos Aires province, the stronghold of the landowning classes, their retinue of *estancia* workers, while usually loyal enough, had a very limited influence on the outcome. The conservative forces that offered the most congenial political home for most large landowners found it almost impossible to escape the fate of a permanent minority party; paradoxically, their hopes were now pinned on the industrial suburbs of the now federalized city of Buenos Aires, and in the countryside their most solid bases were in districts with comparatively divided land property patterns (such as the vineyards in the *partido* of San Nicolás and the dairy belt around Exaltación de la Cruz).

The landed classes' lack of electoral clout doesn't mean that they had lost, or had never enjoyed, the awesome political clout common wisdom attributed to them. But the electoral debacle of the conservative forces confirms that the source of that clout was not in the landowners' ability to use their position in the rural economy to fashion a social order that would have made of them the natural leaders in the countryside.

By then the landed elite were both less and more than that: they had finally become, as Olivera had wanted, the first estate in the realm. They had at least partially acquired the features anticipated in Olivera's idealized portrait; among old landowning families the self-conscious, half-ashamed feelings Nicolás Anchorene had harbored toward the rustic source of his affluence had been replaced by an intense pride in their territorial empires, where they built massive residences that served as monuments to their own success. (From the 1920s on, Chapadmalal, the palatial master's residence in the Martinez de Hoz *estancia* on the Atlantic shore, regularly lodged illustrious guests of the state, from the Prince of Wales down.) For those who had prospered in other branches of the economy the possession of a substantial *estancia* offered the only unimpeachable proof that they had indeed reached the top.

Even before the landed classes reached their final apotheosis, their recognized social eminence had achieved equally recognized political conse-quences. In 1857, in the series of articles in which Mitre prospected the articulation of his Party of Freedom with the different sectors of Buenos Aires society, he described the landed interest not as a group whose militant support he had received or even aspired to receive, but rather as one placed above the political sphere, whose approval was more essential for achieving political legitimacy than even the most enthusiastic support of less eminent social actors.[17]

It is then not surprising that those members of the landed elite who cared to enter politics found it easy to reach eminent (if not always influential) positions in the Conservative (and for that matter, the Radical) Party. Even then, however, their political roots were not in rural society. In the 1920s and in both parties the substantial landowners were mostly found in the *grupo metropolitano*, based in the city of Buenos Aires, enjoying the privileged connections with the national political elite and foreign economic interests that came with their acknowledged place at the summit of the national socioeconomic hierarchy. But not even in the pastoral districts did that national preeminence protect them from the successful political challenges coming from locally rooted rivals of humbler social extraction.[18]

Thus the political eminence the landed elite could obtain for the asking was a less effective political asset than would appear at first glance. How much this was the case became evident only when the conflictive dimension (always present in the link between the landed elite and the state) was again brought to the fore in the course of the twentieth century.

The tensions between the landed elite and the state had gradually lost intensity during the last quarter of the previous century. As the anti-Rosista exiles had rightly anticipated, the propertied classes were the first beneficiaries of the gradual elimination of arbitrary practices in the administration and the judiciary. The elimination of areas of conflict was favored not only by the end of the Indian wars but by the impact of economic progress on the rural lifestyle and by the rise in affluence, which by putting an end to chronic fiscal penury suppressed the most effective stimulant for governmental arbitrariness. This gradual attenuation of an inveterate conflict was expected to give way to its total elimination when, after decades of socioeconomic progress, Argentina would finally be ripe for the replacement of an only nominally representative government with one truly elected by the citizenry.

When the electoral reform of 1912 lent substance to the universal franchise nominally adopted at the very start of the post-Independence era, it was soon discovered that political democratization didn't limit autonomous state power. The Radical regime brought to power in 1916 was as devoutly committed as its predecessor to the path to growth that had achieved such a signal success for a century; otherwise, the compact it offered the properties and landed classes was partially reminiscent of the one Rosas (who had been clearly committed to export-led growth) had forced on them.

This is perhaps the kernel of truth behind the otherwise preposterous description of Irigoyen as the new Rosas, much favored by his political enemies. Irigoyen's opponents couldn't reconcile themselves to his building an unbeatable electoral machine with resources that, as they monotonously reminded the public, should have gone instead to productive investments in infrastructure (such as grain elevators and silos or a national road network). Such investments, given the existing socioeconomic conditions, would of course have concentrated their benefits at the top. True, the Radical administration knew better than to tax heavily or otherwise to cut the profits and revenues of the landed interests. (Irigoyen spared landed wealth from taxation as much as had preceding regimes.) But it was bad enough, as landowners saw it, that Irigoyen used the taxes that were collected, plus foreign loans, for the expansion of the state bureaucracy, and for a substantial rise in the salaries of state employees, thus contributing not a little to the formidable expansion of the urban middle class during the twenties.

The political dangers implicit in the specific mode of political insertion of the Buenos Aires landed classes were by then becoming painfully clear. In the nineteenth century the intermittent conflict with the state had opposed the propertied classes, with the landed elite at their core, to the political power elite, while other sections of society were apparently happy to be left on the margin. Under the new conditions of the twentieth century, however, with a more complex society and with political participation extending to ever wider sections of that society, nonelite groups were not passive spectators any more, and their new presence strengthened the hand of the state in its renascent tug-of-war with the landed and properties classes. It is therefore difficult to agree to the widespread notion that the rise to power of the Radical Party didn't introduce any significant changes in the relationship between the state and these classes. The distribution of the federal budget was no trivial matter to disagree on, not when that budget was gradually approaching the level of total Argentine exports.

When the cataclysm of 1929 destroyed the world economic order that had sustained the exceptional success of the Argentine export economy, that ambiguous relationship didn't immediately lose its central place in the national life of Argentina. The agony of the society created by more than a century of export-induced prosperity was to prove a messy and protracted affair, and that society enjoyed an even longer afterlife in the national self-image. More than half a century after the end of that Argentine era, in *La República perdida*, a documentary film that offers the version of Argentine recent history currently shared by the two largest national parties, the faith in the omnipotence—though certainly not the benevolence—of the landed classes and their organization, the *Sociedad Rural Argentine*, remains as strong as ever.

NOTES

1. Sergio Bagú, *Evolución histórica de la estratificación social en la Argentina.* Caracas, 1969, 75–76.

2. H. S. Fern, "Britain's Informal Empire in Argentina," *Past and Present* 10, no. 4 (1954): 4.

3. Félix Luna, *El 45. Crónica de un año decisivo.* (Buenos Aires, 1971), p. 437.

4. See Samuel Amaral, "Trabajo y trabajadores rurales en Buenos Aires a fines del siglo XVIII," Juan Carlos Garavaglia, "¿Existieron los gauchos?," Jorge Gelman, "¿Gauchos o campesinos?," in *Anuario IEHS* 2 (Tandil, 1987), pp. 33–70, in which the authors discuss the viewpoints of Carlos A. Mayo. Ricardo Salvatore and Jonathan Brown take a different approach when studying conditions in Uruguay in "Trade and Proletarianization in Late Colonial Banda Oriental: Evidence from the Estancia de las Vacas, 1791–1805," *Hispanic American Historical Review* 67, no. 3 (Aug. 1987): 431–60. See also the polemic between these authors and Gelman in Jorge Gelman, "New Perspectives on an Old Problem and the Same Source: The Gaucho and the Rural History of the Colonial Rio de la Plata," *HAHR* 69, no. 4 (Nov. 1989): 175–32 and Salvatore and Brown, "The Old Problem of Gauchos and Rural Society," *Hispanic American Historical Review* 67, no. 3 (Aug. 1987): 733–45.

5. Mario Góngora, *Origen de los "inquilinos" en el Chile central* (Santiago: Editorial Universitaria, 1960).

6. Juan Carlos Garavaglia, "Economic Growth and Regional Differentiations: The River Plata Region at the End of the Eighteenth Century, *Hispanic American Historical Review* 65, no. 1 (1985): 51–89.

7. Ricardo Levene, "Riqueza, Industrias y Comercio Durante el Virreinato," in Academia Nacional de la Historia, *Historia de la Nación Argentina*, 2nd ed., vol. 4 (Buenos Aires: Editorial El Ateneo, 1940), sect. 1, 266.

8. On this point, see Tulio Halperin Donghi, *Guerra y finanzas en los origenes del estado Argentino (1791–1850)* (Buenos Aires: Editorial de Belgrano, 1982), 12.

9. Rosas repeatedly stated his political objectives on these terms; see, among others, his confidential remarks to the Uruguayan representative, Santiago Vázquez, on the occasion of his taking the oath of office for the first time as governor of Buenos Aires in 1829, in Julio Irazuta, *Vida política de Juan Manuel de*

Rosas a través de su correspondencia, 2d ed., vol. 1 (Buenos Aires: Editorial Albatros, 1940), sect. 1, 197.

10. Ernesto J. A. Maeder, *Evolución demográfica Argentina de 1810 a 1869* (Buenos Aires: EUDEBA, 1969), 33–35.

11. Eduardo Olivera, "La exposición de Birmingham," in Olivera, *Miscelánea* (Buenos Aires: Compañia Impresora de Billetes de Banco, 1910), 7–23.

12. On Hernández's contribution to the *ruralista* campaign, see Tulio Halperin Donghi, "*El Rio de la Plata* y la formulación de una ideología ruralista en la Argentina," chap. 6 in Halperin Donghi, *José Hernández y sus mundos* (Buenos Aires: Sudamericana-Di Tella, 1985), 231–88.

13. Eduardo Olivera, "Banco rural," in *Anales de la Sociedad Rural Argentina* 1, no. 4 (1866): 111.

14. Tulio Halperin Donghi, *loc. cit.*, 256–58, n. 11.

15. Juan Manuel de Rosas, *Instrucciones a los mayordomos de estancias* (Buenos Aires: Huemul, 1951), 56–57.

16. See on this point his letters to Vicente González, manager of his *estancia* Los Cerrillos and his political agent in the *partido* of Monte and the southwest of the province, published by Ernesto H. Celesia in his *Roses, aportes para du historia* (Buenos Aires: Peuser, 1954), 447–82.

17. Mitre published the series of articles he described as a *curso de política aplicada a la práctica* ("El Partido Gubernamental," May 15, 1857) in his paper *Los Debates*.

18. Richard J. Walter, *The Province of Buenos Aires and Argentine Politics, 1912–1943* (Cambridge: Cambridge University Press, 1985), 48–49.

Authoritarianism, Political Culture, and the Formation of the State

Landowners, Agrarian Movements, and the Making of National Politics in Nineteenth-Century Mexico and Peru

Florencia E. Mallon

We now possess myriad explanations for the failure of democracy in Latin America, as well as for the rise of authoritarianism; and the two, for obvious reasons, often go together. Some of these harken back to Latin America's colonial heritage and, in a distressingly antihistorical examination of the past, emphasize "Iberian" or "centralist" traditions, as if simply declaring the existence of a cultural tradition were enough to explain multiple and often contradictory political outcomes.[1] Guillermo O'Donnell, initially combining Robert Dahl and dependency theory, theorized that the form and timing of industrialization in Latin America resulted in a new increase (rather than further decrease) of the cost of inclusionary politics—the well-known extension of Dahl's polyarchy graph. Out of this grew perhaps the most influential modern-day explanation for authoritarianism, which highlighted capital-intensive industrialization and the inability of sociopolitical systems associated with it effectively to incorporate presures from below.[2] But as authoritarianisms have given way almost everywhere to new parliamentary regimes, apparently not due to the original factors identified in the bureaucratic-authoritarian literature, new and more contingent explanations—often resembling grocery lists of variables—have also emerged to claim a place in the literature.[3]

A major problem with this literature is its lack of historical depth, both in the shortness of the historical period considered relevant and in the failure to use a historically sophisticated methodology. On the first count, only events occurring after the depression of the 1930s are examined. On the second count, the structural conditions given by late, dependent, and capital-intensive industrialization are considered a sufficient explanation for particular forms of politics. Clearly, both forms of superficiality need correction, and the approaches suggested in this volume begin to do precisely this.

Regional Political Cultures, State Formation, and Authoritarianism

In line with the overall project of the volume, it seems to me that any historically grounded and methodologically sophisticated analysis of democracy and authoritarianism in Latin America must range broadly in time period while intricately examining the forms of class conflict and alliance that help form, reproduce, and challenge political institutions. Only such an analysis has the potential to move us beyond the quandary between overly structural and overly narrative or contingent models, which emerge in the literature as opposite sides of the same coin. Methodologically, we need to expand Barrington Moore's theory on landlord power, coerced labor, and authoritarianism to consider contingent, on-the-ground variations in labor relations, class conflict and alliance, and the composition of the power blocs emerging during periods of state formation. In terms of time period, some of the essays in this volume shift our historical focus back to the period of agricultural export expansion (1880–1930), while others—including my own—move even further back to the immediate post-Independence years. Indeed, it seems to me that the crucial period for analyzing the rise of exclusionary political institutions is what I call elsewhere the "long nineteenth century"—the period between the Great Andean Civil War (1780), which signalled the crisis of the colonial system, and the depression of the 1930s. It was during this very long century that Latin America underwent the twin great transformations of the transition to capitalism and nation-state formation. To focus only on the later period within these great transformations is to underrepresent the importance of earlier events in the final outcomes.[4]

But I also wish to suggest that politics played an analytically more autonomous role in the transformations than has heretofore been allowed. Though the expansion of export agriculture was key to the consolidation of state power, the success of export production was itself conditioned by previous struggles among classes, racial or ethnic groups, and regions to create a more centralized state out of the scattered fragments left by the destruction of the colonial political system. In this earlier process, the interaction between political and economic dimensions was constant and complex, with issues of social control and labor relations at the very heart of the conflicts. At the same time, however, the conflicts could not be reduced to labor relations or class struggle, and we cannot ignore their more purely political and ideological dimensions.

During this long nineteenth century, struggles to centralize power in Mexico and Peru involved negotiation and conflict among regional political cultures, which were themselves being formed in regionally and historically specific struggles over the control of resources and people, and the meaning of actions, events, and relationships. Defined as combinations of beliefs, practices, and debates around the accumulation and contestation of power, these regional political cultures set the contours within which the broader class or ethnic negotiations and alliances necessary to the formation of the state could occur. At the same time, however, political cultures were themselves internally conflictual and variable, and once regions became involved in the making of a national politics the process would have a reciprocal effect on the regional cultures themselves.

Such a focus on regional political cultures in the shaping of national politics provides new elements for a rethinking of how authoritarianism and democracy got constructed in Latin America. As Evelyne Huber points out in her introduction, a close look at Latin America encourages us to consider the historical variety of authoritarian and democratic experiences as well as to question whether there exists the kind of definitive line between democracy and authoritarianism that Moore established. Just as no class—perhaps least of all the bourgeoisie—has played an inherently democratic role, the bourgeois revolution does not emerge as the only possible path to a democratic outcome. In such a flexible and contingent context, the explanation for democracy or authoritarianism must be sought in the historically specific forms taken by the interactions and negotiations among evolving regional political cultures, where emerging national elites, politics, and states were constructed in the intersections among and be-tween these multiple negotiations.

In this essay, I focus on two regions where large estates dominated economic production: Morelos, Mexico, and Cajamarca, Peru. I treat mainly the period of attempted state consolidation in the mid-nineteenth century, and especially the conflicts that emerged in both regions during periods of foreign intervention (roughly 1860–1870 in Mexico, 1880–1890 in Peru). I also range forward and backward in time to make broader analytical connections. I examine quite minutely the socioeconomic and political conditions that defined regional struggles over these years and attempt to tie these conflicts to emerging political trends at the national level.

As we see from an examination of nineteenth-century Mexico and Peru, Latin American states-in-formation already had quite a record of repression against social movements by the takeoff of export production in the 1880s. The impact of such experiences on the possible forms of state consolidation, ongoing until the 1930s, would of necessity be dramatic, and certainly predisposed both countries toward political relationships that fell short of our definitions of democracy. But equally important, the particular forms of confrontation, negotiation, inclusion, and repression that state makers used in their ongoing interactions with regional and popular political cultures would help define the success or failure of democracy. For if we agree with Corrigan and Sayer that state formation is a process of cultural revolution, the consolidation of democracy must entail, in addition to formal participation, the elaboration of a common social and moral project in which most people have some kind of stake. The inability to construct such a project can be partially explained by pointing to earlier exclusions; later processes of repression then become, at least in part, the result of previous inabilities to envision and build a common future.[5]

Ultimately, I also demonstrate the importance of going beyond the distinction between authoritarianism and democracy, to a deeper and more dynamic understanding of how particular forms of either get constructed. In nineteenth-century Mexico and Peru, while the authoritarian option was exercised in both cases, its form was quite distinct in each. Mexican and Peruvian state makers could attempt to make national politics on the basis of exclusion, thus leading to authoritarianism; but its character and potential for future evolution was conditioned by the relative strength of radical popular movements and their effect on the internal conformation of regional political cultures. Equally important, popular political cultures and their capacity to generate radical movements would in turn be conditioned by the particular state forms and export economies that emerged in each case.

Bandits, Liberal Guerrillas, and the Great Estate in Morelos, 1855–1867

When Juan Alvarez took Mexico City in mid-1855, initiating the Liberal Revolution that would forever change the contours of Mexican politics, he had behind him the organized strength of national guard battalions from the districts of El Sur—that large swatch of territory extending from coastal Guerrero and southern Michoacán, in the west, through the district of Cuernavaca in the present-day state of Morelos. Most recently armed in the 1840s, during the U.S.–Mexican war, and again in 1854, these national guard battalions were based in the villages of the area and served under respected local leaders. They would once again serve the cause of liberalism in 1856, when the Tetecala national guard battalion, from Cuernavaca district, played a key role in defeating Puebla's conservative uprising.[6]

At the same time, however, the owners of sugar cane haciendas in Cuernavaca and Morelos—two districts that by 1850 constituted a key resource base for the state of Mexico and the federal government—were understandably upset by the existence of autonomous national guard battalions in the pueblos bordering their estates. In March 1856, while these battalions were still in Puebla putting down the Conservative rebellion against the Liberal government, a group of *hacendados* wrote personally to President Ignacio Comonfort, requesting that the government place additional federal troops in their districts to protect them from their own returning national guards. Only in this way, they emphasized, would it be possible to prevent caste war and the "plague of socialism." And interestingly enough, despite the role played by national guardsmen in the protection of the Liberal state, Comonfort acceded to the landowners' request, sending troops into Cuernavaca and Morelos districts in April 1856 and giving permission for a generalized repression of national guard battalions between June and August of that same year.[7]

Unravelling the puzzle of why Liberal power holders knowingly allied with landowners who aided their enemies rather than relying on their own Liberal supporters forms the central thread of my narrative. To solve this riddle, it is necessary to find out why the Liberal movement in El Sur was such a powerful military ally in the original taking and consolidation of power, yet a problematic and unreliable one in processes of institutionalization and unification. Once we answer that question, we will also be that much closer to knowing why most Mexican Liberals in the second half of the nineteenth century, whatever their rhetoric, consistently centralized power and repressed social movements and political dissent. The choice to repress with blood, rather than to negotiate differences electorally or in Parliament, was made, ironically, by the very politicians who spouted federalism and free speech. In many ways it was they, rather than the Morelos landowners or other Mexican Conservatives, who took the lead in constructing Mexican authoritarianism.

The place to begin is with a closer look at the internal composition of the regional political culture that had been evolving in El Sur, through a series of struggles and reorganizations of sociopolitical space, since the late eighteenth century. Between 1810 and 1840 regional strongmen Juan Alvarez and Vicente Guerrero, surviving populist leaders from the wars of Independence, constructed a radical federalist coalition composed of peasant villages, local caciques, provincial elites, and urban artisans and petty merchants. They drew on the traditions of popular rebellion and anticolonialism built up in the region since the 1780s, which had combined resistance to the Bourbon reforms with a strong hostility to Spanish merchants, landowners, and state officials. In the post-Independence years, continued Spanish control of larger properties and important commercial networks gave additional meaning to the Independence slogan *Mueran Los Gachupines*. By the 1830s, conflicts within villages over municipal versus *república* forms of politics and communal landholding intermingled with struggles among local notables and provincial leaders over taxation, municipal autonomy, and rentals of municipal land. For politicians with their eyes on Mexico City, these conflicts fed into an intensifying debate between centralist and federalist models of political organization, as diverse factions attempted to broaden their coalitions in order to become contenders in the struggle to "make" national politics.[8]

Peter Guardino convincingly shows that rural conflicts in Guerrero between 1820 and 1850 were not mainly about land—at least not in the sense familiar to historians of the later nineteenth century. In many areas the unifying factors seem to have been resistance to taxation and to political centralization, as rural populations struggled to limit the head taxes levied on them and to maintain or achieve some degree of municipal autonomy. In both the 1830 civil war and the conflicts of the 1840s, these issues interlocked with anti-Spanish and anti-foreign mobilizations, for villagers often interpreted the 1820s legislation expelling Spaniards as also legitimating the expulsion of non-Indians from municipal government and village lands. And in the cases where land was a factor, the conflicts were generally not between communities and haciendas but instead between municipal governments and *oficiales de república* over the ownership of communal lands.[9]

In the districts of Cuernavaca and Cuautla Morelos (what is today the state of Morelos), on the other hand, issues of municipal autonomy, taxation, and anti-Spanish feeling intermingled by the 1840s with more recognizable forms of hacienda-community conflict. Part of the difference had to do with the history of commercial production in this region. Already in the late colonial period, the confrontation between haciendas and communities in the districts of Cuernavaca and Morelos had been based on competition between two market-oriented and relatively dynamic systems of production. In the villages, peasants produced fruits and vegetables for the Mexico City market as well as subsistence crops. People moved back and forth among a variety of urban occupations, commerce, agriculture, and occasional wage labor. The *hacendados*, for their part, were interested not in using coercion to retain a resident labor force but in enlisting the aid of state officials in their struggles to discipline labor and neutralize competition from the village economies. This meant cooperation from local political and judicial authorities in cutting communities off from access to water and other resources, and sometimes even evicting tenants who would not cooperate with hacienda administrators.[10]

These issues reemerged with greater intensity in the 1840s, when a new commercial expansion revived and deepened existing enmities and rivalries. Indeed, between 1848 and 1850, and again in 1856, alliances of village and hacienda peasants, urban artisans, small merchants, and national guards confronted the great estates throughout the district of Cuernavaca and in parts of Cuautla Morelos. They battled large landowners over issues of labor, land, and water. In some particularly dramatic or violent cases, such as on the haciendas Chiconcuac, Dolores, and San Vicente in 1856 and 1860, national guards were also implicated in raids or murders on hacienda territory. Throughout these years, whether fomented by the landowners themselves or by jumpy local officials, rumors flew back and forth about racial or caste war, and about a general conflagration or campaign against the landowners or large merchants of the districts.[11]

Despite regional variation, what unified the various local alliances into a broader radical coalition was the common need, felt throughout the villages of El Sur, to confront the reorganization of power set into motion by the transition from *república* to municipal government. As would become clear by the 1840s, federalism allowed for greater municipal autonomy in the working out of these local issues, where control over land, revenue, and political office was being contested along lines of ethnicity, age, class, and geographical space. Centralists, by contrast, tended to support the consolidation of larger municipalities and their control by mestizo or white *vecinos*, with predictable consequences at the community level. Thus peasants in Guerrero and Morelos—whether confronting the encroachment of the hacienda, manipulation by corrupt municipal officials, higher rates of taxation, or some combination of them all—could agree on the need to fight for a decentralized polity in which municipalities could work through these new issues in a relatively autonomous fashion.[12]

By the 1840s, then, the combined practices and experiences of the previous generation came together to generate a broad agrarian movement in Guerrero and neighboring areas. What catalyzed the movement in Guerrero was a worsening of land conflicts in the Chilapa area, in combination with generalized protests against an increase in the head tax. In Cuernavaca and Morelos around the same time, as already mentioned, conflicts over land, markets, water, and other resources had been intensifying along with municipal and taxation issues. In Mexico City as well, the political stakes began rising rapidly in the 1840s, as regional, economic, and sociopolitical conflicts among elite factions reverberated against, and formed the backdrop for, broader attempts to consolidate the kind of national political alliance that could build and retain state power. And the final element in the mix was the growing crisis with the United States, which by the second half of the decade led to war and foreign occupation.[13]

Particularly in the Morelos area, the broad agrarian movement of the 1840s fed into and mingled with Alvarez's guerrilla resistance to the U.S. occupation. This was certainly the case in Cuernavaca district, where the Tetecala national guard commander, José Manuel Arellano, an Alvarez appointee, led his battalion in an offensive against the haciendas Chiconcuac, San Vicente, and Miacatlán, removing or replacing boundary markers to dramatize hacienda expansionism. That this movement occurred in 1848, while U.S. troops were still stationed in nearby Cuernavaca city, did not amuse Alvarez, who chastised Arellano severely, writing to him that his commission did not entitle him to get involved in other people's affairs. While temporary, the rift between Alvarez and Arellano reflected in part the different contours of the agrarian movement in the Guerrero and Cuernavaca subregions of El Sur, as well as the lesser direct influence of Alvarez in the latter.[14]

But a deeper question emerged as well: even if landowners, provincial notables, villagers, and townspeople could all agree on the need for federalism and could represent this unity through the creation of national guard battalions, in the end they might develop quite different visions of what the final goals of federalist policy might be. If for federalist politicians and notables like Alvarez the ultimate goal was national power, or at least the ability to negotiate participation in a national coalition, for villagers and townspeople the more direct issues were social justice, access to resources including land, and the responsiveness of local political institutions. It was the negotiated convergences between these two visions, and the working out of the contradictions between them, that ultimately generated—by the mid-1850s—the Alvarista form of radical federalism qua liberalism that would propel the Ayutla revolution. For the federalist and Liberal politicians gathering around Alvarez, it was precisely the need to find allies outside their social class that forced them to take seriously the issues being discussed in the pueblos and communities of El Sur. And in 1855, taking these issues seriously turned out to be a key component in winning Mexico City.[15]

In relation to their allies in El Sur, therefore, the Liberal statemakers who came to power in 1855 faced a difficult dilemma. On the one hand, politically and militarily it was the national guards born of previous struggles who constituted the most reliable Liberal allies. Without them Mexico City would not have been taken in mid-1855; without them Puebla could not have been reconquered six months later. And yet on the other hand, taking autonomy, land, and social justice seriously radicalized and fomented the agrarian social movements that buttressed and protected the national guards. Already by the second half of the 1840s, rural people throughout El Sur were connecting federalism and political autonomy to their own definitions of citizenship and of a broadly inclusive national polity in which they would be recognized as legitimate participants. Thus many Mexico City politicians viewed their peasant allies with dismay, hoping to disband the national guards as quickly as possible once national power had been assured.[16]

In the districts of Morelos and Cuernavaca, which in the 1850s composed the third district of the state of Mexico, the situation was further complicated by the strategic economic and political importance of the sugar *hacendados*. As a group, these landowners controlled roughly half of the national sugar industry in 1850, and the taxes on their production represented an important resource for any national state. Further, at various points in the previous decade it had become clear that the rural guards, based on the haciendas, were often the most reliable repressive forces in the face of village social movements, for national guards might actually refuse to repress their brothers if the cause of the movement was deemed just. In the end, therefore, Liberal state officials ignored the *hacendados* in Cuernavaca and Morelos at their peril, even if these same *hacendados* gave covert support to the Conservatives. The only alternative would have been support for the entire radical social program emerging in the countryside, something for which the top Liberal leadership proved themselves entirely unprepared when they ousted Juan Alvarez from the presidency.[17]

From the perspective of El Sur, then, the Liberals failed to consolidate their hold on the state because they could not formulate policy to satisfy the agrarian movement that had carried them to power in the first place. Given the state of military technology and communications in the middle of the nineteenth century, moreover, the social movements and national guards in Morelos and Guerrero, and the regional political culture they helped construct, were key elements in any broader negotiations or alliances that might vie for control of the state. In this context Ignacio Comonfort's 1856 decision to honor the landowners' request and repress his national guard allies foreshadowed the alliance he would make two years later with the Conservative Party, serving as interim president after their takeover of Mexico City with the Plan de Tacubaya.[18] It represented as well a key juncture in the liberal path toward authoritarianism in the nineteenth century. Yet the very same agrarian movement that impeded Liberal consolidation continued to make the Liberals unbeatable when they were in opposition. As they proved in the 1858–1861 civil war, and once again during the French Intervention and Second Empire (1861–1867), the national guards in El Sur might not be able entirely to defeat the social forces supporting centralism and conservatism, but they could certainly fight them—and any national government supporting them—to a stalemate.

Indeed, during nearly a decade of violent conflict between 1858 and 1867, the strength of the national guard movement in Guerrero and Morelos continued unabated along the region's western side. In Guerrero, the mountains around the town of Teloloapam and the whole region south of the Mescala River remained unconquered by Conservative and imperial troops. There, and in Alvarez's general headquarters at his hacienda La Providencia, Liberal strategy was formulated and debated and new guerrillas trained.[19] In the district of Cuernavaca, Liberal guerrillas in touch with Alvarez maintained spheres of influence in the sierra de Huitzilac, directly south of Mexico City, and surrounding villages. They also operated in the area near Tetecala and Xochitepec, maintaining headquarters in the *ranchos* in the surrounding mountains. The irony of this was not lost on the imperial government: only a few miles south of the capital city, in the richest sugar estates of mainland Mexico, it was impossible for imperial officials entirely to rid themselves of guerrilla bands.[20]

That this occurred in Cuernavaca should not surprise us. Even earlier, during the Liberal Revolution, the Cuernavaca region had experienced the most intimate and intense integration into the *revolución del sur*. Closest geographically to Alvarez's strongholds in coastal Guerrero, Cuernavacans had also experienced the most intense assault from the hacienda in the 1840s and exhibited the greatest overall concentration of population on haciendas. This was especially true in the area known as the cañada de Cuernavaca, the lowland area located at the center of the district, where expansionist haciendas disputed territory and resources with municipalities that sported the strongest national guard battalions, such as Xochitepec, Tetecala, and Tlaquiltenango. With a few notable exceptions, therefore, the agrarian and national guard mobilizations were concentrated in Cuernavaca district throughout the 1850s. And this tendency would deepen in the 1860s.[21]

A particularly dramatic example of this happened in October of 1863, in the villages of Jojutla, Puente de Ixtla, and Tlaquiltenango, all in the municipality of Tetecala, when a band of approximately one hundred Liberal guerrillas commanded by Vicente Cuenca and Juan Fandiño made the rounds asking for money, horses, and provisions. In Tlaquiltenango, according to local authorities, Cuenca's men politely asked for pasture for their horses and for any money that the local population was able to collect. By contrast, the municipal president of Jojutla was forced to flee to the nearby hacienda of San Nicolás, abandoning the pueblo to the guerrillas because only five or six people appeared to defend the plaza. And in Puente de Ixtla, when Cuenca asked for a conference with the municipal president an hour and a half after attacking the village, the political official agreed. Cuenca then demanded one thousand pesos; the municipal president said they would give nothing until Cuenca's men gave back the agricultural land at the borders of the village that they had been occupying illegally. Cuenca agreed immediately, but after the official saw that Cuenca's men were not living up to the promise and were instead continuing to steal horses, he got together a force of locals and threw the guerrillas out of the town.[22]

As these events make clear, in Cuernavaca district the relationship between the local population and the guerrillas was one of easy and longstanding familiarity. The guerrillas identified themselves clearly with the Liberal cause, maintaining a base in the area's villages and generally taxing populations or individual travellers on the road in a relatively polite and "legal" way. In the sierra de Huitzilac, villages were known for such a complete dedication to the cause that one desperate imperial official was prompted to suggest that several of the pueblos be destroyed and their inhabitants relocated in the cities, in order to make the region a free-fire zone. Near Tetecala, our documents reveal that when the soldiers acted politely and well, they were well cared for. When local authorities demanded that the villages confront them, only a few people showed up. But when the Liberal soldiers took liberties and acted unjustly, the *vecinos* threw them out. In none of these cases, however, were local men willing to collaborate with the repressive forces under the command of the Regencia.

In fact, the repression was ultimately organized from the haciendas, by an alliance of administrators who then demanded support from the government, or by imperial officials, who then demanded aid from the hacienda.[23]

The situation was somewhat different in the eastern part of the Morelos area, in the district of Cuautla Morelos, where local villagers were a great deal more ambivalent about the political factions contesting power. The comparative weakness of the Liberal presence, when combined with the endemic activity of bandit bands called *plateados*, muddied the sociopolitical waters for all parties involved. Manuel Mendoza Cortina, for example, owner of the hacienda Coahuixtla, had an ongoing conflict with a group of peasants living on what he claimed as his property who refused to work on his fields and insisted they had prior claim to a stretch of land they said had been the town of Apatlaco. At various points Mendoza tried to evict them from his estate, accusing them of insubordination and also of harboring or cooperating with *plateados*. In such a case the role of bandits was, at least de facto, supportive of the peasantry's social demands.

In other cases, however, the *plateados* allied with landowners, abusive priests, even abusive political authorities, or they robbed indiscriminately from peasants and small merchants attempting to take their goods to market. Even as early as 1862, Liberal forces in the area got into difficulties with each other because one had accepted into its ranks a number of notorious *plateados*, known for terrorizing local villagers across a band of territory from Ameca in the north through Jantetelco and Jonacatepec in the south. According to the Liberal government's report on the incident, two Liberal forces fired on each other after the bandits in one force, fearful that they would be recognized, began to shoot in an effort to create a diversion. As the local official explained, people in the villages did not fear the bandits when they appeared as such, but only when they managed to masquerade as soldiers of the government.[24]

In the villages of Jantetelco and Jonacatepec, the presence of *plateado* gangs was constant by 1863, aided and abetted by the complicity of village and hacienda notables. Even if the gangs often took the name of "defenders of liberty," their behavior against the local population was quite indiscriminate. When it came to attacking bandits, therefore, the local *vecinos* were willing to collaborate with the Regencia. And that was exactly what happened on December 26, in a place named Rancho Las Piedras belonging to the hacienda Tenextepango, when a force of 120 men organized an ambush of the gang of *plateados* whose custom it was to congregate there. As they stood on the green hillsides to the south of Cuautla, though, sixty imperial cavalry and sixty volunteers from the village of Mapazlán saw pass behind them a guerrilla force of around two hundred infantry, led by Liberal commander Francisco Leyva. "When the men from Mapazlan saw the force," reported the local military commander from Yautepec, "they said they were going back to their village and they refused to attack Leyva even though such an attack would surely have been successful because he did not see them. This is because don Rafael Sanchez, head of the men from Mapazlan, once served under the orders of Leyva.''[25] Thus ended what might otherwise have been an important moral and military victory for the imperial forces of the Regencia, much more so than a routine sweep of the local bandit gang. Also important, however, was that the villagers' refusal to fight against a prestigious Liberal military commander such as Leyva evidenced a clear lack of commitment to the Conservative cause.

In fact, the ambivalence of the Mapazlán *vecinos* both represented and foreshadowed the problems faced by the Regencia and the emperor in the Morelos countryside. Between 1864 and 1866, Maximilian attempted to win over the poor and indigenous classes of Mexican society, those grouped under the euphemism *clases menesterosas*. In addition to the Junta Protectora de las Clases Menesterosas, founded in April 1864 under the presidency of Nahua intellectual Faustino Chimalpopoca, Maximilian put into effect a number of decrees concerning village lands, labor laws, and personal audiences with him, all translated into Náhuatl and all designed to increase his popularity across class and ethnic lines. Yet if villagers attempted to use the laws to their advantage, they ran up against local officials who inevitably supported the cause of the landowners. And when push came to shove, it was precisely upon these officials that the imperial edifice stood. Without exception, if brought face-to-face with local political authorities, the populism of the imperial government quickly melted and disappeared.[26]

An excellent example of the empire's hollow promises occurred in Cuernavaca district between June and August of 1866. Don Juan Núñez, designated protector of the indigenous villages in the district, presented a series of petitions to the imperial government on behalf of the village of Xiutepec and others. In an attempt to get enforcement of an earlier decree removing abusive *alcalde* Sixto Valero, villagers had presented two additional requests to the government over a period of six months. It seems that Valero had been in complicity with local *hacendados*, aiding a process of land accumulation by the haciendas Temixco and Treinta over several years. In the process, several of the area's villages had found that the territorial markers separating them from the great estates had actually reached the outlying houses. But every time an order came down from the government to remove Valero, the departmental council—where he apparently had friends—sat on the order. Núñez thus requested that Valero be removed, and that the land issues affecting his clients be resolved. Within two weeks of the first petition by Núñez, however, his clients were protesting his false arrest. And when the final decree "resolving" the case came from the Junta Protectora, it simply urged the emperor to sign a separate decree protecting a village's *fundo legal,* so that haciendas could not usurp land right up against the houses.[27]

A similar incident occurred in the eastern Morelos area, around Cuautla and Yautepec, that stands as the best proof of the problems encountered by the imperial government in winning the hearts and minds of the agrarian population. In September of 1866 Juan Cataño y Calvo, merchant and small-time miner from Cuautla Morelos, was named president of a Junta Auxiliar de las Clases Menesterosas formed for Morelos. Within days, the word had spread across the villages of the district and, when Cataño was in Jonaca-tepec on business, several of the communities in Zacualpan municipality requested his intervention on land and other issues. Apparently quite enthusiastic about what the imperial government might do for the peasants of the area, Cataño travelled to each of the communities and held assemblies in the plazas, ringing church bells and giving speeches about the mercy and justice awaiting rural people under the empire. People got quite excited, and began giving "vivas" to Faustino Chimalpopoca and Maximilian, setting off firecrackers as part of their celebration. The end result was that Cataño was arrested by the subprefect of Cuautla, along with his son and an aide on the Junta Auxiliar, for stirring up the population and disturbing public tranquility. The case actually reached the imperial authorities in Mexico City, where it became clear that Cataño had been appointed to head a Junta Auxiliar for the municipality of Morelos, while he assumed he had jurisdiction over the entire district. In the end, the Junta Protectora in the capital city fired him from the position for overstepping the boundaries of his authority. Nothing was done for the villages who had presented their petitions to Cataño.[28]

In the end, therefore, imperial policy to protect the rural population actually backfired. While raising hopes about redress of grievances, it had no teeth with which to enforce the socially progressive provisions it contained. Thus it simply opened up peasants and other rural folk to the repression of local authorities, whose first loyalty was often to the landowners in their district. In this context, it is hardly surprising that even in Cuautla Morelos, where the Liberal presence was less constant or organic, neither the conservative nor the imperial governments were able to gain the loyalty and wholesale support of the villages. While both were willing to paint themselves as the protectors of the Indian communities, neither was capable of meeting the deeper sociopolitical challenge presented by the agrarian movement in Morelos.

And that was precisely the point. Liberal presidents and European monarchs were equally incapable of participating in the kind of radical social project presented by the national guards and agrarian social movements of El Sur. The explanation for this inability, however, is not to be found in the landowning class but in the popular movement itself. Given the way in which regional political culture was constructed in Morelos between 1810 and 1860, the rural lower classes claimed enough space and autonomy within it that an alliance with them, from the perspective of any national political faction, became a risky proposition. It was in this sense that we can speak of an unbeatable popular movement in opposition, yet also understand why its demands could not be incorporated into a more mainstream, national-level political project. As would once again become clear after 1867, during the reconstructed Liberal republic, Liberals fearing social upheaval repressed as hard and with as much bloodshed as Conservatives. In Morelos, it was this repression—rather than the landowners' need to underwrite coerced labor—that defined the authoritarian option for the Mexican state. And state makers repressed, not because they were under the thumb of the landowners, but because they could not stomach the alternative.[29]

Landlords, Peasants, and National Resistance in Cajamarca, 1879–1900

In contrast to Morelos, where an economically and culturally strong peasant community had placed significant limits on the landowning class's control of labor and regional politics, constructing a regional political culture around radical federalism and municipal autonomy that directly challenged the *hacendados'* desire for centralism and control over local governments, in the northern Peruvian highland department of Cajamarca the regional oligarchy was firmly in control during the second half of the nineteenth century. One important explanation for this difference lies in the much weaker peasant communal tradition found in Cajamarca, where even before the Spanish conquest communal structures had been imported from the south through conquest by the Incas, rather than having strong native roots. By the time of independence from Spain, even though smallholding villages did exist, they had little if any sense of institutional cohesion, communal land, or communal tradition of struggle. Thus the great estate, even while facing opposition to its process of territorial expansion, had not confronted the type of concerted, powerful, and viable communal resistance its counterpart had faced in Morelos.[30]

A second factor contributing to hacienda dominance was the lack of economic alternatives available in the regional economy during the nineteenth century. Beginning in the late eighteenth century, the decline of the area's *obrajes* encouraged the local economy to turn in on itself. In quite the opposite way from the Morelos region, where the proximity of the Mexico City market generated strong opportunities for commercial production in both hacienda and village economies, highland Cajamarca seems to have remained an economic backwater in the years before the War of the Pacific (1879–1884). Local peasants had few alternatives, whether in the form of markets for their surplus production or opportunities for occasional wage labor in mining or other sectors. The hacienda—and therefore the *hacendado*—was the most powerful social, economic, and political force in local life. The basis for this power was not always direct control over people, but rather a monopoly of the land itself. This is clear from the fact that, while only 30 percent of the department's inhabitants lived on the great estates—which is not all that different from the municipalities in Morelos with the highest concentration of hacienda population—in Cajamarca the great estate controlled over two-thirds of the entire land area. Thus the majority of the region's inhabitants was dependent on the hacienda for access to resources, even in the cases where they did not live directly on the properties.[31]

This combination of economic, cultural, and political conditions generated quite a distinct regional political culture. Those *hacendados* who succeeded in reproducing their position in local society did so by keeping private armies on their estates and developing patron-client relations with the smallholder villages near their properties. Under such conditions, conflict tended to occur among factions loyal to different landlord powerholders, taking the form of contestation between families or clienteles. Ultimately, therefore, while there were cases of peasant resistance against the *hacendados*, the crucial source of conflict in prewar Cajamarca was competition among landlords, as they attempted to establish the most complete hold over their areas in order to maintain and reproduce their status. In stark contrast to Morelos, therefore, neither the landlords nor the villagers were able to build a unified political position: the former fought among themselves for influence and prestige and the latter did not generate an autonomous radical political project.[32]

Systems of land tenure, population patterns, and regional political culture varied substantially in Cajamarca department's northern province of Jaén. A frontier region with a relatively sparse population, where the economy had for a long time been based on the commercial exploitation of tropical crops, Jaén had undergone a significant commercial expansion in the decades before the War of the Pacific (1879–1884). Traders from Chota province and the departments of Piura and Lambayeque entered the area seeking to buy up supplies of cattle, cacao, coffee, cascarilla, and other products. The opportunity to rent a sizable proportion of the existing great estates, which belonged to the state-controlled Beneficencia and were dedicated mainly to the breeding of cattle and sheep, also attracted entrepreneurs from surrounding provinces. The combined effect of commercial expansion and hacienda rentals was that, despite the overall thinness of population in the province, a higher percentage of it was concentrated on haciendas than was usual in the rest of the department: over 40 percent, according to the 1876 census.[33]

For local smallholders and peasants, accustomed to the greater autonomy of a frontier trading economy, the influx of outsiders from Chota associated with large landholding or interprovincial commerce resulted in a distinct perspective on local conflicts over power. Since these outside entrepreneurs were able to expand commercial agriculture mainly by renting lands through the Beneficencia of Jaén, a state-affiliated charitable organization that got access to funds by administering state properties, smallholders tended to equate their presence with the extension of state authority. Scattered evidence further suggests that they saw state incursions—especially in the form of the *contribución personal*, or head tax, as yet another invasion of outsiders that went along with commerce and commercial agriculture. The end result was the construction of a militantly antistate local political culture, whose main project was the removal of exploitative strangers and of an abusive, intrusive state. This political culture would have important implications for the type of movement developing in this province during the War of the Pacific.[34]

In contrast to Jaén, where the landowners renting state properties had a more direct connection to, and dependence on, state officials, in Cajamarca province many landowners defended the sanctity of their properties' boundaries by not allowing state officials to cross into their estates when chasing criminals or collecting taxes. *Hacendados* also hid bandits on their estates in exchange for personal loyalty, and in some cases even protected neighboring peasants who were resisting taxation or conscription. The peasants, for their part, seemed to prefer a local patron's protection against state exaction to the only available alternative, which was to be taxed by the landlord *and* the state. Only when *hacendados* competed with each other for influence did the role of the state become relevant. Indeed, the participation of local landowners in factional battles at the national level before the War of the Pacific can best be explained in the context of local intra-elite competition.[35]

Thus Jaén and Cajamarca provinces each present a distinct prewar pattern of internal conflict as well as a different relationship to the emerging state structure in Lima. In Jaén, interclass hostility over commercial expansion predisposed outside landowners to accept state aid in extending commercial agriculture, while at the same time it increased peasant resistance to state exactions. In Cajamarca, peasants and landowners both viewed the state with suspicion, preferring the existing status quo to an unclear and disruptive form of change. The only exception seemed to be the weaker landowners who were willing to seek state aid in their unequal battle with their stronger colleagues, thus forcing the political involvement of the more influential Cajamarca *hacendados* as well. In contrast to Morelos, then, where a political stalemate between classes made both much more receptive to state involvement, the rural popular classes in Cajamarca were never open to an alliance with the state.

Indeed, the construction of regional political cultures in Cajamarca made it difficult for any group to see the state as a potential ally, for peasants and landowners tended to share a suspicious hostility vis-à-vis the expansion of a state authority they did not think would bring them any benefits. This was in direct contrast to the situation in Morelos, where landowners and peasants had each participated enthusiastically, though on different sides, in the struggles between Liberals and Conservatives to centralize and reproduce state power. The central location of Morelos, moreover, and the importance of the area's economy and revenues, meant that struggles for control of the capital city were often resolved there. Finally, the very strength of the agrarian social movement, and the resulting evenness in the balance of class forces, made the state a welcome participant in local politics. In the northern Peruvian sierra, on the other hand—with the exception of entrepreneurial groups in Jaén—the existence of an effective system of private landowner power diminished the relevance of state interventions for all parties involved.

The final element that helped define this political culture was the specific insertion of the northern Peruvian sierra into the War of the Pacific. When Nicolas de Piérola abandoned Lima to Chilean occupation in January of 1881, he established camp in Jauja and divided the country into three large zones of resistance. The northern zone, under the control of Admiral Lizardo Montero, had its headquarters in Cajamarca. In contrast to the northern coastal departments, which had been subject to Chilean invasion and occupation since 1880, Cajamarca seems to have been spared the presence of Chilean soldiers until mid-1882. Even then the actual occupation, while quite destructive, was short-lived. This did not mean, however, that the political conflicts among Peruvians generated by the war and the occupation did not have a significant impact in the highland department. Indeed, both of the major resistance movements that developed in the region had their origins in intra-elite battles over how best to deal with the Chilean occupation of the country.[36]

Only a few months after he became commander of the northern zone, Montero named Manuel José Becerra subprefect of Chota province. Apparently not a member of the highest landowning elite, Becerra nevertheless seems to have participated in the prewar commercial boom in Jaén, travelling to that province in search of commercial opportunities. During the early part of the war, he had fought as a lieutenant colonel in the fourth division of the Northern Army organized by Miguel Iglesias. Once the formal battle was lost in 1881, Becerra enthusiastically supported the option for continued resistance as represented by Montero and Piérola. There were those with different ideas, however. Shortly after the Chileans refused to recognize Piérola and supported the formation of a new government based in the Lima suburb of La Magdalena and headed by Francisco García

Calderón, political agitation began in Chota, especially around the city of Bambamarca, for recognition of the García Calderón government and immediate peace negotiations. By the time Becerra became subprefect, several outbreaks of violence had already occurred.[37]

The supporters of García Calderón in Chota received a political shot in the arm when Lizardo Montero, encouraged by the energetic intervention of U.S. special envoy Stephen Hurlbut and hoping to achieve peace without territorial concessions, recognized the La Magdalena government in November of 1881. Only a month later, due to the president's exile to Chile, Montero himself succeeded to the presidency. By early February of 1882, Montero had passed his position as commander of the northern region to Miguel Iglesias, a landowner from Cajamarca province who had been in retirement on his estate since the Peruvian defeat in Lima one year before. The combination of Montero's "defection" to the García Calderón camp and Iglesias's appointment to commander generated wild rumors in Chota. It was even said that a battalion was headed for the province to force the payment of war contributions and install a new pro-Magdalena government.[38]

By May 1882 Pierolista subprefect Manuel Becerra was on the run in the province of Jaén, pursued as a rebel by government forces. Until his death in 1885, he led a guerrilla movement that repeatedly eluded both occupation and government forces. Operating mainly along the commercial routes tying the jungle to the coast, especially in the provinces of Chota and Jaén, Becerra's *montonera* was instrumental in preventing collaborationist forces—most notably Miguel Iglesias—from establishing full control in the northern highlands. Its popularity in the region was increased by the fact that its leaders were from an intermediate stratum of Chota merchants, small landowners, and village notables who, while apparently profiting from the prewar boom in Jaén, were never fully incorporated into the local elite.[39]

Even a cursory placement of the *montonera's* operations on a map makes clear that its long-term survival depended on the knowledge of trade routes and resources previously amassed by its leaders. There were two main areas of operation. One centered in Bellavista district, in the jungle area of Jaén province, connecting west to Jaén itself and then much further west to the commercial center of Olmos, on the way down to the coast in the department of Lambayeque. The town of Pimpingos, south of Jaén and en route to the commercial centers of Chota and Cutervo, was also in this first general area. The second base formed a rectangle whose northern, eastern, southern, and western angles were the towns of Querecotillo, Huambos, Llama, and Cachén respectively. Located much further south in the Chota-Cutervo highlands, nearly halfway between Chota and the coastal commercial entrepôts of Ferreñafe, Chiclayo, and Lambayeque, this second guerrilla stronghold was based in the towns from which many of the regulars in Becerra's band originally came. By basing itself in areas familiar to the members of the band, due to previous trade and family connections, Becerra's *montonera* was able to survive through a combination of stealing and marketing commercial goods and seeking the protection of local village notables whom they knew personally. Indeed, local authorities or prominent citizens in the towns and villages through which Becerra passed played a crucial supportive role, providing information, commercializing stolen goods, acquiring arms, and recruiting additional men. Thus Becerra's *montonera* operated like a merchant's army based in the small towns and commercial routes of the region.[40]

Though led by merchants and small landowners, the *montonera* had a much more varied base of support. On one side were the large *hacendados*, mainly from the western corner of Chota and into the department of Lambayeque, who provided crucial commercial connections to the coast. On the other side were the peasant and even Indian populations who provided the fighting men and, particularly in Bellavista, the resources and logistical support for a hideaway when government pressure was high. Taken together, this wide variety of contacts and environments was ideal for the survival of a small guerrilla force. Near the coast, influential landowners and others served as a conduit through which flowed booty in exchange for arms and ammunition. In Chota a base among smallholding peasants and petty merchants provided fighters, occasional refuge, additional commercial connections, and intelligence on troop movements. And in Jaén, Bellavista was the largest producer of cacao in the province, directly on the Marañón River, yet difficult to reach if travelling overland from west to east—all characteristics making it an excellent refuge from armies based in the highlands.[41] The question remaining, though, is how Becerra was able to keep such a broad and varied coalition together. In order to answer it, we must turn to an examination of the movement's internal sociopolitical dynamics.

The actions of Becerra's band helped construct a common political and symbolic arena in which diverse groups could participate according to their own experiences and needs. In Jaén, the band was so successful at stealing commercial cargoes in order to finance itself that it ultimately threatened the expulsion of all large landowners from the province and the destruction of Jaén's Beneficencia. Indeed, by 1884 Jaén's subprefect submitted a desperate report from his hideout in Cutervo, explaining that Becerra, his father-in-law Manuel Vílchez, and other leaders had made it impossible for any merchants from Cutervo or Chota to trade in the province except under threat of violent death. This type of action was clearly attractive to Jaén's petty merchants and smallholders, all of whom had suffered at the hands of state officials and large *hacendados* before the war. Involved in the attempt to commercialize tropical products but facing competition from more power-ful landowners and entrepreneurs, smaller merchants saw in Becerra's band a legitimate way to revenge themselves, even to allow themselves the fantasy that after the war they might take over the more profitable routes. For the Indians and peasants of Jaén, the band's attacks on prominent landowners and its de facto destruction of Jaén's Beneficencia meant a return to the forms of local autonomy they had known before the prewar commercial expansion. In Jaén province, therefore, Becerra was able to unite this variety of sentiments into a powerful movement against the collaborationist Peruvian government and the foreign invader. An impor-tant element of Becerra's impact was his sense of theatre, aptly illustrated by the tale of Becerra riding into one of his local strongholds, appropriating two hundred receipts for the head tax, and tearing them up in the central plaza to general applause.[42]

Becerra's connections with *hacendados* are certainly more difficult to explain, given his movement's hostility to the prominent landowners in Jaén and Chota. The fact that his landlord connections were outside these two provinces, in or near the coastal departments of Piura and Lambayeque, helps to explain part of the contradiction. So does the fact that separate commercial routes connected Jaén to those coastal areas—in particular through the strategic center of Olmos—and that it was not necessary to go through his Chota strongholds. But most importantly, for those *hacendados* supporting Becerra, the state represented an unwelcome interference in their lives. A common antistate sentiment thus unified these landowners with the other participants in Becerra's movement. In this context it is interesting to note that José Mesones, Becerra's strongest *hacendado* ally, had been involved in a major altercation with local authorities in 1880 when these had attempted to draft men from his hacienda.[43]

Becerra's movement was thus a motley coalition of rebellious *hacen-dados*, ambitious merchants, local notables, dispossessed or pauperized peasants, and marginalized frontier producers. What kept them together was a variety of antistate feelings that had emerged, for different reasons within each group, in the prewar and early war period. An antistate sentiment also united Becerra with his village supporters outside Jaén, for as we see in more detail below, many highland villagers had experienced the earlier part of the war as a violent incursion of the Peruvian state, most notably in the form of taxes and conscription. Becerra's opposition to the head tax, and the fact that he fought with a volunteer army, thus made him an attractive ally for villages squeezed by Peruvian or Chilean exactions; people joined him to defend themselves from the incursions of the Peruvian state in the form of head taxes, war contributions, conscription, or commer-cial penetration.

Indeed, the very conditions for the movement's existence were defined by the weakness of the state in the time before the War of the Pacific. This meant that, during a national emergency, state efforts to collect resources and raise an army resulted in violence and aggression against the rural population. In a sense, it was the Peruvian state itself that first acted as a foreign invader in the northern highlands. In reaction to this, a multifaceted alliance emerged among a series of groups and classes: antistate landowners and peasants, Indians resisting commercial penetration, and merchants attempting to marginalize larger landowners from the profits of Jaén's commercial boom. Both Becerra's astute political sense and their common antigovernment position kept them together for the duration, but after his death in 1885 and Caceres's triumph over Iglesias, there was no common vision or project to bind them any longer. In the postwar confusion, it would be the differences among them that would float to the surface.[44]

In contrast to the agrarian radicalism that existed in Morelos, therefore, the oppositional political cuture constructed in the region of Becerra's influence did not include a project, whether implicit or explicit, for the making of a national politics. In the context of the Chilean invasion, of course, and once the Peruvian state began to collaborate with the Chilean army, Becerra's *montonera* became a national resistance movement almost by default. Especially once Chilean forces made incursions into the highlands, the Becerrista coalition proved quite effective in resisting them, while in the process continuing to strike blows against the Peruvian state. But in the long run, such a movement did not present a deep challenge to social control or political consolidation, because without a broader project it would fall apart quite easily once the conjunctural conditions creating it had ceased to exist.

While sharing some similarities with Becerra's movement, the second major center of resistance against the occupation and the collaborationist Peruvian government was located in a very different part of Cajamarca and composed of very different people. Led by José Mercedes Puga, a prominent *hacendado* from southern Cajamarca province, this movement began as a response to Miguel Iglesias's political actions in the period between August and December of 1882. Iglesias and Puga had confronted each other over issues of local power for years before the war, becoming legendary rivals in the province of Cajamarca and lining up on opposite sides of the emerging national factions. Since Iglesias became a Pierolista and Puga a Civilista during the 1860s and 1870s, it was hardly surprising that Piérola called upon Iglesias to organize the northern army in late 1880 during the ill-fated defense of Lima. Puga was even further alienated from the political process when Montero named Iglesias his successor in the north; but it seems that the Chilean invasion of Cajamarca in mid-1882 and the forced contributions placed on the local population began to change Puga's mind. This was especially true given the rather lukewarm defense of the region organized by Iglesias. Thus when Iglesias issued the Cry of Montán, and even more importantly when he organized a constituent assembly in Cajamarca to legitimate his role as national leader, Puga decided to act. As of December 1882, there are references to his participation in a growing rebel movement directly to the south of Cajamarca city, in the area between the districts of San Marcos and Ichocán and the city of Cajabamba.[45]

Ichocán and San Marcos, both centers of rebel activity, were villages with a history of resisting taxation and conscription. In July of 1880, for example, the governor of Ichocán district was attacked by a group of two hundred women and fifty men, armed with stones and sticks, as he attempted to lead a group of conscripts out of the area. During the following year, the authorities encountered major resistance in attempting to tax or draft the local population, often returning from their missions with hands empty. In some cases, people simply retired to the hills; in others, the local inhabitants—mainly the women—took it upon themselves to defend prospective conscripts by attacking the officials. In San Marcos as well there was violent resistance against local authorities, especially with regard to taxation. In October and November of 1882, government representatives had major confrontations with local citizens when they tried to charge the *contribución personal*. The most serious incident occurred on October 25, when over five hundred women and men ambushed the governor and his force, shooting at them and attacking them from the surrounding hills.[46]

Local reaction was understandable given the methods used by the government. Forced conscription, it seems, was quite common. Soldiers entered the villages, breaking down doors in the middle of the night and taking people off at gunpoint. The result was usually that the rest of the population fled the villages, hiding out on the *punas* or in caves, fearing a repetition of the attack. It is of course hard to gauge, on the basis of existing documentation, what proportion of conscripts was taken violently and against their will; but correspondence to the prefect's office is full of letters from individuals begging that recruits taken by force be set free.

Under conditions such as these, with the Peruvian state perceived as the most direct enemy by many villagers, the stage was set for an alliance with several *hacendados* in San Marcos and Ichocán districts, who had also been dragging their feet when faced with draft or war contribution requests. They had hidden possible recruits and criminals within their properties, ignoring official orders to turn men over to local authorities. Since government representatives apparently needed a special warrant to enter haciendas, protecting individuals within the borders of large estates was quite effective. As of the last months of 1882, it seems that landowners in San Marcos and Ichocán districts, most notably the owner of the hacienda La Pauca, José Mercedes Puga, were extending protection within their borders to all peasants resisting state exactions.[47]

This local and contingent alliance was organized around a common antistate position generated by wartime incursions. As the predominant force in the village resistance, both quantitatively and morally, peasant women were fighting to defend their households and families from outside aggression. But the villagers in general also found the alliance with local *hacendados* to be a familiar one, for Puga at least had a long-standing relationship with the inhabitants of Ichocán and San Marcos. As was true in many other parts of Cajamarca, these two villages did not have enough land, especially pasture. Many individuals therefore rented lands from Puga, ostensibly as part of an ongoing relationship of patronage and clientele.[48] This preexisting relation, combined with the need to act in a new emergency situation, formed the glue that held the *montonera* together.

The other important component of Puga's movement was a sizable proportion of the urban Chinese population, particularly from the city of Cajamarca. It is difficult to know at this point why they joined; perhaps because they feared being associated with the coastal Chinese who had rebelled against the *hacendados* and joined with the Chileans, perhaps because their extensive commercial relations in the province had brought them into conflict with members of the anti-Puga faction. Whatever the reasons for their participation, Puga seems to have trusted the Chinese members of his *montonera* implicitly, perhaps in part because their position as outsiders in local society might diminish the possibility of crosscutting loyalties. In addition to acting as his spies in Cajamarca city, it was mainly the Chinese *montoneros* who escaped with him across the Marañón River when he knew he was being pursued by a superior force in November of 1884.[49]

What seems to have held together this complex alliance of landowners, retainers, village peasants, and urban Chinese was a common antistate sentiment, though the reasons for it were understandably different than in the case of Becerra's movement. The village peasantry, and especially the women, had risen up to defend themselves against the outside threat represented by the Peruvian state's efforts to raise funds and men for the war. They had been able to count on the aid of a powerful landowner faction that, for reasons of its own, was also opposing state efforts at taxation. The end result was a powerful and relatively unified *montonera* that was quite effective in confronting the collaborationist Peruvians as well as the occupation forces. In a similar way to Becerra, however, it did not possess a broader project for the making of a national politics.[50]

What distinguished Puga's *montonera* was the strength of its connection to landowner politics and hacienda dynamics. In times of trouble, the most important hideouts were on Puga's properties. The haciendas were also storage places for stolen cattle and the most effective battle sites. And Puga's own motivations were highly colored by his ongoing conflict with fellow *hacendado* Miguel Iglesias, probably more so than by an abstract sense of or commitment to a broader national project. This was also true of those who fought against him.[51]

Indeed, the hacienda-centered political struggles that generated and were reproduced by Puga's *montonera* encouraged ongoing factional and clientelistic battles in the region, both during and after the war. Francisco Baldomero Pinillos, for example, an *hacendado* from Santiago de Chuco who had been involved in border conflicts with Puga before the war, became a rabid Iglesista, leading his own men into battle against Puga's forces and perceiving the entire conflict in localistic terms. He and his sons Serapio and Juan José received commissions in the national guard and, in October 1885, demanded the adjudication of hacienda Uningambal, neighboring on their estate, Sangual, and with which they had been disputing a pasture. As rationale for their demand, they argued that a commander allied with Puga had invaded their property from a base on Uningambal, damaging their estate in a politically motivated reprisal.[52]

In the end, neither Becerra's merchant *montonera* nor Puga's hacienda-oriented movement generated a regional political culture whose overall vision extended outward toward the building of a national politics. Both movements were diverse coalitions of people, held together by an antistate sentiment that in a particular conjuncture prompted them to fight on the nationalist side, but in neither case did events lead them in the direction of elaborating a national project. Though guerrilla commanders allied with Puga or Becerra continued to fight on the Cacerista side in the civil war of 1884–1885, the situation became increasingly muddy after Puga's and Becerra's deaths in 1885, as well as after the defeat of Iglesias. Into the early 1890s, the Cacerista state was unable to come up with an effective strategy for reestablishing control in the region. It would be left to Nicolás de Piérola, and the post-1895 government of national reconstruction, to attempt a return to order in the department of Cajamarca.[53]

In Cajamarca, as in some other areas of the country, Piérola's bid for power was supported by a significant sector of the traditional landowning oligarchy eager to reachieve the prewar status quo; but what that support meant in the north was conditioned by the particular nature of the regional political culture that had emerged in previous decades. Though they had rejected state intervention in the years before the War of the Pacific, by 1895 most landowners in Cajamarca were forced to admit they needed some kind of relationship with a national state. Even though they had not faced an autonomous and militant peasant movement of the kind existing in Morelos, the disorganization and destruction of the Chilean occupation and subsequent civil strife had badly shaken their economic and political control. As Cacerista political officials throughout the north were quick to point out in early 1886, economic dislocation, extended political conflict, and the dispersal of weapons and men from the haciendas had sent shock waves through the regional economy and state institutions. The situation was further exacerbated in the northern sierra by the fact that, after 1890, the increasing demand for labor on the coastal sugar plantations threatened to drive a wedge in the local monopoly of labor power.

When Nicolás de Piérola returned to the presidential palace in 1895, then, he was welcomed warmly by many traditional landowning families in Cajamarca who viewed him as a savior come to reestablish their position in local society. Yet even as they welcomed the state into their areas, landowners in Cajamarca negotiated the terms of the relationship in a very different way than did their counterparts in Morelos.[54]

While in Morelos the emerging Liberal state intervened repeatedly and directly, between 1856 and 1876, to favor the *hacendados* in their relatively even conflict with the villages, in northern Peru the Pierolista consolidation tended to underwrite or rebuild a system of private landowner power. This was possible in part, of course, because of the relative weakness of independent peasant mobilization in the area. It was also possible because the prewar history of class relations had given the landowners a strong territorial and political base from which to work. The end result was an *hacendado*-state relationship that looked a great deal like traditional *gamonalismo*. In exchange for sanctioning the continued privatization of power in the countryside, the government was assured collaboration from local landlords. And the deal seemed to work to a great extent, at least until the 1920s and 1930s. Though banditry and violence became endemic in the region, forcing a massive repression in the 1920s by the national state, until the 1960s the police still had trouble penetrating the borders of the great estates in highland Cajamarca.[55]

Conclusions: Landlords, Popular Movements,
and the Consolidation of the State

Between 1850 and 1890, only the first bases were set in Mexico and Peru for what would become, as of the 1930s and 1940s, more recognizable forms of state. Conditions at the national level were in each case constructed through a series of negotiations among regional political cultures, of which our two examples cannot be considered typical. A comparison of Morelos and Cajamarca, therefore, does not get us to the bottom of the relevant issues nor set any generalizable pattern for either country. What it does do is underline the importance of the popular classes in defining the contours of regional political cultures as well as that of landowner participation in and responses to those cultures. As we have seen for Morelos and Cajamarca, variations in all these factors could affect regional perceptions on the need for, or lack thereof, state intervention in local politics, thus opening up different options for factions attempting to control—or consolidate—state power. And it is in this context that a comparative look at these cases suggests some interesting general hypotheses about the relationship of landowners, agrarian social movements, and regional political cultures to the consolidation of the state, the choice of an authoritarian option, and the particular forms authoritarianism could take.

In Morelos, as we saw, a series of socioeconomic and political coondi-tions made possible the rise of an unusually strong and autonomous popular movement during the nineteenth century. A commercialized and dynamic village economy provided opportunities for peasants outside the haciendas, and in fact resulted in competition for land, labor, water, and other resources between communal and hacienda agriculture. The need to defend village resources against pressure from the great estate was indeed an important factor in maintaining and reproducing communal solidarity in Morelos, even if less crucial to the villagers' allies in other areas, Guerrero in particular. In their ongoing battles for federalism, municipal autonomy, lower taxes, and occasionally continued access to land, peasant villages throughout El Sur actively sought allies beyond their localities, building bonds with small merchants, artisans, and peons as well as with federalist provincial elites and other power holders. In so doing, they began to fashion their own project for the making of national politics, supporting the winning coalition that took national power in 1855 and again in 1867 with the defeat of the empire.

In opposition to this popular agrarian movement, the sugar *hacendados* in Morelos maintained a united front and, from early on, recognized the importance of state aid in repression and social control. Though centralist and politically conservative throughout the midnineteenth century, land-owners also petitioned Liberal governments and used their control of revenue as a weapon to press their case. In combination with the Liberals' need to reproduce their own power and control, this financial pressure helped build an alliance of conservative *hacendados* and liberal state makers in a common project of popular repression. The end result was a centraliza-tion of power through the exclusion of the popular movement; in other words, authoritarianism.

In Cajamarca, by contrast, and despite differences among the subre-gions, no strong or autonomous popular movement emerged in the nine-teenth century. I have already suggested some reasons for this, including the lack of an economic or politicocultural basis for communal autonomy. This dispersion of popular resistance allowed landowners also to remain divided, fighting local battles over surplus, resources, and power among themselves. A system of private landowner power emerged, where multi-class factions battled with each other; there was no perceived need for state support in social control.

During the War of the Pacific, the social movements that resisted the Chilean invasion were in fact multiclass, antistate alliances with no overall project for the making of national politics. More than anything else it was the destruction and disorganization caused by the wars, both international and civil, that ultimately led to a convergence of interests between local landowners and the reemerging state. In the case of Cajamarca, however, this convergence was negotiated through the recreation of a system of private landowner power. The result was a decentralization of power, with no clear popular project to exclude. Repression was localized; no centralized authoritarian state emerged. Instead, through the 1920s and 1930s, ongoing and localized confrontations among clientelistic factions, along with generalized banditry and privatized violence, were the rule. Yet in contrast to existing interpretations of these events, which tend to explain them by pointing to the "traditional" sociopolitical dynamics that underlay them,[56] my analysis suggests that banditry, clientelism, and private violence were the result of a particular renegotiation of power between regional political cultures and an emerging national state.

Attempts to create national politics in Mexico and Peru, therefore, interlaced quite distinctly in the two regions, as struggles for national power involved and helped reorganize local coalitions. Morelos, an area of strategic economic and geographic importance to events in the capital, where differences between subregions were negotiated through the construction of a common popular political culture and a unified *hacendado* class, played a crucial role in defining national political options throughout the second half of the nineteenth century. Radical federalism, as it was constituted in the villages of El Sur, was central to the ideological and political debates surrounding the 1855 Liberal revolution. In this sense we can say that, even as it was repressed, southern popular political culture was inscribed in the very foundations of the modern Mexican state. Cajamarca's highland region, on the other hand, was less central than Morelos, both geographically and economically, yet it did have an important political role in the broader factionalism and civil war of the 1880s, because Miguel Iglesias was from the area. This form of involvement in national power struggles, however, further deepened the differences between provinces or subregions that had already been heightened in factional struggles between clientelistic followings. Thus neither the landowning elites nor the popular classes had a unique effect on the making of modern Peruvian politics.

The regimes that finally consolidated state power in late-nineteenth-century Mexico and Peru were the Porfiriato (1876–1910), emerging from conflicts internal to liberalism after the defeat of the empire, and the so-called Aristocratic Republic, set into motion by Nicolás de Piérola between 1895 and 1899 and institutionalized under his successors (1899–1918).[57] In both cases, the general policy themes were economic development, modernization, and social control. Yet given the distinct historical experiences of the two societies in the previous period, what each of these themes meant was quite different in each case. So was the potential of each political system for continuity and change in the twentieth century.

The strength of popular agrarian mobilization in Morelos—and in other parts of central Mexico, such as highland Puebla[58]—during the 1860s and 1870s meant that Porfirio Díaz initially gained power at the head of a coalition that included agrarian social movements. The consolidation of his regime through the early 1890s, repressive and authoritarian as it was, was based in part on strategic negotiations with these regional political constituencies. Diaz's increasing reliance on landowners and foreign capital, his resulting abandonment of his village allies, and his consequent need to increase repression, all helped generate a political crisis in the early twentieth century. His ex-allies in the villages of central Mexico then advanced an agrarian and radical federalist agenda between 1910 and 1917, turning an intraelite squabble and palace revolt into a social revolution.

These agrarian social movements also forced the consolidation of a new kind of Mexican state in the postrevolutionary period. Built on the destruction of the landowning class as such and on the selective incorporation of popular aspirations and organizations into the state itself, the new state was hegemonic in the sense that its rule was built on a combination of coercion and consent. Yet it would never be democratic. Quite the contrary: from the 1930s to the 1970s, one of the dramatic achievements of the postrevolutionary Mexican state was the combination of incorporation and authoritarianism.[59] A look at Morelos's regional political culture, which has played such a major role in the construction of both nineteenth- and twentieth-century states, suggests that this combination has its roots in the intense strength and autonomy of the popular agrarian movement.

In Peru, the Pierolista state was consolidated between 1895 and 1899 through a policy of divide and rule in which each region received relative autonomy, represented in localized control by landowning oligarchies and regional power holders. The one region where this model was somewhat modified was in the central highlands, where a strong agrarian movement prompted a Morelos-style solution in 1895 and beyond. Yet in contrast to Mexico, repression and exclusion were not part of a general centralization of power, nor did the depth or breadth of agrarian social movements force even a glimmer of strategic negotiation. Quite the opposite: in Peru until the end of the 1960s the exclusion of agrarian social movements, and the repression that accompanied it, was relived over and over again each time a crisis accompanied by agrarian unrest raised the possibility of a new alternative. Authoritarianism without incorporation, based on a more "colonial" model of regionalization and the fragmentation of power, continued to be the order of the day.[60]

Only during the first phase of the military revolution (1969–1975) did President Juan Velasco Alvarado experiment with a form of inclusionary yet authoritarian politics, *a la mexicana*, prompting some scholars to analyze the regime with terms like "hegemony" and "corporatism."[61] But its failure would become painfully apparent in the second half of the 1970s, as the strength of the popular movements it unleashed quickly overstepped the boundaries of the political system it had created. Ironically, the return to "democracy"—in the form of elections and a parliamentary system—was accompanied in the 1980s by increasing violence and the militarization of the highlands. Despite electoral forms, the construction and reconstruction of "colonial" fragmentation—in stark contrast to the hegemonic if authoritarian model of Mexican integration—has reemerged at the center of contemporary Peruvian politics. Outside of Lima, in the 1980s, the Peruvian state existed mainly in military form.[62]

If we are to conceptualize the many paths to democracy and authoritarianism in a more nuanced way, therefore, we need to think of class alliance and political culture, not only as terms coined to analyze dominant class battles, but most importantly as concepts that allow us to think historically about the role of different popular classes and movements in the making of national politics. In this sense, as recent work on Europe has begun to show, the various paths to authoritarianism or democracy are clearly constructed on more than a dominant-class level, on more than whether landowners and industrialists, *hacendados* and the bourgeoisie, agree or disagree, fight or ally, in the formation of the state.[63] The option for authoritarianism—and the specific form it takes—depends also on the capacity to negotiate or incorporate the demands of popular political movements and cultures. Distinguishing among authoritarianisms according to the history and form of exclusion and inclusion, therefore, becomes as important as defining the conditions under which authoritarianism can arise. Specifically for Mexico and Peru, such distinctions help us understand the present as well as the past. For even if both countries have generally lived under authoritarian regimes, this alone cannot explain why today, in the midst of bone-crushing crisis, only the Peruvian state is in an advanced state of decomposition.

NOTES

This essay is part of a broader work. A different version of some of the materials presented here appeared in chapters 5 and 7 of Florencia E. Mallon, *Peasant and Nation: The Making of Postcolonial Mexico and Peru* (Berkeley and Los Angeles: University of California Press, 1995). The research on which it is based was conducted in Peru in 1981, on a Social Science Research Council Postdoctoral Grant, and in Mexico in 1984–1985, funded by a Fulbright Faculty Research Fellowship and the Graduate School of the University of Wisconsin-Madison.

Writing and revision was done with the help of a Romnes Fellowship, University of Wisconsin-Madison, and an NEH Fellowship for College Teachers. The final preparation of the manuscript was done while I was a fellow at the Center for Advanced Study in the Behavioral Sciences, Stanford, California (1990–1991).

Abbreviations

ACDN	Archivo de Cancelados de la Defensa Nacional, Mexico City
ADC	Archivo del Departamento de Cajamarca, Cajamarca, Peru
AGN(M)	Archivo General de la Nación, Mexico City
AHDN	Archivo Histórico de la Defensa Nacional, Mexico City
AHM	Archivo Histórico Militar, Lima, Peru
BNM, LAF	Biblioteca Nacional de México, Colección Lafragua, Mexico City
BNP	Biblioteca Nacional del Perú, Lima, Peru
GOB [TP]	Gobernación [Tranquilidad Pública]; Archivo General de la Nación, Mexico City
II IMP	Segundo Imperio: Archivo General de la Nación, Mexico City
JPCM	Junta Protectora de las Clases Menesterosas; Archivo General de la Nación, Mexico City

1. See, for example, Richard Morse, "Toward a Theory of Spanish Government," *Journal of the History of Ideas* 15, no. 1 (1954): 71–93; Glen Dealy, "Prolegomena on the Spanish American Political Tradition," *Hispanic American Historical Review* 48, no. 1 (Feb. 1968): 37–58, and *The Public Man: An Interpretation of Latin American and Other Catholic Countries* (Amherst: University of Massachusetts Press, 1977); Claudio Veliz, *The Centralist Tradition of Latin America* (Princeton: Princeton University Press, 1980); and Peter Smith, "Political Legitimacy in Latin America," in *New Approaches to Latin American History*, ed. Richard Graham and Peter H. Smith (Austin: University of Texas Press, 1974), 225–55.

2. For the original formulation, see Guillermo A. O'Donnell, *Modernization and Bureaucratic-Authoritarianism: Studies in South American Politics* (Berkeley: Institute of International Studies, 1973). For some of the later extensions, discussion, and revisions, see O'Donnell, "Tensiones en el estado burocrático-autoritario y la cuestión de la democracia," Documento CEDES/G. E. CLACSO/ Nº 11 (Buenos Aires: Centro de Estudios de Estado y Sociedad, 1978), and *1966–1973: El Estado Burocrático Autoritario* (Buenos Aires: Ed. de Belgrano, 1982); James M. Malloy, ed., *Authoritarianism and Corporatism in Latin America* (Pittsburgh: University of Pittsburgh Press, 1977); and David Collier, ed., *The New Authoritarianism in Latin America* (Princeton: Princeton University Press, 1979).

3. Some of these can be found in Guillermo O'Donnell, Philippe Schmitter, and Laurence Whitehead, eds., *Transitions from Authoritarian Rule: Latin America* (Baltimore: Johns Hopkins University Press, 1986); and in Larry Diamond, Juan J. Linz, and Seymour Martin Lipset, eds., *Democracy in Developing Countries* (Boulder, Colo.: Lynne Rienner, 1988).

4. For my first formulation of the concept of the long nineteenth century, see Florencia E. Mallon, "Editor's Introduction," *Latin American Perspectives* 13, no. 1 (winter 1986): 3–17. Other discussions of this periodization occurred at the Conference on Latin American History's panel on "The Middle Period of

Latin American History, " American Historical Association, Washington, D.C., December 1987, where I presented "Peasants and the 'National Problem' during the 'Middle Period' of Latin American History: Alternative National Projects in Mexico and Peru, 1850–1910."

5. Philip Corrigan and Derek Sayer, *The Great Arch: English State Formation As Cultural Revolution* (Cambridge, Mass.: Basil Blackwell, 1985).

6. BNM, LAF 839: "Ejército de operaciones sobre Puebla: Parte general," 23 Mar. 1856. For a more detailed analysis of the formation and activities of the national guard battalions, see Florencia E. Mallon, "Peasants and State Formation in Nineteenth-Century Mexico: Morelos, 1848–1858," *Political Power and Social Theory* 7 (1988): 1–54.

7. Mallon, "Peasants and State Formation," 21–22, 24–30.

8. This paragraph is based on Peter Guardino, "Peasants, Politics, and State Formation in Nineteenth Century Mexico: Guerrero, 1850–1855" (Ph.D. diss. [history], University of Chicago, 1992) and on Florencia E. Mallon, *Peasant and Nation: The Making of Postcolonial Mexico and Peru* (Berkeley: University of California Press, 1995), chap. 5.

9. Guardino, "Peasants, Politics, and State Formation," especially chaps. 3, 4, and 5. *Oficiales de república* were the political authorities in charge of administering the older institutions of *cabildo* government set up during the colonial period, in many cases "domesticated" by local ethnic hierarchies to represent Indian communal interests. The municipalities organized after Independence in some cases came to compete with these older forms, providing mestizos or outsiders with a possible avenue to local influence or power.

10. Horacio Crespo, coord., *Morelos: Cinco siglos de historia regional* (Mexico City and Cuernavaca: Centro de Estudios Históricos del Agrarismo en México and Universidad Autónoma del Estado de Morelos, 1985); Cheryl English Martin, "Haciendas and Villages in Late Colonial Morelos," *Hispanic American Historical Review* 62, no. 3 (1982): 407–27, and Martin, *Rural Society in Colonial Morelos* (Albuquerque: University of New Mexico Press, 1985).

11. Mallon, "Peasants and State Formation," 8–10, 12–14, passim; ACDN, Expediente de Francisco Leyva; Mallon, *Peasant and Nation*, chap. 5.

12. Guardino, "Peasants, Politics, and State Formation"; Mallon, "Peasants and State Formation."

13. Mallon, "Peasants and State Formation," and *Peasant and Nation*, chap. 5; Cecilia Noriega Elío, *El Constituyente de 1842* (Mexico City: Universidad Nacional Autónoma, 1986); Charles Hale, *Mexican Liberalism in the Age of Mora* (New Haven: Yale University Press, 1968).

14. For the incident with Arellano, see Leticia Reina, *Las rebeliones campesinas en México (1819–1906)* (Mexico City: Siglo XXI Editores, 1980), 157–61. The comparison of Alvarez's influence in Morelos and Guerrero is based on Guardino, "Peasants, Politics and State Formation," and Mallon, "Peasants and State Formation."

15. Mallon, "Peasants and State Formation"; Reina, *Las rebeliones campesinas*; Fernando Díaz y Díaz, *Caudillos y caciques* (Mexico City: El Colegio de México, 1972). I have borrowed the concept "radical federalism" from Peter Guardino, "Peasants, Politics and State Formation," especially chapter 4. He argues quite convincingly, at various points in his dissertation, that it was radical federalism rather than liberalism that propelled Juan Alvarez into the presidency in 1855.

16. Mallon, "Peasants and State Formation"; Guardino, "Peasants, Politics and State Formation," chap. 5, discusses the development of a radical political culture in El Sur during the 1840s, especially an alternative definition of citizenship.

17. Mallon, "Peasants and State Formation."

18. On the ambivalence of liberals, as evidenced by Comonfort, see ibid. On Comonfort's contradictory role during the Conservative takeover, see Jan Bazant, *A Concise History of Mexico: From Hidalgo to Cárdenas, 1805–1940* (London and New York: Cambridge University Press, 1977), 76–77. For more on the contradictory politics of these years, see Bazant, "Mexico from Independence to 1867," in *The Cambridge History of Latin America*, vol. 3, ed. Leslie Bethell (Cambridge and New York: Cambridge University Press, 1985); and Richard Sinkin, "The Mexican Constitutional Congress, 1856–1857: A Statistical Analysis," *Hispanic American Historical Review* 53, no. 1, (1973): 1–26.

19. On Teloloapam in particular, and the western side of the Morelos-Guerrero region more generally, see AGN(M), GOB: Legajo (hereafter Leg.) 1126 (2): "Autoridades del distrito de Bravos, zona de Teloloapam, al Gobernador de Cuernavaca," 14 Aug. 1864; Expediente (hereafter Exp.) 18: "Oficio de los vecinos de Acapetlahuaya, distrito de Teloloapam, desde México," Aug. 1864, and "Informe de la autoridad política de Cuernavaca," 3 Jan. 1865; AHDN, XI/ 481.4/9450: "Gobierno del Imperio: Movimientos y cuentas diversas militares, 1864," ff. 211–13: "Solicitud de los vecinos de varios pueblos del distrito de Teloloapam a los Regentes del Imperio," Istapan, 13 Dec. 1863; D/481.4/9536: "Gobierno del Imperio, Año de 1864. Movimiento de fuerzas Imperiales"; D/ 481.4/9526: "Gobierno del Imperio. Año de 1864. Cuernavaca.-Movimiento de fuerzas"; XI/481.4/9532: "Gobierno del Imperio. Año de 1864. Movimiento de tropas imperiales durante el año de 1864"; D/481.4/9449: "Gobierno del Imperio. Año de 1864. Armamento pedido por varias autoridades y distribución de él"; D/481.4/9541, ff. 30–32: "Representacion de los mineros de Taxco al Ministro de Guerra y Marina, pidiendo fuerzas para su zona," 7 Jan. 1864, ff. 162–62v: "El Comandante Militar de Cuernavaca al subsecretario de Guerra y Marina, transcribiendo parte de Iguala," 29 Jan. 1864; AGN(M), GOB [TP]: 3ª/866/4/1: "Correspondencia del Prefecto Político del Departamento de Iturbide al Ministro de Gobernación," Feb.–Oct. 1866, 3ª/866–67 (1)/ 2 [49]: "Expediente sobre la comisión especial de D. Abraham Ortiz de la Peña en Teloloapam," began 2 Apr. 1866, and "Correspondencia del Prefecto Político del Departamento de Iturbide con el Ministro de Gobernación," Cuernavaca, Jan.–Apr. 1866; 2ª/865 (2)/1 [51]: "Oficio del Prefecto de Iturbide, Gerardo Gómez, al Ministerio de Gobernación, comunicando novedades de la semana anterior," Cuernavaca, 5 June 1865, and "Oficio del Prefecto Político de Iturbide al Ministerio de Gobernación, sobre novedades," Cuernavaca, 24 July 1865. AGN(M), GOB: Leg. 1162(2), Exp. 18, 1865: "Información del Prefecto Político de Iturbide sobre la tranquilidad Pública," Cuernavaca, 20 Jan.–20 Mar., 1865; II IMP: Caja 14: "Oficio de Abraham Ortiz de la Peña, transcribiendo oficio del Crel. Carranza sobre la situación en la zona del Mescala," 2 Oct. 1866. On Alvarez's general headquarters on the hacienda La Providencia, see AGN(M), GOB: Leg. 1423, Exp. 4: "Prefecto Político de Iturbide al Ministerio de Gobernación, transcribiendo parte del subprefecto de Teloloapam," 6 Nov. 1866.

20. For the sierra de Huitzilac, see *Periódico Oficial del Imperio Mexicano* 2, no. 13 (30 Jan. 1864): 1; *El Pájaro Verde*, 9 Feb. 1864, p. 2; AHDN, D/481.4/8864:

"En el pueblo de Huitzilac es derrotada la fuerza del traidor Galván. . . ." 2 Oct. 1862, D/481.4/9541, f. 91: "Proclama de Francisco Leyva a los ciudadanos del 3er distrito," Huitzilac, Oct. 1863; ff. 92–93: "Carta de Francisco Leyva a Domingo Montañes, administrador de la hacienda San José," Huitzilac, Nov. 1863; ff. 125–25v: "Parte del Comandante Militar de Cuernavaca al Subsecretario de Guerra y Marina, transcribiendo parte del Comandante Militar de Tetecala sobre la derrota de gavillas en la sierra de Huitzilac," 28 Jan. 1864; ff. 164–64v: "Comandante Militar de Cuernavaca, Felipe N. Chacón, al Subsecretario de Guerra y Marina," 29 Jan. 1864; D/481.4/9540, "Gobierno del Imperio. Año de 1864. Movimiento de Fuerzas, incluyendo la División Márquez," f. 65: "Oficio del Comandante Militar de Iturbide, E. Vargas, al Ministerio de Guerra y Marina," Cuernavaca, 30 Dec. 1864; AGN(M), GOB: Leg. 1161(2), Exp. 18: "Oficio del Ministro de Guerra al Ministro de Gobernación, sobre un oficio del Comandante Militar de Cuernavaca," Mexico City, 29 Jan. 1865; "Oficio del Prefecto de Iturbide al Ministerio de Gobernación," Cuernavaca, 20 Feb. 1865; and AGN(M), GOB: Leg. 500(3), Exp. 1: "Tranquilidad Pública, Iturbide: Oficios varios del Jefe político del territorio de Iturbide sobre las gavillas de facciosos que operan en la zona," Cuernavaca, Jan.–June 1860. For the rest of the district of Cuernavaca, see AHDN, D/481.4/9541, ff. 89–90: "Circular de Francisco Leyva, Comandante Militar del 3er Distrito del Estado de México, desde su cuartel general en Los Hornos," 18 Dec. 1863; ff. 94–95v: "Parte del Comandante Militar Interino Abraham Ortiz de la Peña al Ministerio de Guerra y Marina, sobre encuentro con liberales," Cuernavaca, 21 Dec. 1863; ff. 75–76v: "Subprefecto de Tetecala al Prefecto de Cuernavaca, sobre ataque a Ixtla," 25 Oct. 1863; ff. 77–78: "Subprefecto de Tetecala al Prefecto de Cuernavaca, transcribiendo oficio del Presidente Municipal de Jojutla," 25 Oct. 1863; ff. 79–79v: "R. Hernández, administrador de la hacienda San Nicolás, al Subprefecto de Tetecala," 25 Oct. 1863; ff. 130–31: "Proclama del Teniente Coronel Amado Popoca a los habitantes del cantón de Tetecala," Campo de Nespa, Dec. 1863; ff. 132–32v: "Teniente Coronel Amado Popoca, Jefe Político y Comandante Militar de Tetecala, transcribiendo circular de Francisco Leyva," Campo de Nespa, 20 Dec. 1863; D/481.4/9526, ff. 2–2v: "Comandante Militar de Cuernavaca al Ministerio de Guerra y Marina, sobre conspiración en Tepoztlán," 15 June 1864; ff. 52–53v: "Oficio del Administrador General de Peajes al Subsecretario del Ministerio de Hacienda, transcribiendo partes del recaudador de peajes en San Mateo Xalpa, camino a Cuernavaca," 21 Dec. 1864; El Pájaro Verde, 16 Jan. 1864, p. 2; 16 Jan. 1865, p. 3; 24 Feb. 1865, p. 3; AGN(M), GOB: Leg. 1144(1), Exp. 2: "Queja de vecinos del barrio de Nexpa, municipalidad de Jojutla, sobre terrenos," 29 Apr. 1865–17 Jan. 1866; II Imperio, Caja 74: "Resumen de hechos para S.M. el Emperador, N° 1216," 7–12 Aug. 1865; GOB: Leg. 1423, Exp. 4: "Oficio del Visitador Imperial de Iturbide al Subsecretario de Gobernación," Cuernavaca, 17 Dec. 1866; GOB: Leg. 1161(2), Exp. 18: "Oficio del Prefecto Político de Iturbide al Ministerio de Gobernación, dando cuenta de hechos en su territorio," Cuernavaca, 13 Jan. 1865; "Varios oficios del Prefecto Político de Iturbide a Gobernación, sobre una conspiración en Tepoztlán," Cuernavaca, 25–26 Feb. 1865; and GOB [TP]: 2ª/865/(1)/2[53]: "Expediente formado sobre un desorden en Coatlán, Morelos, en que el Alcalde Municipal de Coatlán del Río, D. Guadalupe Rubio, se queja de los procedimientos del Juez de Letras de Tetecala," Cuernavaca, 25 Aug. 1865.

21. Mallon, "Peasants and State Formation." For cases of hacienda-community conflict in the districts of this area, see Alejandro Villaseñor, Memoria política

y estadística de la prefectura de Cuernavaca presentada al Superior Gobierno del Estado Libre y Soberano de México (Mexico City: Imprenta de Cumplido, 1850), 7, 18; AGN(M), GOB: Leg. 1786 (2), Exp. 6: "Solicitud de los vecinos del barrio de Amilcingo, pueblo de Huasulco, municipalidad de Zacualpan Amilpas, al Emperador," 22 Dec. 1865; JPCM, IV: Exp. 15, ff. 146–46v: "Irineo Nava, del pueblo de Acatlipa, compensión de Cuernavaca, y Juan Nuñez, apoderado del estado de Iturbide, al Emperador," 1 June 1866; ff. 140–41v: "Solicitud de los Concejales del Ayuntamiento de Xiutepec al Emperador," 2 June 1866; ff. 147–48v: "Miguel Rojas, alcalde propietario y otros vecinos de S. Bartolomé Atlacholoaya, con Juan Nuñez, apoderado del estado de Iturbide, al emperador," 2 June 1866; ff. 144–45v: "Solicitud de Juan Nuñez, representando los pueblos de Xiutepec, San Francisco Izacualpan, Tesollucan, Xochitepec, Acatlipa, Cuentepec, Teclama, Alpuyecan, Ahuehuecingo y Atlacholoaya, de la comprensión de Cuernavaca," 3 June 1866; ff. 154–55: "Resolución de la Junta Protectora sobre el caso de Xiutepec y otros," 24 Aug. 1866; JPCM, IV: Exp. 20, ff. 190–92v: "Solicitud de los vecinos de Amayuca a S.M. el Emperador," 6 June 1866; f. 193: "Certificado de Leandro Alcazar, Teniente de Alcalde de Amayuca," 5 June 1866; II Imperio, Caja 95: "Solicitud de los alcaldes auxiliares de algunos pueblos de la zona de Cuernavaca, protestando la aprehensión del apoderado de Iturbide, D. Juan Nuñez," 16 June 1866. Under such circumstances of hacienda-community tensions, it is not surprising that people in the villages would be responsive to proclamations that called for a defense of the freedoms won during Independence, against the "slavery" then existing on the haciendas of the *cañada*. See especially AHDN, D/481.4/9541, ff. 130–31: "Proclama del Teniente Coronel Amado Popoca a los habitantes del cantón de Tetecala," December 1863.

22. AHDN, D/481.4/9541, ff. 75–76v: "Subprefecto de Tetecala al Prefecto de Cuernavaca, sobre ataque a Ixtla," 25 Oct. 1863; ff. 77–78: "Subprefecto de Tetecala al Prefecto de Cuernavaca, transcribiendo oficio del Presidente Municipal de Jojutla," 25 Oct. 1863; ff. 79–79v: "R. Hernández, administrador de la hacienda San Nicolás, al Subprefecto de Tetecala," 25 Oct. 1863.

23. On the suggestion to make pueblos in the sierra de Huitzilac a free-fire zone, see AGN(M), GOB [TP]: 2ᵃ/865 (2)/ 2 [51]: Oficio del Prefecto Político de Iturbide al Ministerio de Gobernación, sobre los Ranchos que Ayudan a los disidentes," Cuernavaca, 24 July 1865. On the organization of repression by the haciendas, see Alejandro Villaseñor, *Memoria política y estadística de la prefectura de Cuernavaca presentada al Superior Gobierno del Estado Libre y Soberano de México* (Mexico City: Imprenta de Cumplido, 1850), Anexo Nº 8; and AHDN, D/481.4/9541, ff. 79–79v: "R. Hernández, administrador de la hacienda San Nicolás, al subprefecto de Tetecala," 25 Oct. 1865. On government attempts to tax the haciendas to finance the government, including its activities of social control, see AGN(M), Leg. 500, Exp. 2: "Quejas de los hacendados del 3ᵉʳ Distrito del Estado de México al Gobernador del Distrito y al Presidente de la República, sobre un nuevo impuesto directo a la producción," Aug.–Sept. 1862. On the general issues of the *hacendados'* role in repression, see also Mallon, "Peasants and State Formation."

24. On the case of Apatlaco and the hacienda Coahuixtla, see AGN(M), GOB: Leg. 1126. Exp. 3, 1864: "Expediente formado sobre la expulsión de varios habitantes de la Hacienda Coahuixtla," Morelos, Apr.–May 1864; Leg. 1161(1), Exp. 10, 1865: "Manuel Mendoza Cortina, dueño de la hacienda Coahuixtla, contra los vecinos del llamado pueblo de Apatlaco, sobre expulsión de la

hacienda," Cuautla y México, Dec. 1864–May 1865; Leg. 1144(1), Exp. 2, "Vecinos del Real de la hacienda Coahuixtla protestan la transacción que en julio celebró el apoderado de ellos con el dueño de la hacienda," 12 Sept. 1865; II Imperio, Caja 48: "Lista de individuos que el administrador de la hacienda Coahuixtla quiere expulsar," 1 Dec. 1864; copied by Prefectura de Cuautla Morelos, Feb. 1865. For the incident with the liberal forces, see AHDN, D/481.4/8927, ff. 5–5v: "Oficio del Coronel Rafael Cuellar al Ministerio de Guerra y Marina, transcribiendo oficio del comandante Lucio Maldonado, desde Ayotla," 16 July 1862; ff. 8–12: "Oficio del Comandante Militar del 3er distrito del estado de México al Ministro de Guerra y Marina, transcribiendo oficio del Comandante Militar de Morelos sobre los sucesos en Totolapa contra Maldonado," 20 July 1862; and ff. 19–19v, 21–21v: "Informe de Comandante Militar del 3er distrito del estado de México al Ministro de Guerra y Marina sobre los sucesos en Totolapa," Yautepec, 5 Aug. 1862. More generally on the activities of the *plateados*, see *El Pájaro Verde*, 29 Jan. 1864, p. 2; 9 Feb. 1864, p. 3; 7 Apr. 1864, p. 3; 25 Apr. 1864, p. 3; AHDN, XI/481.4/8879, ff. 13–13v: "Oficio del Comandante Principal de Morelos al Ministerio de Guerra y Marina, participando los asesinatos cometidos por los plateados de Jantetelco," Morelos, 25 Mar. 1862; D/481.4/8860: "Comandancia Militar de Morelos. Partes sobre acciones militares," 1862, ff. 1–3, 8–10; D/481.4/8755, ff. 1–1v: "Oficio del Comandante Militar del 3er distrito del estado de México al Ministro de Guerra," Mexico City, 25 June 1862; D/481.4/8860: "Comandante Principal de Cuernavaca al Ministro de Guerra, transcribiendo parte del jefe político de Jonacatepec sobre encuentro con los plateados," 20 Oct. 1862; D/481.4/9541, ff. 64–64v: "Ayuntamiento de la villa de Jonacatepec a la Regencia del Imperio, pidiendo ayuda con los 'bandidos,' " 23 Sept. 1863; D/481.4/9449: "Gobierno del Imperio. Año de 1864. Armamento pedido por varias autoridades y distribución de él"; AGN(M), II Imperio, Caja 59: "Oficio del Gobernador y Comandante Militar del 3er distrito del estado de México al Ministro de Relaciones Exteriores y Gobernación," Cuernavaca, 23 May 1863; GOB: Leg. 1161(1), Exp. 10: "Correspondencia del Subprefecto de Cuautla Morelos con el Ministerio de Gobierno, sobre la situación en Jonacatepec y Chiautla," 2–9 Mar. 1865; GOB: Leg. 1126, Exp. 3, 1864: "Expediente sobre si se les debe dar armas a los vecinos de Jantetelco para defenderse de los plateados," Jantetelco, 31 Aug. 1864; "Oficio de los hacendados del distrito de Cuautla al Emperador," 1 Oct. 1864; II Imperio, Caja 81: "Oficio del Cura Tomás Luis G. Falco pidiendo indulto para un grupo de plateados del distrito de Morelos," and "Oficio del Arzobispo de México sobre el párroco D. Luis F. Falco," 24 Sept. 1865; GOB [TP]: 2ª/865 (1)/2[53]: "Oficio del Prefecto Político de Iturbide al Ministro de Gobernación, sobre el enjuiciamiento del Comisario Suplente de Zacualpam," Cuernavaca, 29 July 1865.

25. On *plateados'* use of liberty and the liberal cause, see *El Pájaro Verde*, 15 Nov. 1864, p. 2. On the case of Mapazlán and the hacienda Tenextepango, see AHDN, D/481.4/9541, ff. 101–02: "Oficio del Comandante Militar de Cuernavaca, Felipe Chacón, transcribiendo parte del comandante militar de Yautepec," 7 Dec. 1863, and ff. 107–107v: "Oficio del comandante militar de Cuernavaca transcribiendo parte del comandante militar de Yautepec," 30 Dec. 1863; the quote is on f. 107.

26. For the imperial decrees on the Junta Protectora de las Clases Menesterosas, see AGN(M), JPCM, Exp. 20, ff. 196v–97: "Decreto del Emperador creando la Junta Protectora de las Clases Menesterosas," Chapultepec, 10 April 1865; f. 197: "Decreto del Emperador autorizando a la Junta Protectora a formar juntas

auxiliares en todos los municipios del Imperio," 19 July 1865. For other imperial laws on issues relevant to the peasantry, see JPCM, IV, Exp. 20, ff. 197–97v: "Circular del Ministro de Gobernación sobre las tierras de colonización," 14 Sept. 1865; ff. 197v–98v: "Decreto del Emperador sobre los trabajadores del campo," 1 Nov. 1865; ff. 198v–99v: "Decreto del Emperador sobre diferencias sobre tierras y aguas entre los pueblos," 1 Nov. 1865; f. 200: "Decreto del Emperador sobre daños y perjuicios de animales en pastos y sembrados," 25 June 1866; ff. 200v–202: "Ley del Emperador sobre terrenos de comunidad y de repartimiento," 26 June 1866. For cases in which pueblos attempted to use imperial laws in their favor, see AGN(M), II Imperio, Caja 83: "Alcalde auxiliar de Temoaca y vecinos de la municipalidad de Zacualpan al Juez de 1ª Instancia de Jonacatepec, pidiendo se oficie al Director del Archivo General para que saque testimonio de las mercedes de tierras, previa cita a los pueblos colindantes," 18 Oct. 1866; "Oficio del Juez de Paz de Cuernavaca al Director del Archivo General del Imperio," 23 Aug. 1866; II Imperio, Caja 43: "Solicitud de Audiencia con el Emperador, de la Comisión del Estado de Guerrero," Mexico City, 28 May 1866; JPCM, I, Exp. 9, ff. 236–50: "Solicitud de 110 vecinos del pueblo de S. Mateo Atlatlahucan sobre el terreno de S. Diego Tepantongo," 21 Mar. 1865; JPCM, IV, Exp. 20, f. 193: "Certificado de Leandro Alcazar, Teniente de Alcalde de Amayuca," 5 June 1866; ff. 190–92v: "Solicitud de los vecinos de Amayuca al Emperador," 6 June 1866; GOB: Leg. 1786(2), Exp. 6: "Solicitud de los vecinos del barrio de Amilcingo, pueblo de Huasulco, municipalidad de Zacualpan Amilpas, al Emperador," 22 Dec. 1865. On the limits of cooperation by local authorities, and the dependence of the Junta Protectora on them, see AGN(M), JPCM, IV, Exp. 15, ff. 142–43: "Oficio de Aguilar, desde Xiutepec, a Dn. Juan Nuñez," 1 June 1866; ff. 140–41v: "Solicitud de los Concejales del Ayuntamiento de Xiutepec al Emperador," 2 June 1866; ff. 154–55: "Resolución de la Junta sobre el caso de Xiutepec y otros," 24 Aug. 1866; Exp. 20, ff. 194–94v: "Informe y resolución de Faustino Chimalpopoca a la Junta," 24 Aug. 1866; AGN(M), II Imperio, Caja 95: "Solicitud de los alcaldes auxiliares de algunos pueblos de la zona de Cuernavaca, protestando aprehensión del apoderado de Iturbide, Dn. Juan Nuñez," 16 June 1866.

27. AGN(M), JPCM, IV, Exp. 15, ff. 146–46v: "Solicitud de Irineo Nava, del pueblo de Acatlipa, comprehensión de Cuernavaca, y Juan Nuñez, apoderado del estado de Iturbide, al Emperador," 1 June 1866; ff. 142–43: "Oficio de Aguilar, desde Xiutepec, a Dn. Juan Nuñez," 1 June 1866; ff. 147–48v: "Miguel Rojas, alcalde propietario y otros vecinos de S. Bartolomé Atlacholoaya, con Juan Nuñez, apoderado del Edo. de Iturbide, al Emperador," 2 June 1866; ff. 140–41v: "Solicitud de los Concejales del Ayuntamiento de Xiutepec al Emperador," 2 June 1866; ff. 144–45v: "Solicitud de Juan Nuñez, representando los pueblos de Xiutepec, S. Francisco Izacualpan, Tesollucan, Xochitepec, Acatlipa, Cuentepec, Teclama, Alpuyecan, Ahuehuecingo y Atlacholoaya, de la comprensión de Cuernavaca," 3 June 1866; ff. 154–55: "Resolución de la Junta sobre el caso de Xiutepec y otros," 24 Aug. 1866; and AGN(M), II Imperio, Caja 95: "Solicitud de los alcaldes auxiliares de algunos pueblos de la zona de Cuernavaca, protestando aprehensión del apoderado de Iturbide, Dn. Juan Nuñez," 16 June 1866.

28. AGN(M), JPCM, V, Exp. 26, ff. 215–18v: "Solicitud e informe de Juan Cataño y Calvo, vocal presidente de la Junta Auxiliar Protectora de las Clases Menesterosas de Cuautla Morelos," 13 Sept. 1866; GOB: Leg. 1786(2), Exp. 6: "Expediente formado en ocasión de la prisión de Juan Cataño y José María

Portela, sobre prisión arbitraria por el subprefecto de Cuautla," 13 Sept.–29 Oct. 1866; JPCM, V: Exp. 37, ff. 268–71: "Solicitud de los vecinos de San Pablo, Cuernavaca, pidiendo que Juan Cataño y Calvo los represente en un litigio de terrenos," 23 Nov. 1866.

29. The connection between liberal authoritarianism and the repression of popular movements is best analyzed in Mallon, "Peasants and State Formation." For a more detailed examination of the interaction of state making and popular political cultures, see Mallon, *Peasant and Nation*, passim.

30. Carmen Diana Deere, "Changing Relations of Production and Peruvian Peasant Women's Work," *Latin American Perspectives* 4, nos. 1–2 (winter and spring 1977): 48–69; "The Development of Capitalism in Agriculture and the Division of Labor by Sex: A Study of the Northern Peruvian Sierra" (Ph.D. diss., University of California. Berkeley, 1978); and *Household and Class Relations: Peasants and Landlords in Northern Peru* (Berkeley: University of California Press, 1990), part 1; and Lewis Taylor, "Main Trends in Agrarian Capitalist Development: Cajamarca, Peru, 1880–1976" (Ph.D. thesis, University of Liverpool, 1979).

31. Taylor, "Main Trends," 17–23.

32. *Ibid.*, 27–32; Lewis Taylor, "Los orígenes del bandolerismo en Hualgayoc, 1870–1900," in *Bandoleros, abigeos y montoneros: Criminalidad y violencia en el Perú, siglos XVIII–XX*, ed. Carlos Aguirre and Charles Walker (Lima: Instituto de Apoyo Agrario, 1990), 213–47; ADC, Particulares, 1880–89: "Carta del hacendado Daniel Silva Santisteban al Subprefecto de la provincia," Hacienda Chonta, 21 Apr. 1881; Gobernadores del Distrito de San Marcos, 1854–99: "Oficio del Gobernador José Castañaduy al Subprefecto," n.d.; "Oficio del Gobernador José Castañaduy al Subprefecto," 13 Dec. 1881; Prefectura, 1880–85: "Circular del Prefecto P. J. Carrión al Subprefecto del Cercado," 1 Sept. 1881; Particulares, 1880–89: "Oficio de Manuel María Arana, hacendado de La Laguna, al Subprefecto," Cajamarca, 1 Jan. 1881; Prefectura, 1880–85: "Resolución del Jefe Superior del Norte, comunicado por el Prefecto Tadeo Terry al Subprefecto del Cercado," 19 Oct. 1881; "Decreto del Prefecto Tadeo Terry sobre la solicitud de Dn. Carlos Montoya Bernal, apoderado de María Arana," 15 Oct., 1881; Subprefectura de Cajamarca, 1880–85: "Oficio del Subprefecto Manuel B. Castro a las autoridades de su dependencia," 22 Sept. 1881; and Particulares, 1880–89: "Oficio de la Abadesa del Convento de Religiosas Descalzas Concebidas de Cajamarca, al Prefecto," 28 Oct. 1884.

33. Taylor, "Main Trends," 13–14, 16, 19; ADC, Subprefectura de Jaén, 1880–89: "Marjesí de las Rentas de la extinguida Beneficencia de la Provincia de Jaén presentada por el Subprefecto Baltazar Contreras," 15 Mar. 1885 ; Particulares: "Solicitud de Manuel Collazos al presidente de la República Miguel Iglesias," Lima, 3 Nov. 1885; Subprefectura de Jaén, 1880–89: "Informe del Subprefecto Arróspide sobre la provincia de Jaén," 2 May 1887.

34. ADC, Subprefectura de Jaén, 1880–89: "Oficio del Gobernador de San Felipe al Subprefecto de Jaén," 29 Apr. 1880; "Oficio del Subprefecto de Jaén al Prefecto," Pucará, 10 Dec. 1882; Subprefectura de Chota, 1880–89: "Oficio del Subprefecto de Chota al Prefecto del Departamento," 12 May 1884; "Oficio del Subprefecto de Chota al Prefecto del Departamento, transcribiendo oficio del gobernador del distrito de Llama," May 1884 ; Subprefectura de Jaén, 1880–89: "Oficio del Subprefecto de Jaén al Prefecto," Cutervo, 15 Oct. 1884; "Marjesí de las Rentas de la extinguida Beneficencia de la Provincia de Jaén presentada por el Subprefecto Baltazar Contreras," 15 Mar. 1885.

35. Taylor, "Los orígenes del bandolerismo"; ADC, Gobernadores del Distrito de San Marcos, 1854–99: "Oficio del Gobernador Manuel María Lazo al Prefecto," 8 Apr. 1880; "Oficio del Gobernador José Castañaduy al Subprefecto," n.d.; "Oficio del Gobernador José Castañaduy al Subprefecto," 13 Dec. 1881; Prefecturas, 1880–85: "Oficio del Prefecto Leonardo Cavero al Subprefecto del Cercado," 13 May 1881; and "Oficio del Gobernador Manuel Rubio al Subprefecto," 15 May 1882.

36. Jorge Basadre, *Historia de la República del Perú*, 6th ed. (Lima: Editorial Universitaria, 1968), vol. 6, 272–80, 406–11; Patricio Lynch, *Segunda Memoria que el Vice-Almirante D. Patricio Lynch presenta al supremo Gobierno de Chile* (Lima: Imp. de la Merced, 1883–84), vol. 2, 94–100; and Nelson Manrique, "La ocupación y la resistencia," *Reflecciones en torno a la Guerra de 1879*, ed. Jorge Basadre et al. (Lima: Francisco Campodónico-Centro de Investigación y Capacitación, 1979), 277–78.

37. On Becerra's previous position, see AHM, Colección Vargas Ugarte, Legajo 54: "Organización del Ejército del Norte dictada por el General Miguel Iglesias," Lima, 3 Jan. 1880. On his being named subprefect of Chota and on his support for continued resistance, see ADC, Subprefectura de Chota, 1880–89: "Oficio del Subprefecto Manuel J. Becerra al Prefecto, acusando recibo de la copia del oficio de Montero," 22 May 1881. On the outbreaks of violence, see Subprefectura de Chota, 1880–89: "Oficio del Subprefecto Domingo Lacerna al Prefecto," 30 Apr. 1881. On Becerra's commercial connections in Jaén, see Florencia E. Mallon, "Nationalist and Antistate Coalitions in the War of the Pacific: Junín and Cajamarca, 1879–1902," in *Resistance, Rebellion and Consciousness in the Andean Peasant World, 18th to 20th Centuries*, ed. Steve J. Stern (Madison: University of Wisconsin Press, 1987), p. 270, n. 6.

38. Jorge Basadre, *Chile, Peru y Bolivia independientes* (Barcelona-Buenos Aires: Salvat Editores, S.A., 1948), 492–96; Basadre. *Historia de la República del Perú*, vol. 8, 344–57; Nelson Manrique, *Campesinado y Nación: Las guerrillas indígenas en la guerra con Chile* (Lima: C.I.C.-Ital Perú S.A., 1981), 219; Manrique, "La ocupación y la resistencia," 294–97; ADC, Subprefectura de Chota, "Oficio del Subprefecto Manuel J. Becerra al Prefecto," 4 Feb. 1882.

39. ADC, Subprefectura de Chota, 1880–89: "Oficio del Subprefecto Eulogio Osores al Prefecto," 25 May 1880; "Terna para gobernador del distrito de Cutervo, presentada por Manuel A. Negrón," Chota, 28 Mar. 1881; Subprefectura de Jaén, 1880–89: "Oficio del Subprefecto J. de la R. Salgado al Prefecto," 20 May 1882; "Oficio del Subprefecto de Jaén Baltazar Contreras al Prefecto," 10 Sept. 1885; BNP, D3712: "Oficio N° 3: Prefecto de Cajamarca Miguel Pajares, al Director de Gobierno," Cajamarca, 1883.

40. ADC, Subprefectura de Jaén, 1880–89: "Oficio del Subprefecto J. de la R. Salgado al Prefecto," Pucará, 1 Apr. 1883; Subprefectura de Chota, 1880–89: "Oficio del Subprefecto de Chota al Prefecto del departamento," 12 May 1884; "Oficio del Subprefecto de Chota al Prefecto del departamento, transcribiendo oficio del gobernador del distrito de Llama," May 1884; Subprefectura de Jaén, 1880–89: "Oficio del Subprefecto de Jaén al Prefecto," Cutervo, 7 Sept. 1884; "Oficio del Subprefecto de Jaén al Prefecto," Cutervo, 15 Oct. 1884; Subprefectura de Chota, 1880–89: "Oficio del Subprefecto de Chota Timoteo Tirado al Prefecto," 6 Feb. 1884; Subprefectura de Jaén, 1880–89: "Oficio del Subprefecto de Jaén al Prefecto del Departamento," Cutervo, n.d.; Subprefectura de Chota, 1880–89: "Oficio del Subprefecto de Chota Timoteo Tirado al Prefecto," Bamba-

marca, 26 May 1884; "Oficio del Subprefecto de Chota al Prefecto del Departamento," 18 Dec. 1884; Subprefectura de Jaén, 1880–89: "Oficio del Subprefecto de Jaén al Prefecto," Cutervo, 6 Feb. 1885; "Oficio del Subprefecto de Jaén al Prefecto," Cutervo, 14 Feb. 1885; Subprefectura de Chota, 1880–89: "Oficio del Subprefecto de Chota al Prefecto," 27 Mar. 1885; Subprefectura de Jaén, 1880–89: "Oficio del Subprefecto de Jaén al Prefecto," Cutervo, 13 May 1885; "Oficio del Subprefecto de Jaén Baltazar Contreras al Prefecto," 10 Sept. 1885; Particulares, 1880–89: "Oficio de Baltazar Contreras al Alcalde Pedro Ceballos," Cutervo, 25 May 1885.

41. ADC, Subprefectura de Jaén, 1880–89: "Oficio del Subprefecto J. de la R. Salgado al Prefecto," Pucará, 1 Apr. 1883; Subprefectura de Chota, 1880–89: "Oficio del Subprefecto de Chota al Prefecto," 12 May 1884; "Oficio del Subprefecto de Chota al Prefecto del Departamento, transcribiendo oficio del gobernador del distrito de Llama," May 1884; "Oficio del Subprefecto de Chota Timoteo Tirado al Prefecto," Bambamarca, 26 May 1884; "Oficio del Subprefecto de Chota al Prefecto," 18 Dec. 1884; Subprefectura de Jaén, 1880–89: "Oficio del Subprefecto de Jaén Baltazar Contreras al Prefecto," 10 Sept. 1885; "Oficio del Subprefecto de Jaén al Prefecto," Cutervo, 14 Feb. 1885; "Oficio del Subprefecto de Jaén al Prefecto," Cutervo, 13 May 1885; Particulares, 1880–89: "Oficio de Baltazar Contreras al Alcalde Pedro Ceballos," Cutervo, 25 May 1885; "Oficio de Nicolás Tellos, Hacienda Llaucan, al Prefecto del Departmento," 18 Nov. 1885; Subprefectura de Jaén, 1880–89: "Informe del Subprefecto Miguel Arróspide sobre la provincia de Jaén," 2 May 1887; "Informe del Subprefecto Miguel Arróspide sobre el Presupuesto para 1889," 16 Apr. 1888.

42. The desperate report from Jaén's prefect is found in ADC, Subprefectura de Jaén, 1880–89: "Oficio del Subprefecto de Jaén al Prefecto," Cutervo, 15 Oct. 1884. The description of Becerra tearing up receipts for the head tax is found in "Oficio del Subprefecto de Jaén al Prefecto," Cutervo, 7 Sept. 1884. See also "Oficio del Subprefecto de Jaén al Prefecto," Cutervo, n.d.; "Oficio del Subprefecto de Jaén al Prefecto," Cutervo, 3 Nov. 1884; Particulares: "Solicitud de Manuel Collazos al presidente de la República Miguel Iglesias," Lima, 3 Nov. 1885; Subprefectura de Jaén, 1880–89: "Oficio del Subprefecto de Jaén Baltazar Contreras al Prefecto," 10 Sept. 1885; "Oficio del Subprefecto de Jaén al Prefecto," Cutervo, 6 Feb. 1885; "Oficio del Subprefecto de Jaén al Prefecto," Cutervo, 13 May 1885.

43. ADC, Subprefectura de Chota, 1880–89: "Oficio del Subprefecto Eulogio Osores al Prefecto," 25 May 1880; Subprefectura de Jaén, 1880–89: "Oficio del Subprefecto de Jaén al Prefecto," Cutervo, 13 May 1885.

44. ADC, Subprefectura de Jaén, 1880–89: "Informe del Subprefecto Arróspide sobre la provincia de Jaén," 2 May 1887.

45. Taylor, "Main Trends," 81–82; Manrique, *Campesinado y Nación*, 218–22; Basadre, *Historia de la República del Perú*, vol. 8, 408–12; AHM, Colección Vargas Ugarte, Legajo 54: "Organización del Ejército del Norte dictada por el General Miguel Iglesias," Lima, 3 Jan. 1880; ADC, Subprefectura de Cajamrca, 1880–85: "Oficio del Subprefecto Serna al Prefecto," 19 Feb. 1882; Gobernadores del Distritio de San Marcos, 1854–99: "Oficio del Gobernador Manuel Rubio al Subprefecto de Cajamarca," 28 Dec. 1882; "Oficio del Gobernador Manuel Rubio al Subprefecto," 25 Jan. 1883.

46. ACD, Gobernadores del Distrito de Ichocán, 1856–99: "Oficio del Gobernador Santos G. Cobán al Prefecto," Distrito de Ichocán, 18 July 1880; "Oficio

del Gobernador Santos G. Cobán al Subprefecto," 18 Sept. 1881; "Oficio del Gobernador Santos G. Cobán al Subprefecto," 12 Dec. 1881; Gobernadores del Distrito de San Marcos, 1854–99: "Oficio del gobernador Manuel Rubio al Subprefecto," 25 Oct. 1882; "Oficio del gobernador Manuel Rubio al Subprefecto de la provincia," 12 Oct. 1882; "Oficio del gobernador Manuel Rubio al Subprefecto de la provincia," 20 Sept. 1882; "Oficio del gobernador Manuel Rubio al Subprefecto de Cajamarca," 27 Oct. 1882; "Oficio del gobernador Manuel Rubio al Subprefecto de Cajamarca," 31 Oct. 1882.

47. ADC, Gobernadores del Distrito de San Marcos, 1854–99: "Oficio del Gobernador Manuel María Lazo al Prefecto," 8 Apr. 1880; "Oficio del Gobernador José Castañaduy al Subprefecto," n.d., 1881; "Oficio del Gobernador José Castañaduy al Subprefecto," 13 Dec. 1881; "Oficio del Gobernador Lizardo Zevallos al Subprefecto," 26 June 1881; "Oficio del Gobernador Manuel Rubio al Subprefecto," 15 May 1882; Subprefectura de Cajamarca, 1880–85: "Oficio del Subprefecto Manuel Castro al Prefecto," 28 Oct. 1881; "Oficio del Subprefecto Serna al Prefecto," 19 Feb. 1882.

48. ADC, Gobernadores del Distrito de San Marcos, 1854–99: "Oficio del Gobernador Manuel Rubio al Subprefecto," 15 May 1882; Alcaldías de los distritos de Cajamarca, 1855–99: "Oficio del Alcalde Pedro W. Zevallos al Prefecto," Ichocán, 31 July 1883. It is interesting, in this context, to note the presence of two women in auxiliary combat roles in Puga's *montonera* in 1884: AHM, Paquete 0. 1884.6, Prefecturas: "Oficio de Gregorio Relayze, Comandante General de la División de Operaciones en el Norte, al Ministro de Estado en el Despacho de Guerra y Marina," Cajabamba, 27 May 1884.

49. On conflicts between members of the Chinese community and "Peruvians" in Cajamarca, see ADC, Corte Superior de Justicia, Causas ordinarias, Leg. #58: "El asiático Wing-Walon con Don Justiniano Guerrero sobre cumplimiento de un contrato," Cajamarca, 15 Oct. 1881; Leg. #62: "D. Manuel Rubio con el asiático Colorado sobre pago de cantidad de soles," Cajamarca, 11 Jan. 1882: Leg. #54: "Dn. Juan Chavarria con Dn. Luis Maradiegue, sobre entrega de dos caballos," Cajamarca, 19 May 1880. On the participation of Chinese men in Puga's *montonera*, see ADC, Alcaldías de los distritos de Cajamarca, 1855–99: "Oficio del Alcalde Pedro W. Zevallos al Prefecto," Ichocán, 31 July 1883; Particulares, 1880–89: "Solicitud de Francisco Deza, asiático, al Prefecto del Departamento," Cajamarca, 7 Dec. 1883; and AHM, Correspondencia General, Paquete 0.1883.1 [*sic*]: "Oficio del Comandante en Jefe de las fuerzas del Norte al Ministro de Estado en el Despacho de Guerra y Marina," Cajamarca, 6 Jan. 1884.

50. For a very different kind of involvement by women during a period of war, see Florencia E. Mallon, "Constructing Third World Feminisms: Lessons from Nineteenth-Century Mexico (1850–1874)," Women's History Working Papers Series, Number 2, University of Wisconsin, Madison, 1990.

51. AHM, Correspondencia General, Paquete 0.1883.1: "Oficio del Comandante en Jefe de las fuerzas del Norte al Ministro de Estado en el Despacho de Guerra y Marina," San Marcos, December 1883; "Oficio del Comandante en Jefe de las fuerzas del Norte al Ministro de Estado en el Despacho de Guerra y Marina," Cajamarca, 9 Dec. 1883; Colección Recavarren, Manuscritos, Cuaderno 10, 72–73: "Oficio de José Mercedes Puga a Recavarren," Hacienda Huagal, 18 July 1883; Ordenes Generales y Correspondencia, Paquete 0.1883.2: "Oficio del Jefe de las fuerzas expedicionarias al distrito de la Asunción," Cajamarca, 6 May

1883; BNP, D3710: "Nota dirigida por el Prefecto y Comandante General del Departamento de la Libertad D. Z. Relayze adjuntado documentos relativos a la invasion de la provincia de Huamachuco por el caudillo Dr. José Mercedes Puga," Trujillo, 29 Mar. 1885.

52. BNP, D3710: "Nota dirigida por el Prefecto y Comandante General del Departamento de la Libertad D. Z. Relayze adjuntando documentos relativos a la invasion de la provincia de Huamachuco por el caudillo Dr. José Mercedes Puga," Trujillo, 29 Mar. 1885; AHM, Paquete 1885 s/n: "Oficio de la Prefectura y Comandancia General del departamento de La Libertad, firmado por Juan N. Vargas, al Oficial Mayor del Ministerio de Guerra y Marina," Trujillo, 7 Nov. 1885; BNP, D7974: "Expediente sobre la petición hecha por Josefa Hoyle vda. de Pinillos y Ana Hoyle de Loyer para que se declare sin lugar la solicitud de los Sres. Pinillos sobre la confiscación de la Hda. 'Uningambal,' " Trujillo, 3 Oct. 1885; Archivo Piérola, Caja (Antigua) Nº 53: Correspondencia Oficial y Particular: "Carta de M. Serapio Pinillos a Nicolás de Piérola," Santiago de Chuco, 16 Apr. 1896.

53. For Puga and Becerra's deaths, see ADC, Particulares: "Solicitud de Manuel Collazos al presidente de la República Miguel Iglesïas," Lima, 3 Nov. 1885; and BNP, D3710: "Nota dirigida por el Prefecto y Comandante General de la Departamento de la Libertad D. Z. Relayze adjuntando documentos relativos a la invasion de la provincia de Huamachuco por el caudillo Dr. José Mercedes Puga," Trujillo, 29 Mar. 1885. On lack of Cacerista control in the area, see BNP, D3980: "Memoria que presenta el Prefecto de Lambayeque, Crel. Federico Ríos, al Ministro de Gobierno, Policía y Obras Públicas sobre el estado del Departamento de su mando," Chiclayo, 26 Apr. 1886; D11375: "Expediente sobre el oficio dirigido por el Prefecto del departamento de Cajamarca, Jacinto A. Bedoya, al Director de Gobierno, pidiéndole el aumento de la fuerza pública en esa plaza," Cajamarca, 21 Oct. 1889; D5156: "Memoria del Subprefecto de Cajamarca, Tomás Ballón, al Prefecto del Departamento," Cajamarca, 3 June 1892; and D7611: "Notas sobre el envio de una expedición a Gorgor con el fin de capturar a Román Egües García y Cia," Cajatambo, 7 Dec. 1895. On the Cacerista commanders fighting during the civil war, see BNP, D3704: "Inventario de los daños causados en la casa prefectural de la ciudad de Cajamarca por las montoneras comandadas por el Dr. José Mercedes Puga," Cajamarca, 11 Jan. 1884; D3995: "Memorial elevado al Ministro de Gobierno por los vecinos de la villa de Supe. . . ," Supe (Provincia de Chancay), 13 Feb. 1884; D3797: "Oficio dirigido por el Prefecto del departamento de la Libertad a la Dirección de Gobierno, adjuntando documentos relativos a las correrías de la montonera capitaneada por Romero," Trujillo, 9 May 1885; AHM, Paquete 0.1884.2: "Carta del gobernador del distrito de Huánuco, Pedro P. Reina, al prefecto y comandante general del departamento," 17 Mar. 1884; Paquete 0.1884.6 (Prefecturas): "Oficio del Prefecto y Comandante General del Departamento de Lambayeque al oficial mayor del Ministerio de Guerra y Marina," Chiclayo, 9 July 1884; Paquete 0.1884.1: "Oficio de Fernando Seminario al coronel jefe de la expedición," Pariamonga, 30 Nov. 1884; Paquete 1885 s/n: "Oficio de M. Mondoñedo, designado jefe superior político y militar de los departamentos de Piura, Lambayeque y Cajamarca, por don Andrés A. Cáceres, al alcalde del distrito de Chongoyape," 1 May 1885.

54. On support for Piérola in the Cajamarca area, see BNP, Archivo Piérola: Copiador Nº 16, 1889–90: Correspondencia Oficial y Particular, Norte, "Oficio de Piérola al Presidente del Comité Departamental de Trujillo, José María de la

108 *Florencia E. Mallon*

Puente," 3 July 1889; Caja (Antigua) N° 41, 1892–95: "Cartas de Nicolás Rebaza y Santiago Rebaza Demóstenes, de Trujillo, felicitando a Piérola y communicándole ser partidarios fervorosos de él. . . ," 28 Mar. 1895; "Carta de Vincente González y Orbegoso a Piérola," Hacienda Motil, 12 Apr. 1895; "Carta de Rafael Villanueva a Piérola," Cajamarca, 13 Apr. 1895; Caja (Antigua) N° 45, 1895: "Carta de José María de la Puente a Piérola," Trujillo, 13 July 1895; "Carta de Isidro Burga a Piérola," Cajamarca, 17 June 1895; "Oficio de Isidro Burga a Cruz Toribio Cruz," 29 May 1895; and s/n Correspondencia Oficial y Particular: "Carta de Miguel Iglesias a Nicolás de Piérola," Hacienda Udima, 18 July 1895. On the difficulties of control after the war, see Taylor, "Main Trends," 86–87, 103–15,177–79; AHM, Paquete 0.1885.2: "Oficio de J. Borgoño al Ministro de Guerra y Marina," Trujillo, 3 Jan. 1886; and "Oficio del Prefecto del Departamento de Piura al señor oficial mayor del Ministerio de Guerra," 15 June 1886.

55. In Peru, the term *gamonalismo* has generally been used to designate the system of regionalization of power in which local powerholders, most often *hacendados*, delivered the loyalty of "their" areas in return for support from the central state in maintaining their personal control in their regions. On the endemic nature of violence in the area, see BNP, Archivo Piérola, Caja (Antigua) N° 50 (1895–99): "Carta de Rafael Villanueva a Piérola," Cajamarca, 27 June 1897; "Carta del Prefecto de Cajamarca, Belisario Ravinez, a Piérola," Cajamarca, 21 June 1897; "Carta del Prefecto de Cajamarca, Belisario Ravinez, a Piérola," Cajamarca, 20 June 1897; "Carta del Prefecto de Cajamarca, Belisario Ravinez, a Piérola," Cajamarca, 24 May 1897; "Carta de Rafael Villanueva a Piérola," Cajamarca, 1 Feb. 1897; "Carta del Prefecto de Cajamarca, Belisario Ravinez, a Piérola," Cajamarca, 11 Jan. 1897; "Carta del Prefecto de Cajamarca, Belisario Ravinez, a Piérola," Cajamarca, 28 Dec. 1896. On banditry, see John Gitlitz, "Conflictos Políticos en la Sierra Norte del Perú: La Montonera Benel Contra Leguía, 1924," *Estudios Andinos* 9, no. 16 (1980): 127–38; Taylor, "Main Trends," 106–15; Lewis Taylor, *Bandits and Politics in Peru: Landlord and Peasant Violence in Hualgayoc, 1900–1930* (Cambridge, U.K.: Centre of Latin American Studies, 1987); and especially Taylor, "Los orígenes del bandolerismo." Rodrigo Montoya commented to me in personal conversation, Lima 1981, about the difficulties the police had encountered entering the boundaries of Cajamarca's haciendas as late as the 1960s.

56. See especially the works by Lewis Taylor already cited: "Main Trends;" *Bandits and Politics*; and "Los orígenes del bandolerismo."

57. The literature on both regimes is quite extensive. For Peru, a good starting point is Basadre, *Historia de la República del Perú*, vols. 11–12, and Manuel Burga and Alberto Flores Galindo, *Apogeo y crisis de la República Aristocrática*, 2d. ed. (Lima: Ediciones Rikchay Peru, 1981). For Mexico, see Daniel Cosío Villegas, *Historia Moderna de México* (Mexico City: Editorial Hermes, 1956), and Friedrich Katz, "Mexico: Restored Republic and Porfiriato, 1867–1910," in *The Cambridge History of Latin America*, vol. 5, ed. Leslie Bethell (Cambridge and New York: Cambridge University Press, 1986), 3–78.

58. For highland Puebla in the 1860s and 1870s, see Mallon, *Peasant and Nation*, chaps. 2, 3, 4, 8.

59. On the presence of agrarian social movements in Porfirio Diaz's early coalition, see Florencia E. Mallon, "The Intricacies of Coercion: Popular Political Cultures, Repression, and the Failure of Hegemony in Nineteenth-Century Mexico and Peru," (paper presented at the Conference on "State Formation,

Popular Culture and the Mexican Revolution," Center for U.S.-Mexican Studies, La Jolla, California, 27 February–2 March, 1991). The classic treatment of the popular revolution in Mexico is still John Womack, Jr., *Zapata and the Mexican Revolution* (New York: Knopf, 1968); see also Arturo Warman, . . . *y venimos a contradecir: Los campesinos de Morelos y el estado nacional*, 2d. ed. (Mexico, D.F.: Ediciones de la Casa Chata, Centro de Investigaciones Superiores del INAH, 1978). For the "new" popular interpretation of the Mexican Revolution, see Alan Knight, *The Mexican Revolution*, 2 vols. (Cambridge and New York: Cambridge University Press, 1986). For new approaches to the impact of popular culture on the Revolution, see Ana María Alonso, "Gender, Ethnicity and the Constitution of Subjects: Accommodation, Resistance and Revolution on the Chihuahuan Frontier" (Ph.D. diss., University of Chicago, 1988); Maria Teresa Koreck, "Space and Revolution in Northeastern Chihuahua," in Daniel Nugent, ed., *Rural Revolt in Mexico and U.S. Intervention* (La Jolla, Calif.: Center for U.S.-Mexican Studies, Monograph Series 27, 1988), 127–48; and Daniel Nugent, "Land, Labor and Politics in a Serrano Society: The Articulation of State and Popular Ideology in Mexico" (Ph.D. diss., University of Chicago, 1988). On incorporation and authoritarianism, see (as examples of a much larger and broader literature) Arnaldo Córdova, *La política de masas del cardenismo* (Mexico City: Ediciones Era, 1974); and *La ideología de la revolución mexicana* (Mexico City: Ediciones Era, 1973); and *La revolución y el estado en México* (Mexico City: Ediciones Era, 1989); Paul Friedrich, *The Princes of Naranja* (Austin: University of Texas Press, 1986); and José Luis Reyna and Richard S. Weinert, eds., *Authoritarianism in Mexico* (Philadelphia: Institute for the Study of Human Issues, 1977).

60. Mallon, *Peasant and Nation*, chap. 9 and 10.

61. See, for example, Alfred Stepan, *The State and Society: Peru in Comparative Perspective* (Princeton: Princeton University Press, 1978); Abraham F. Lowenthal, ed., *The Peruvian Experiment* (Princeton: Princeton University Press, 1975); and Abraham F. Lowenthal and Cynthia McClintock, eds., *The Peruvian Experiment Reconsidered* (Princeton: Princeton University Press, 1983).

62. The failure of the Peruvian military regime in the 1970s was perhaps best symbolized in the violent repression of the peasant movement in Andahuaylas in 1974; see Rodrigo Sánchez E., *Toma de tierras y conciencia política campesina* (Lima: Instituto de Estudios Peruanos, 1981). On more recent events in Peru, see (as examples of a broader literature) *NACLA Reports*, Speical Issue on Peru, December 1990; Alberto Flores Galindo, *Tiempo de plagas* (Lima: El Caballo Rojo Ediciones, 1988); Carlos Degregori, "Los hondos y mortales desencuentros," and Nelson Manrique, "Sendero Luminoso."

63. For a review of recent literature, see John D. Stephens, "Democratic Transition and Breakdown in Western Europe, 1870–1939: A Test of the Moore Thesis," *American Journal of Sociology* 94, no. 5 (March 1989): 1019–77. For a thoughtful consideration of these issues for South America, see Evelyne Huber Stephens, "Capitalist Development and Democracy in South America," *Politics and Society* 17, no. 3 (1989): 281–352.

Agrarian Systems and the State: The Case of Colombia

Frank Safford

Some Preliminary Considerations

Barrington Moore, in his stimulating thesis on the agrarian origins of dictatorship and democracy, begins his analysis with European history as his paradigm. As he moves to Asian cases, the discussion becomes increasingly complicated by phenomena (e.g., caste in India) that are extraneous to his initial formulations relating to the commercialization of agriculture in England and the postures of landed nobilities on the European continent. Indeed, as Evelyne Huber and John Stephens point out in their conclusion, one of his Asian cases, Japan, does not actually fit the category into which Moore inserts it.

Moore never seriously attempts to address the question of how Latin American states might fit into the paradigm that he elaborates from his reading of European history. Perhaps he is wise not to do so. Several facts make applying Moore's analysis to Latin America problematic from the outset. First, there is the fundamental problem of the history of the state itself. In his European, and indeed his Asian, cases Moore is dealing with polities with long histories of independent existence, which provide bases for analysis of a certain depth. The various pieces of what is now Latin America were, until circa 1810–1825, colonial dependencies. This fact complicates, or at least alters, the use of a Moorean analysis over a long historical run. During the three centuries of colonial rule, the imperial states of Spain and Portugal did use their authority to coerce and control rural labor, in accord with the needs of the Iberian states and of colonial elites. It seems clear that colonial elites did have a good deal of influence on whether labor coercion might be used and what forms it might take. On the other hand, it would be difficult to contend that the colonial elites or their interests had any important bearing on the political conformation of the Iberian monarchies. It thus becomes difficult to apply to the Hispanic American colonial period the analyses of landowner power alliances so much featured in Moore's treatment of his European cases.

This is not to say that the coercion of colonial labor had no relationship whatever to the political character of the Iberian states. For example, the flow of American bullion, produced by labor coerced in various degrees, helped the kings of Castile to free themselves from any sort of effective parliamentary control in Spain itself. Thus, during the centuries in which the need for revenue forced the kings of England increasingly to concede power to their Parliament, Spanish monarchs were able to dispense with the Cortes and so to avoid a similar development of the bases of republican government from the sixteenth through the eighteenth centuries. But this long-standing, not to say hoary, explanation of the divergent development of parliamentary government in Great Britain versus monarchical absolutism in Spain represents a very different proposition than Moore's scheme, which so much emphasizes commercialized versus coercive forms of agriculture.

The Moore thesis, then, becomes possibly relevant to Latin America only when separation from the Iberian monarchies permitted the emergence of independent states, in which local interests presumably played a more clearly determinative, or at least important, role in the formation of state policy and the conformation of the state itself. For a number of reasons however, it becomes difficult to apply the Moorean approach to Spanish American states even in the post-Independence era, at least in the ways in which Moore applies it to Europe and Asia. As Evelyne Huber and John Stephens note elsewhere, the states with which Moore deals were constituted monarchies; the revolutionary, or counterrevolutionary, dramas with which he deals occurred within frameworks of established authority. The newly constituted states of Spanish America, with some temporary exceptions, adopted imported republican forms, so that at least in their formal norms the systems were not supposed to be authoritarian or dictatorial. Of course, the reality frequently proved to be far different from the formally established constitutional norms. The constitutional norms in some countries often were violated by military or caudillesque seizures of power and, in some cases, as in Rosas's Argentina, by dictatorial government. In Colombia, however, the constitutional forms were generally observed.

Because the republican form was rather quickly accepted as the Spanish American norm, and because in Colombia the republican forms were generally observed, the relevant question for Colombia, within the Moore framework, is not how agrarian systems affected governmental forms, but rather, how agrarian systems may have affected the actual exercise of power. More specifically, to what degree were landed interests able to enlist republican government as an enforcer of coercive labor systems in agriculture?

For Colombia, as in many other parts of Spanish America, this question is of dubious applicability for the years before 1880, because there, as elsewhere in the region, the central government lacked the authority or power to enforce its will in the provinces. In Colombia, as in many parts of Spanish America, the new republic through most of the nineteenth century remained fiscally weak. Partly for this reason, the republic in Colombia, like other post-Independence governments in Spanish America, was fragile. Colombia's government, unlike those of Mexico, Peru, or Bolivia, was not frequently overthrown; in the nineteenth century, the national government changed hands by force only twice, in 1854 and 1861. But it suffered frequent armed challenges from its provinces.

At least until about 1880, if not longer, Colombia, like most of the other newly constituted states, was too weak to control its outlying provinces. Political instability and lack of revenues weakened the capacity to rule effectively. Slow communications over vast and topographically obstructed territories further diminished the effective authority of the central government. Colombia's national government, like most of the republics of Spanish America, was too weak to be able to offer landowners any effective aid in controlling labor. Possibly landowners recognized this fact; in most places they appear not to have expected any help from the national government.

Another problem diminishes the applicability of Moore to much of Spanish America in the years before 1880. In most of Spanish America populations were sparse and scattered, and overland transportation, usually conducted on the backs of horses and mules, was costly. Interregional trade therefore was relatively slight and sluggish, and the stimulus of internal demand was weak indeed. External trade was also small in scale, significant only in a few regions of Spanish America—western Cuba (still under Spanish rule), coastal Venezuela, the Littoral of the Rio de la Plata. Among the factors limiting external demand before 1850 was the fact that Great Britain, the principal western trading nation, drew a great part of its tropical commodities preferentially from British dependencies. In a situation in which internal markets were slight and circumscribed and external demand weak, there was little to motivate landowners to coerce rural labor into production. Furthermore, in these slack economic conditions landowners in most places tended not to be a specialized and politically organized group; it is often difficult, therefore, to trace their influence, as a distinctive group, on state policy. All of these phenomena were especially characteristic of Colombia.

After 1880, however, much of this changed, at least in some Spanish American countries. Expansion of agricultural exports after 1880 meant that there was increased demand for labor; therefore, if landowners were likely to use coercion to control rural labor, this was the time they were most likely to do so. Export expansion after 1880 also brought increased revenues to central states through the growth of customs collections. Increased external demand for exported primary materials also induced the construction of railway nets, which further strengthened the effective reach of national governments. Finally, the more vigorous economies stimulated by export expansion helped to encourage the specialization of large landowners and their organization into effective and politically active interest group associations. Associations of large landowners played particularly prominent roles in the politics of Chile and Argentina in the period 1880–1930.[1]

Furthermore, it is possible to point to a number of Spanish American cases in which landowners producing crops for export did make use of state power to coerce rural labor in the period after 1880. The best-known case is that of Porfirian Mexico. There the pattern is clearly demonstrated. Progress toward laying a rail network and export expansion in the 1880s provided the economic basis for a stronger national government, whose greater power enabled it more effectively to maintain rural order. Most particularly, the Mexican national state lent its assistance in the enslavement of Yaqui Indians in the northwestern state of Sonora and their transportation to Yucatán, where they were put to work on plantations producing henequen fiber for export. This was only the most flagrant and publicized of various forms of state-backed labor coercion employed in support of export agriculture in southern Mexico.[2] Another salient example of the systematic coercion of rural labor during the post-1880 export expansion is that of Guatemala, discussed briefly in this volume by Lowell Gudmundson. It therefore seems appropriate to look, as this volume does, particularly at the period of export expansion after 1880 for indications of the applicability of the Moore thesis in Spanish America.

The Case of Colombia: The Argument

The Moore thesis does not appear to apply very well to Colombia before 1880, even if adapted to fit Spanish American conditions. Before 1880 the Colombian economy was too inert, its economic elites too diffuse, and its central government too weak for the government to play a perceptible role in the discipline of agricultural labor. To the degree that state coercion was used to control rural labor before 1880 (and, as yet, not much evidence of this has surfaced), it was used by local authorities acting more or less without reference to the national government. Whether because of patterns of cultural domination or because of the leverage of economic power, in many parts of the country estate owners appear to have been able to dominate local labor without resorting to overt coercion.

After 1880 the economy became somewhat more active and integrated, its economic elites more specialized and organized, and the national state gradually somewhat stronger. As Paul Oquist aptly notes, Colombia in the nineteenth century had a weak state but a strong structure of social domination. By contrast, in the 1920s and 1930s Colombia's structure of social domination weakened somewhat, while the state became relatively stronger.[3] The question of a state role in the coercion of labor thus comes most clearly into play in the 1920s and 1930s. The years from the 1880s to perhaps the beginning of the 1920s may be considered a transitional period from an invertebrate economy and a weak state to the beginnings of a more vital economy and a more energetic state.

Nonetheless, Colombia after 1880 continued in various ways to defy categorization in Moorean terms. Modes of production were so regionally variegated that they cannot be squeezed into one pattern or even a few patterns. Agriculture in some places depended upon traditional modes of domination and in other places was becoming increasingly commercial. While some traditional estates (along with many *minifundia*) remained in such places as highland Boyacá, commercial cultivation of coffee was coming to the fore successively in the Santander region, in southern and western Cundinamarca and Tolima, in Antioquia and Caldas, and in the Cauca Valley. Though coffee was the most general commercial crop, modes of production in coffee varied from region to region and even within single localities. Large estates tended to dominate in the coffee-producing districts of the eastern cordillera, particularly in Cundinamarca and the Santanders. But many small and medium growers existed in all regions and were the principal producers in such western departments as Caldas and the Cauca Valley. One consequence of this variegation was a tendency for spokesmen even within the coffee industry to disagree about appropriate government policies affecting agricultural modes of production. Such divisions as did exist within the most powerful groups representing commercial agriculture opened up some possibility for choice in the elaboration of national policy.

The large coffee growers, whatever their regional base, were, in many cases, urban businessmen, mostly merchants.[4]. They ran their agrarian enterprises in a capitalist spirit, with considerable attention to profit maximization. While in some regions they might make use of modes of production that could be considered precapitalist, many of them were also open to the argument that the coffee industry ought to move in the direction of using wage labor, and by the 1920s a number increasingly were relying on wage labor.[5]

If modes of production in Colombian agriculture between 1880 and the 1930s were a mix of precapitalist and capitalist forms, so also the relationship between the state and landowners was ambiguous and inconstant. During the 1880s the national state adopted land policies intended to protect small farmers from the depredations of large land entrepreneurs, but it still lacked the power to make these measures effective. During the 1920s the national state became stronger and, even under Conservative governments, began to intervene more effectively in the defense of the property rights of individual smallholders. On the other hand, at the end of the 1920s, a

Conservative government used massive force to repress strikes by agricultural workers. During the 1930s Liberal governments adopted a more conciliatory attitude toward collective movements by rural workers.

Whatever party held the national government and whatever the policy of the national government, municipal and departmental authorities remained largely responsive to local estate owners, supplying them with police support in the repression of tenant farmers and agricultural workers in moments of emergency. Although the use of repression by local authorities continued into the 1930s, the counterpressure of the attitudes and policies of modernizing and reformist political leaders at the national level opened at least the possibility for some tenant farmers and rural workers to achieve greater economic autonomy. By and large, however, there has remained a significant disjuncture between the political superstructure of the national state and what goes on at the local level. The national state may adopt socially democratizing rhetoric and policy without being able to effect any significant change in relations of production in the greater part of the country.

These last comments seem to reverse the relationship between agrarian structure and the character of the state as posited by Moore. Moore saw the agrarian structure as affecting the political character of the state. Here I note the development of social democratic tendencies of the national state, and its ineffectuality in reforming agrarian structures. Whatever the causal direction of the statement, however, the central point is the substantial separation of the formal state superstructure from local agrarian bases.

Colombia's Topography and Social Structure

In considering the case of Colombia, it is important to bear in mind its geographic circumstances. The three branches of the Andes running south to north through Colombia divide the country into several major zones. To the east of the eastern cordillera are the vast and practically unpopulated lowland plains (the *llanos orientales*), and farther south lie the tropical valleys of the Caquetá and Putumayo, flowing into the Amazon. The highlands of the eastern cordillera have been through most of Colombian history the most densely populated part of the country. Between the eastern and central cordilleras lie the plains of the Upper Magdalena Valley and the swampy lowlands of the Lower Magdalena, ultimately giving way to the plains and swamps of the Caribbean coast. Between the central and western cordilleras is the fertile but isolated Cauca Valley. Squarely in the central cordillera itself is the broken terrain of greater Antioquia. Finally, west of the western cordillera are the still more isolated Pacific lowlands. Each of these major zones in turn is divided into many smaller subsegments, the lowland plains by multiple rivers, the mountainous areas by crosscutting ridges and rivers. Colombia's topographic features divided the country into many small pockets of settlement, many more or less isolated economic niches.

This topographic fragmentation was reinforced by the fact that the whole country lies in the tropical zone. In the tropics temperatures remain generally uniform throughout the year in any given place and vary primarily according to altitude. This means that most major regions of the country are capable of producing, at one altitude or another, virtually all of the crops that might be grown in any other major region. And where mountains make possible local variations of temperature, a good deal of product complementarity is possible within a single subregion. Within the space of a relatively few miles, potatoes, wheat, and wool might be produced in the highlands; cotton, sugar cane, tobacco, yuca, and cacao in lower, warmer regions; and maize and cattle virtually everywhere. The combination of mountainous terrain and tropical climate thus makes possible a good deal of *local* complementarity among economic niches at different altitudes. By the same token, however, these geographic features, until well into the twentieth century, obstructed the development of much of a national market or even very vital larger regional ones. Sparse, diffuse, and fragmented as it was, Colombia's population was able to feed itself largely with locally obtainable crops; accordingly, there was too little trade, or perceivable potential trade, to stimulate or support significant improvements in over-land transportation. Further, when improvements were made in mule trails (the principal overland transportation links until the twentieth century), tropical rainstorms quickly wiped them away. Colombia's mountainous terrain and tropical climate thus combined to make the country, in the words of Luis Eduardo Nieto Arteta, a series of economic archipelagoes.[6]

Colombia's mountainous topography and tropical climate tended not only to fragment its population and economy, they also made it difficult for the country to engage effectively in exporting agricultural commodities. During the colonial period and the nineteenth century the bulk of the population lived in the highlands of the interior, which were deemed not only more comfortable but also a good deal more salutary than the hot, humid coastal lowlands. Transportation costs from the interior to the coast, until at least the end of the nineteenth century, made it difficult for products from the interior to compete in European or North American markets. Only those commodities that had a very high value in relation to their volume and weight could successfully be exported from the interior. During the colonial period and the first half of the nineteenth century, Colombia's exports consisted overwhelmingly of gold, so valuable that it easily could withstand the cost of being packed by mule to navigable rivers.

In the last quarter of the eighteenth century Bourbon viceroys and other administrators sought to encourage the development of other exports besides gold. The most successful of these exports were produced in areas close to the Caribbean, which helped to limit transportation costs. During the 1780s and into the 1790s small amounts of cotton and dyewoods from the Caribbean coastal provinces were exported, as was cacao from the plains of Cúcuta, which could be sent out via Lake Maracaibo. The interior exported only tiny quantities of cinchona bark and cotton in these years. Despite efforts to promote exports of commodities other than bullion, in the decade from 1784 to 1793 gold and silver still accounted for more than 90 percent of the registered exports from the port of Cartagena to Spain.[7] The figures on registered exports from Cartagena to Spain cannot be taken as completely accurate indicators of exports from the viceroyalty: an unmeasured amount of contraband exporting of dyewoods occurred through the secondary ports of Santa Marta and Riohacha; on the other hand, a large proportion of Colombia's gold production also was shipped out as contraband gold dust. So the official figures from the port of Cartagena may even underestimate the significance of gold as the principal export of the viceroyalty at the end of the colonial period.

During the first half of the nineteenth century, gold continued to be Colombia's principal export. Independence-era disruptions reduced gold production, but some nongold exports, like cinchona bark and cotton, virtually ceased, only to reemerge temporarily in the 1850s in the case of cinchona bark and in the 1860s, during the Civil War, in the case of cotton. Colombia's most significant agricultural export from the middle of the 1840s through the 1860s was tobacco, mostly produced in a small zone in the Upper Magdalena River Valley. Tobacco, and occasionally cotton and indigo, grown in the Upper Magdalena could be exported at relatively low cost on boats or rafts floated down the river. But for most of these commodities Colombia was a secondary producer, successful only when for some reason supplies from more effective exporters were interrupted.

Consequently, Colombia was a notably weak exporter by comparison to other Latin America countries. Before 1870, Colombia generally ranked no higher than seventh as an exporter, though it had the third largest population in the area. In the 1830s and 1840s exports per capita were in the range of 1.50 to 2.50 dollars, between 1850 and 1870 in the range of three to four dollars. Even during the period of erratic export growth between 1850 and 1870, Colombia's exports per capita were less than a third of those of Argentina, Chile, and Peru.[8]

Given the lack of export possibilities, a real national market, or even well-integrated regional markets, agriculture in the highland interior functioned at a rather indolent pace. During the first half of the nineteenth century many foods were produced primarily for local markets, and in small quantities, by peasant farmers. In the eastern highlands, before the breakup of Indian community lands (*resguardos*) between the 1830s and the 1860s, peasant cultivators provided Bogotá and other towns with garden crops.[9] Larger Creole landowners tended to concentrate on raising livestock, though some also grew wheat, using rather antiquated methods. (Eugenio Diaz, a writer of socially descriptive fiction in the middle of the nineteenth century, describes landowners on the Sabana de Bogotá as still using horses to thresh wheat.) The markets of wheat growing regions in the eastern highlands (Pamplona, Tunja, Tundama, Bogotá) by the 1850s were limited to immediately surrounding provinces.[10] North American wheat flour had taken most of the market on New Granada's Caribbean coast during the eighteenth century, and by the middle of the nineteenth century it had penetrated far into the interior. Wheat flour from the eastern cordillera, which had reached the western province of Antioquia during the eighteenth century, was no longer being sent there in the 1850s.[11]

Domestic agriculture by and large was considered not a very good way to make money. Profits were generally slight and often nonexistent. Francisco Vargas, a merchant in Bogotá in 1850–1880, thought that only a complete dolt would dedicate himself to farming. The import trade seems, in fact, to have been a much more likely way to accumulate capital. During the nineteenth century, the wealthiest people in Colombia, certainly in terms of liquid capital, were merchants in Antioquia, who accumulated capital largely in commerce, as factors of gold from the region's many placer mines and suppliers of gold as foreign exchange for merchants in other regions.[12]

Large landowners in Colombia before 1880 formed part of a rather diffuse and economically unspecialized dominant class. For many, farming was only one of several occupations, which might include the practice of law or commerce or a military position. As landowners they were not particularly wealthy, in terms of their capacity to mobilize liquid capital. Landowners could be said to exist as an identifiable group. In the early 1830s when Colombia was experiencing a severe economic crisis, juntas of merchants and landowners were consulted as to possible remedies. But other than at times of such emergencies, landowners were neither organized nor politically articulate. In many places they may have been locally cohesive, but neither on a national or a regional level did they exist, as a coherent, self-conscious group. Regionally dispersed across Colombia's fractious topography, they did not, and could not, articulate a national interest-group position and only occasionally did they speak formally as regional or local interest groups.[13] At least in the realm of national politics landowners depended for information and direction on city men, who were in the nerve centers of political action in the national and provincial capitals. Those who made the policies of the national government (and also those at the provincial level) were more or less professional politicians—mostly lawyers and some merchants, military officers, clergy, and literati. Many of these politically active people owned some land, but many, probably most, of these did not think of themselves primarily as landowners, but rather, more honorifically, as public servants or political leaders.

Although landowners did not form an organized special interest group, in various ways national policies implicitly attended to their interest. But the picture is quite mixed. On the whole, large landowners in the nineteenth century seem to have been favored as much (and probably more) by the weakness of the Colombian government as by policies intended to favor them. Throughout the nineteenth century the Colombian government was notably unable to collect the revenues necessary to make it an effective state. This revenue weakness stemmed fundamentally from the feebleness of the economy in general and of foreign trade in particular. Paucity of foreign trade limited income from customs duties, the easiest kind of tax to collect.[14] Slight foreign trade also limited the wealth even of the Colombian upper classes.[15] As a result, it proved politically and practically impossible to collect much in the way of direct taxes. During the 1820s the early republican government sought to subject property owners to a direct tax on the value of properties. This tax failed, however, as the national government lacked the mechanism, and probably the political strength, to enforce it. On the other hand, landowners did not go untaxed. Until 1849 they paid a tithe on gross agricultural production. In addition, in time of civil war they were subject to frequent irregular exactions by the armies of rebels and of national or regional governments, who were particularly given to seizing horses, mules, cattle, and farm workers.

Several government policies appear to have helped affluent Colombians to accumulate land. One was the national policy of dividing Indian community lands (*resguardos*), initially legislated in 1810, reiterated in 1821, and put into execution in much of the country from the 1830s through the 1860s. Some upper-class Colombians took advantage of this process to accumulate large holdings. It should be noted, however, that the division of Indian community lands was not something particularly advocated by established landowners, and in some regions, notably the Cauca, landed aristocrats came to oppose the division of Indian lands because of its impact on the indigenous population.[16]

Probably more important to the accumulation of large landholdings was the wholesale alienation of public lands during the nineteenth century. During most of the century large tracts of public lands could be obtained at little cost through the purchase of depreciated government bonds. Once again, however, it is not clear that the alienation of public lands in this manner was motivated primarily by a desire to aid large landowners. The principal aim of the policy from the 1820s to 1870 was to try to use public lands to prop up the credit of the national government. Public lands also were ceded in large grants to attract colonies of foreign immigrants and to encourage the improvement of overland communications. Although some very large holdings were appropriated before 1870, many of the tracts claimed between 1820 and 1870 were not developed and were abandoned when later laws required effective exploitation. Actual appropriation of these lands occurred particularly in the 1870s, when a temporary market for cinchona bark provided for the first time a strong economic motivation. From the 1870s and 1880s onward, national laws increasingly emphasized effective exploitation as the basis for land claims and offered protection to squatters actually using the land, as against the claims of large land entrepreneurs.

Whatever the intentions of policies on public lands, at no point in the nineteenth century was the government able effectively to enforce its writ in frontier areas. Usually men of power and money got their way—through violence, in the courts, or with the aid of local authorities. This fact frustrated the good intentions of the national laws of the 1870s and 1880s. In the accumulation of public lands, as well as in other matters, there was a disjuncture between the policies of the national government and what really happened at the local level.[17]

Our picture of relations of production in Colombian agriculture for the period from 1810 to 1880 is rather sketchy, as not much research has yet been done for this period.[18] So it is not possible to say very much about the use of state coercion of rural labor during this period. Negro slavery continued to exist in the Cauca region, although dwindling in scale, up to the time of complete abolition at midcentury. Presumably coercion came into play in the enforcement of that institution, but it is not clear that the resources of the national state were employed. In general, one may suggest, there were several reasons why the state's use of coercion in support of existing relations of production was unlikely to come into play. In some regions, such as highland Boyacá, a deep rooted pattern of Spanish cultural dominance over a humbled indigenous peasant population made overt coercion unnecessary. In most places, landowners appear to have been able to enforce their authority without the assistance of the state. Secondly, except in a few isolated pockets like tobacco-producing Ambalema (1845–1865), in most parts of the country an inert, fragmented economy created only a weak demand for labor. The tendency of upper-class landowners to devote much of their land to cattle raising further reduced labor demand. In these circumstances, there was little occasion to seek to control labor through coercion. Finally, had there been such occasion, the national state was too weak to have been much use to local landowners.

Agrarian Structures in the Coffee Era, 1880–1930

Examining the relationship of Colombia's agrarian structure to its political system becomes most relevant with the onset of the coffee era after 1870.

Coffee gave Colombia, for the first time, an agricultural export that came to have some scale and an enduring market. Expanding coffee exports increased the scale of foreign trade as a whole, enlarging government revenues and thereby making possible for the first time a somewhat effective central government. The coffee trade provided much of the underpinning for the country's first successful banks (1870–1885). Coffee as freight stimulated the construction of many of the country's railways[19] and provided the economic base that encouraged more than two hundred million dollars in foreign loans in the 1920s, most of which helped to finance rail and highway construction. The coffee industry itself, as well as the construction of railways and highways, increased demand for labor, particularly in the 1920s. Consequently, in that decade the question of retaining and controlling labor became a pressing private concern and a public issue. The expansion of coffee also sparked interest in previously uncultivated forest lands, over which large land entrepreneurs and poor squatters came into conflict. Coffee enriched planters and merchants, who organized associations (beginning with the Sociedad de Agricultores de Colombia in 1906) to press the government to protect their interests. For their part, rural laborers and settlers also came to organize and to seek government protection, particularly in the 1920s and 1930s. A stronger and more assertive national government ultimately came into play as a referee and participant in the developing conflicts between large landowners and rural labor.

The following discussion of agrarian structures and their relationship to political authority makes several general points. First, it is not possible to speak of a single mode of production in Colombian agriculture. Agrarian systems varied according to the type of crop produced; and, even in the case of a single commodity, like coffee, predominant labor arrangements varied regionally. Furthermore, within any given region there tended to be a mix of large, medium, and small producers. In addition, agrarian modes of production were not static; they changed significantly, at least in the case of coffee, in the course of the first four decades of the twentieth century. The overall trend in the twentieth century, which seems to have accelerated in the 1930s and 1940s, was toward the replacement of service tenants with wage workers in agriculture.

With regard to the actions of the state, there continued to be a substantial disjuncture between national authorities, on the one hand, and local authorities, on the other. In general, municipal authorities deferred to large property owners and supported their interests; at the national level, peasants and rural workers might have a hearing, at least some of the time, particularly when competitive politics induced political elites to take an interest in them. Sometimes national political leaders displayed at least a rhetorical interest in protecting rural workers; more frequently the rhetoric masked a de facto defense of existing economic power.

Modes of production in Colombian agriculture varied both regionally and within each region. In highland regions with peasant populations of notably indigenous origins, as in Nariño and Cauca in the South, and Boyacá and Cundinamarca in the eastern cordillera, social relations were marked by expressions of servility of the rural poor in their dealings with the dominant class. Nonetheless, relations of production in such regions varied a good deal. In highland Boyacá, more or less precapitalist forms, particularly service tenantry, were still common in the middle of the twentieth century. Haciendas dedicated mostly to cattle and sheep controlled much of the land and in many areas obtained much of their labor from service tenants. But in many localities the large estates also were surrounded by a plethora of *minifundia*, whose owners grew potatoes and grains and raised sheep on their own land and also hired themselves out.[20] But even in Boyacá, generally thought of as one of the poorer and more economically archaic parts of Colombia, labor forms varied. In some parts of Boyacá tenants were sharecroppers (e.g., Moniquirá); in others they paid a combination of money rent and labor service (e.g., Tibaná, Garagoa, Chiquiza); in still others, though more rarely, and particularly in frontier areas, they paid only money rents (e.g., Miraflores).[21]

In contrast with Boyacá, where service tenantry was common, plantations producing bananas or cotton on the Caribbean coast or sugarcane in the Cauca Valley depended on wage labor.[22] In such regions, however, there were many small independent farmers at the margins producing foods for local consumption. In the Santa Marta banana region the rural poor alternated between wage labor and farming, usually as squatters at the margins—when loss of wage work forced them into independent farming, or loss of land pushed them back into wage work.[23]

Because of the dynamism of the coffee industry and its role as the country's chief agricultural export after 1880, owners of coffee estates and merchants dealing in coffee played important roles in Colombian politics. Owners of large coffee plantations generally were well connected and politically influential—much more influential than the owners of more stagnant highland estates. After 1900 large planters controlled the chief agricultural interest group associations, first the Society of Coffee Producers (1904), then its successor the Society of Agriculturalists of Colombia (1906), and finally the National Federation of Coffeegrowers of Colombia (1927). A number of coffee growers, as individuals, figured among the chief leaders of the two traditional parties. The Conservative eminence, Jorge Holguin, in the 1920s owned at least five large plantations with a total of nearly 1,500,000 trees in Cundinamarca. Influential Liberals such as the Camacho Roldán family and Eustacio de la Torre had Cundinamarca estates of 200,000 and 320,000 trees, respectively. The Ospina family, which produced two twentieth-century Conservative presidents of the republic, possessed at least six large plantations in Antioquia totalling some 900,000 trees.[24] Alfonso López Pumarejo, the son of one of the country's largest coffee merchants who himself carried on in the trade, became the chief standard bearer of the Liberal Party, and twice national president, from the early 1930s until the middle of the 1940s. If any Colombian economic interest group might expect particular protection from the government, it would be coffee growers.

The coffee industry, further, is of particular interest for the Moore hypothesis because a number of conflicts between landowners and rural labor erupted in some coffee-producing areas in the 1920s and 1930s. These battles exposed and illuminated the character of the labor systems used in the conflicted areas. Further, they raise the question of how the political system would respond when the owners and the labor force in the country's most important export industry confronted each other. Would the government come to the aid of property owners by repressing rural labor? Or would it seek to conciliate the labor force? Given Moore's hypothesis, one might expect the state to adopt a repressive stance where landowners depended upon precapitalist or coercive modes of production, or a more conciliatory or democratic stance in the case of more capitalist forms. In the event, the modes of production in use in the coffee industry were quite mixed, and so was the government's response to conflict.

The modes of production of Colombian coffee varied a good deal from region to region. In the first three areas to begin coffee production on some scale—Northern Santander-Santander, Cundinamarca, and Antioquia—large coffee plantations, many owned by merchants or other urban absentees, were a very visible presence. By contrast, in some areas of somewhat later entry into coffee production, such as Caldas and el Valle del Cauca, large units were less common (the largest with not many more than one hundred thousand trees), and small to medium-sized production units played a much more important role in total production. (See tables 1 and 2.) Indeed, in the regions where large estates were relatively prominent—even in Cundinamarca, where large coffee haciendas were most numerous—they were surrounded by many small producers, as is indicated by the small mean size of coffee planting. (See tables 3 and 4.)

The labor systems employed on the large coffee estates, also varied regionally. Each of the three major regions that led the way in coffee production had a somewhat different form of tenant producer. In Santander, the first Colombian region to produce coffee on some scale, the predominant mode of production was sharecropping, with the crop generally divided equally between landowner and grower. Marco Palacios describes this arrangement between landowner and cultivator as a "purely economic relationship," in which the cultivator remained independent and did not live under "personal subjection." Such a system, he suggests, is

TABLE 1—Distribution of Coffee Production, by Property Size in
Major Coffee-producing Departments (1925)

Departments	More than 35 Hectares	3 to 35 Hectares	Less than 3 Hectares
Eastern			
Santander			
% of farms	3.2	28.8	78.0
% of trees	48.0	37.7	14.3
Cundinamarca			
% of farms	5.0	23.0	72.0
% of trees	55.0	32.0	13.0
Tolima			
% of farms	2.6	30.1	67.3
% of trees	38.5	46.5	15.0
Western			
Caldas			
% of farms	0.6	27.1	72.3
% of trees	10.4	61.2	28.4
Valle del Cauca			
% of farms	0.3	16.7	83.0
% of trees	7.2	53.3	39.5

Source: Absalón Machado C., "Incidencias de la economía cafetera en el
desarrollo rural," in *El agro en el desarrollo histórico colombiano: Ensayos de economía
política* (Bogotá: Editorial Punta de Lanza, 1977), 192–97, based on Diego
Monsalve, *Colombia cafetera* (Barcelona: Artes Gráficas, S.A., 1927).

characteristic of a region in which there is evident economic inequality but
in which a relative racial and cultural homogeneity engenders some sense
of identification between owner and cultivator.

In southern and western Cundinamarca, as well as in Tolima, on the
other hand, the larger coffee estates, from the 1870s into the 1920s, depended for much of their labor on service tenants called *arrendatarios*, who
were granted the right to grow food on plots of land in return for a
stipulated amount of work on the estate. Palacios argues that service
tenantry, a more dependent relation of production than the sharecropping
of northern Santander, was an economic expression of the cultural and

TABLE 2—Coffee Farms and Size of Plantings in Major Coffee-producing Departments (1932)

Department	Number of Coffee Farms	Mean Size of Coffee Planting	
		In Hectares	No. of Trees, @ 1200 per Hectare
Antioquia	28,589	2.23	2,676
Caldas	40,174	1.95	2,340
Cundinamarca	13,812	2.70	3,240
N. Santander	7,972	3.13	3,756
Tolima	12,771	4.70	5,640
Santander	3,045	6.12	7,344
Valle del Cauca	20,069	1.90	2,280
Total or mean	**149,206**	**2.38**	**2,856**

Source: Marco Palacios, *Coffee in Colombia, 1850–1970: An Economic, Social and Political History* (Cambridge: Cambridge University Press, 1980), 229, table 31, derived from Federación Nacional de Cafeteros de Colombia, *Boletín de Información y Estadística*, no. 5, February 1933.

social distance between the Bogotá elite and the servile Indo-mestizo peasant population they recruited from the highlands of Boyacá and Cundinamarca.[25]

It should be noted, however, that, though service tenantry was a distinguishing characteristic of Cundinamarca coffee estates, it was far from the only system in use. All coffee estates made some use of wage workers, particularly during harvests, and many depended heavily on wage workers at all times. To judge from the case of Viotá, larger estates in Cundinamarca in the 1920s tended to rely more heavily on service tenants than smaller ones, which tended to use more wage labor (*jornaleros*). But even some large estates (two to three hundred thousand trees), as a matter of policy, relied more on wage labor than on service tenants.[26]

In Antioquia, a third system, employing *agregados*, predominated. Palacios characterizes the Antioquia system as being between Santanderean sharecropping and Cundinamarca's *arrendatario* pattern on the scale of servility. In fact, however, to judge from his brief description, Antioquia's *agregados* must have been less independent than the Cundinamarcan *arrendatarios*, since Antioquia's estate owners kept the *agregados'* homes separate

TABLE 3—Coffee Trees and Very Large Plantations in Colombia's
Largest Coffee-producing Departments (ca. 1925)

Department	Number of Coffee Trees	Plantations with 100,000–299,999 Trees	Plantations with 300,000 Trees or More
Antioquia	78,435,450	53	3
Caldas	66,713,025	14	0
Cundinamarca	52,951,810	72	13
N. Santander	40,008,530	25	3
Tolima	35,991,726	37	2
Santander	26,956,913	31	3
Valle del Cauca	24,611,730	2	0
Total	325,669,184[a]		

Source: Diego Monsalve, Colombia cafetera (Barcelona: Artes Gráficas, S.A., 1927).
[a]The total number of coffee trees in all of Colombia at this time was 351,378,715.

from their plots, thus preventing the consolidation of a family economy like that developed by Cundinamarca's service tenants.[27]

While large units using service tenants were characteristic of Cundinamarca, in much of the western part of the country—particularly in Caldas (including the present day Quindío) and the Cauca Valley—small to medium farms were the predominant producers. In these regions, where the subjugation of agricultural workers by large estates was not typical, the dominant mode was one of familial self-exploitation.[28] Familial self-exploitation, of course, did not produce labor conflict; hence, there may be a tendency to idealize the result. In any event, that mode of production did not pose a political problem that the government had to confront.

Throughout the period from the 1880s through the 1930s, planters and public commentators debated what labor system ought to be used on coffee estates. In the 1870s the earliest planters in Cundinamarca (in the region of Sasaima and Villeta, northwest of Bogotá) were committed to the use of service tenants.[29] By the 1890s, however, there were strong advocates of wage labor, and their numbers increased in the 1920s and 1930s. In the municipality of Viotá, southwest of Bogotá, most estates used service tenants, but some estate owners in the 1920s were still experimenting with sharecropping while others persisted in favoring wage labor.[30]

TABLE 4—Distribution of Coffee Farms by Number of Trees in
Major Coffee-producing Departments (1932)

Department	Fewer than 5,000 Trees	5,000– 20,000 Trees	20,000– 60,000 Trees	60,000– 100,000 Trees	100,000 or More Trees
Eastern					
N. Santander	5,128	2,416	352	38	38
Santander	1,500	1,128	303	51	63
Cundinamarca	12,474	922	257	68	91
Tolima	9,610	2,670	369	62	60
Western					
Antioquia	24,434	3,531	518	65	41
Caldas	36,475	3,411	260	23	5
Valle del Cauca	18,477	1,514	71	3	4
Total					
(All departments)	129,556	16,921	2,226	324	321
% of farms	86.75	11.33	1.49	0.22	0.21
% of trees	48.79	24.67	12.57	5.51	8.46

Source: Charles Bergquist, *Labor in Latin America* (Stanford: Stanford University
Press, 1986), 299.

In the debate over labor systems on coffee estates, discussion tended in
the past, and in historical scholarship continues today, to focus on the
service tenantry system used in Cundinamarca. This focus on Cundinamarca has occurred in part because its coffee regions were close to Bogotá
and thus relatively well known to national elites and to such counter elites
as labor, Communist, and other Left organizers. Further, Cundinamarca's
coffee zone, as the scene of notable rural conflict in the 1920s and 1930s,
attracted attention both at the time and among scholars more recently.
Colombian critics of service tenantry on Cundinamarca's coffee estates often
characterize it as "feudal" and an outmoded remnant of Colombia's colonial
heritage. Some recent students of the coffee industry have perpetuated this
image by emphasizing its precapitalist character. But those who have looked
most closely at the *arrendatario* system in Cundinamarca depict it as a much
more complex and ambiguous institution.

Marco Palacios makes a gesture toward the colonial heritage thesis by noting that the service tenants in Cundinamarca were mostly recruited from the highlands of Boyacá and Cundinamarca, where peasant servility was deeply engrained. Palacios, however, argues that the institution, while not completely capitalist, was not really feudal either, and he depicts the service tenant more as an entrepreneur than a *peón*. (He points out that by the middle of the seventeenth century the peasants of the eastern highlands, while servile in mien, were showing tendencies to individualist agrarian capitalism.) Michael Jimenez, in his intensive study of Viotá, emphasizes much more than Palacios the tendency of estate owners and administrators to coerce and abuse their service tenants, but he too documents the entrepreneurial aspect of the *arrendatarios*. Jimenez believes that the *arrendatario* system, rather than being a feudal remnant of Colombia's colonial heritage, developed in response to specific economic problems, most particularly the need to contend with fluctuating external markets and perennial scarcities of labor and capital.[31]

The *arrendatario* system in Cundinamarca coffee estates appears to have evolved in tenor over time. The use of *arrendatarios* as a labor force in Cundinamarca may well have had its origin in the *colono* system, which was employed to make initial clearings of coffee lands. A *colono* generally was expected to clear a certain tract of land; in return he would have the right to grow food crops on the land he had cleared for a few years. Not infrequently, a *colono* was required to plant coffee on part of the land he cleared, caring for the coffee bushes until they became productive.

In places where coffee cultivation was already established, the service tenant was granted the right to grow basic food crops on a plot of land in return for providing a specified amount of labor service, for the most part in the care and harvesting of the landowners' coffee trees. In its early phase on Cundinamarca coffee haciendas (ca. 1870–1910), the *arrendatario* system had several functions. First, in a period of relative labor scarcity, the system served as a means of capturing and holding workers, particularly during the harvest period when labor was most in demand.[32] (The fact that the *arrendatarios* were thought of as laborers tied to the hacienda is suggested by the fact that in the early phases they were also called *peones de asiento*). Second, in a time of acute capital scarcity the system helped to hold down wage payments; as *arrendatarios* were compensated in part through the use of plots of land, they could be paid lower monetary wages than day laborers. Third, the food grown by *arrendatarios* could be used to feed the estate labor force as a whole, in this way reducing transportation costs for food consumed on the estate and in general holding down monetary expenditures.[33]

Both Palacios and Jimenez stress the ambiguities of the *arrendatario* system on coffee estates. Jimenez describes the arbitrary maltreatment of *arrendatarios* by estate owners and their administrators, including the sexual abuse of peasant women. At the same time, estate owners placed some service tenants in positions of trust, as *hombres de confianza;* most *mayordomos* (foremen), for example, were also service tenants. The high handed and arbitrary behavior of estate owners and their managers probably played an important role in provoking protest among service tenants. But underlying the conflict were two elements: 1) the contradictions in the *arrendatario's* economic relations with the estate, and 2) the changing economic conditions of the 1920s and 1930s.

Some perceptive Colombians who witnessed the conflicts of the late 1920s and the 1930s noted the general contradiction in the status of the coffee *arrendatarios:* they were at once renters and wage workers, both entepreneurs and *peones.*[34] Conflict with estates occurred in part because, while *hacendados* to a degree accepted the entrepreneurial thrust of the service tenants, the estate owners also often treated the *arrendatarios* as if they were only wage workers.

The *arrendatarios* were small entrepreneurs in many ways. The size of their plots varied, and some had plots too large to farm without the aid of wage workers. The larger tenants therefore employed day laborers, and in so doing competed with the estate for wage labor. Often *arrendatarios* also might hire day laborers to fulfill their labor obligations to the estate, so that they could attend to their own enterprises.[35] In the Tequendama area *arrendatarios* often sold the foods grown on their plots in local markets. Some ran small country stores. Many illegally produced *aguardiente* or *guarapo* (cane liquors) for local sale. Some had mule teams.[36]

Sometimes landowners encouraged, collaborated in, or at the very least tolerated these small *arrendatario* enterprises. Effective food supply by service tenants was in the interest of the estate, as was the provision of mule freight. Some large estates permitted service tenants to run stores on the estate itself. And they acquiesced in the illegal production of cane liquors. But in various ways *arrendatario* enterprise could bring service tenants into conflict with the estate.

Some kinds of conflict were particularly characteristic of the 1920s, when rapid economic expansion brought more acute labor scarcities and rising prices. The growth of coffee cultivation itself created part of the increased demand for labor, as coffee production more than quadrupled between 1905 and 1929. In addition, foreign investment in Colombia for the first time became somewhat significant in these years. United Fruit, which moved into the Santa Marta region at the beginning of the century, was said to have invested seventy million dollars by 1928.[37] United States oil companies from 1918 to 1928 invested another estimated forty-five million dollars. Both types of enterprises offered higher wages than those prevailing in rural areas and thus helped to press labor demand upward. But the most significant impact on the labor market in the interior of the country came from public works projects in the 1920s, fueled in part by twenty-five million dollars in payment by the United States government for the seizure of Panama (1923–1926) and by nearly two hundred million dollars in bonds floated in the United States by Colombia's national, departmental, and municipal governments (mostly during 1926–1928).[38] At the same time, Colombia's larger cities were growing rapidly, both drawing off part of the rural labor force and increasing the demand for food.

The combination of increased labor demand and rising prices provided a favorable environment for labor organization during the 1920s. Port, transportation, and oil workers were among the more militant of those organized, but organization also extended to agriculture in some areas, most notably on the banana-growing plantations of Santa Marta and in some coffee-growing areas in Cundinamarca and Tolima.

In a context of labor scarcity and rising food prices, estates and service tenants came into conflict in various ways. Given rising food prices, *arrendatarios* were especially likely to withhold their labor from the estate, to compete with the hacienda in the employment of scarce day laborers, and to sell the food they produced in markets outside the estate. All of these things it was in the interest of the haciendas to oppose. Estates sought to enforce the labor obligations of service tenants and to deter the sale of crops outside the hacienda.

One of the central issues in conflict between estate owners and service tenants was the cultivation of coffee on the *arrendatarios'* plots. From the earliest years of coffee planting in Cundinamarca, *hacendados* had forbidden their service tenants to plant coffee on their plots. Malcolm Deas says that in the early years the prohibition was aimed at preventing workers from stealing coffee. If only the estate was permitted to produce coffee, then it could be assumed that all coffee found on the estate belonged to it.[39] By the 1920s some estates permitted at least some service tenants to have their own coffee bushes. But this clearly was a concession with which landowners were not entirely comfortable. With the labor scarcity and rising food prices of the 1920s, new reasons for forbidding tenants to have their own bushes came to the fore. If coffee cultivation proliferated among the tenants, it was likely to reduce their food production. At least as important, if service tenants grew coffee, at harvest time they would deny their labor to the estate and would compete with it in hiring day laborers.[40]

The issue of *arrendatarios'* growing their own coffee trees was also related to another pressing question—the service tenants' concern to be compensated for improvements on their plots if landowners discontinued their tenure. Service tenants perennially complained that they were under-compensated, or not compensated at all, for improvements when they lost their plots. The issue became particularly heated in the 1920s when rising prices increased the value of service tenants' improvements and landowners were unwilling to pay for improvements at these higher values.[41] Coffee cultivation by the *arrendatarios*, however, made the issue particularly acute. If the improvements consisted of coffee bushes, their value would be much greater than that of the land itself. Because landowners felt they could not afford to pay the increased value that the coffee trees represented, they contended that allowing tenants to plant coffee was equivalent to losing ownership of the land.[42]

With the onset of the Depression, many of the issues of the 1920s continued in a greatly changed context. As international coffee prices plunged, the Colombian economy shrank. Large coffee producers, many of whom had borrowed heavily in the 1920s to finance coffee expansion, found themselves in tight financial straits. On the other hand, in partial compensation, their bargaining power with rural labor was strengthened by massive umemployment. The scarcity of agricultural labor ended as men drawn off into public works in the 1920s were laid off and returned to rural areas. In the context of falling coffee prices, financial pressures, and an increased supply of labor, one of the primary concerns of estate owners was to reduce their labor costs by jacking up the work requirements and reducing the economic liberties of *arrendatarios*. In the context of the Depression, and with greater availability of labor, estates became less tolerant of *arrendatario* use of estate resources, such as the cutting of timber or even cultivation on marginal lands. The ultimate enforcement weapon of estate owners was to expel service tenants from their plots.

In the Tequendama region of Cundinamarca, where service tenantry played an important role, much of the conflict between estate owners and rural labor focused on the relationship between the estate and the *arrendatarios*. Many issues were in play, but the two most important ones had to do with defining the labor obligations of service tenants and securing their right to compensation for improvements. Service tenants particularly insisted that their labor obligations be written into fixed contracts so that estates could not arbitrarily jack them up. And they sought the support of the state in enforcing compensation for improvements in case of expulsion. Ultimately they came to claim full property rights to plots they had cultivated.

Aside from the Tequendama region, another area of conflict in Cundinamarca was that of Sumapaz, which lies on the other side of the cordillera to the southeast. The conflict in the Sumapaz zone was somewhat different in character because it was more of a frontier zone than the Tequendama. The Tequendama region had long been controlled by large estates, some with roots in the colonial period and most with relatively clear titles. Large estates in the Tequendama usually had substantial areas of uncultivated forest in their higher reaches. But the region was a relatively settled one. By contrast, in the more recently colonized Sumapaz area, landowners' rights to the land they claimed were less clearly established and larger areas claimed by estates were uncultivated forest. Consequently, whereas conflicts in the Tequendama tended to focus on labor conditions in general and the complaints of service tenants in particular, the conflict in Sumapaz centered more on property rights, with agricultural workers asserting that much of the territory claimed by large estates actually was illegally held public land, which they might settle and possess as homesteaders. The conflict between estates and squatters in Sumapaz was but one of the better known cases of a quite general problem.[43] Though the Tequendama and Sumapaz conflicts differed in emphasis, they tended ultimately to converge: in both cases, peasants came to assert property rights to land claimed by haciendas but left unexploited by them.

Still another area of conflict was in southern Tolima. Here, as in Sumapaz, the conflict tended to be between landowners and *colonos* for the control of land in a newly developing frontier area. The conflict was, if anything, even more violent than in Sumapaz, with considerable use of police and departmental forces to evict *colonos*.[44]

Agrarian Issues and the State in the Twentieth Century

Until the 1920s, the national state in Colombia was too weak to have a significant impact on issues relating to large landowners and rural labor. Most matters, whether they involved disputes over land between large land speculators and peasant squatters, or questions of labor discipline on large estates, were handled privately (sometimes with the use of violence) by the large landowners themselves. If it was necessary to turn to the government for support, mayors and local judges generally were the ones who handled such matters, usually, if not invariably, deciding them in accord with the wishes of dominant landowners in the region. (Governors appointed mayors from panels of nominees proposed by local landowners.)[45]

Occasionally, however, conflicts between landowners and peasants reached a scale that local authorities could not handle by themselves. Particularly during the 1930s, in an atmosphere of crisis, landowners called upon departmental governments, often for the eviction of peasant *colonos* in conflict with large estates over claims to land. During the early 1930s departmental guards were mobilized and used to evict squatters, often with a good deal of violence, in various departments, most notably in Cundinamarca and Tolima.[46]

Generally, landowners could depend upon departmental governors to lend a sympathetic ear, and departmental guards generally provided enough force to handle such local issues as might emerge. During the 1920s and 1930s, however, the national government increasingly became involved in rural issues. Several factors brought the national state more actively into play. The belief that public lands ought to be granted only to those that would put them into effective production, already incorporated in national policy in the 1880s, was still more forcefully asserted by elements of the political elite in the post-World War I years. Laws of 1917 and 1926 aided smaller occupants of public land by simplifying the process of making land claims. Further, a 1926 Supreme Court decision undermined the claims of large land speculators by declaring that property would be considered public land if those who claimed it could not show clear documentation that it had been granted by the state.[47] This decision apparently had the effect of encouraging squatters to challenge the claims of large land magnates.

In the 1920s, also, increased revenues and changing notions about the functions of the state encouraged the national government to play a more active role in issues relating to the use of land and the supply and control of labor. This change was particularly reflected in the activities of the Ministry of Industries and its National Labor Office, created in 1923. Initially the mission of the National Labor Office was to collect information on labor conditions, in city and countryside alike. In 1927 its mandate was broadened to include labor mediation; in the same year the National Labor Office sent regional inspectors throughout the republic.[48] In the late 1920s and 1930s the labor office played a very important role in informing the national political elite, most of whom were urbanites, about rural realities. It also was very active in mediating collective conflicts between peasants and landowners. The Conservative regimes of the 1920s thus created a bureaucratic entity that ultimately, under Liberal governments in the 1930s, would serve as the instrument of a policy of at least some responsiveness to peasant demands.

How did this stronger, more effective national government respond to agrarian issues? One might imagine that its policies overwhelmingly would favor estate owners, as a number of large landowners, particularly those who were urban absentee owners, were active in politics. In addition, large landowners were represented by organized pressure groups, particularly the Society of Agriculturalists of Colombia (after 1906) and the National Federation of Coffeegrowers of Colombia (after 1927). On the whole, however, the national government sustained the interests of large landowners less resolutely than one might expect.

There were several reasons for this. First, an element in the political elite, particularly in the Liberal Party, was both essentially urban and susceptible to social democratic tendencies. Francisco José Chaux, minister of industries in the government of Enrique Olaya Herrera (1930–1934), the first Liberal government since the 1880s, was an outstanding example of Liberals of this sort. Chaux and his agents in the Ministry of Industries in the early 1930s played a critical role in turning the national government away from repressive modes and toward conciliatory mediation between landowners and peasants. Another exemplar of this type was Carlos Lleras Restrepo, in the 1930s a young and aspiring Liberal politician who, fearing broad social revolution, sought peaceful resolution of rural conflicts.

It was also possible for the national government to adopt relatively moderate policies on rural issues because spokesmen for large landowners' organizations were not always unanimous in support of repressive or reactionary policies. Difference of opinion among landowner spokesmen probably reflected in part the diversity of modes of production in Colombian agriculture. While large estates making use of service tenants were characteristic of Cundinamarca coffee estates, by the 1920s Cundinamarca was not the most important coffee-growing region. At that time, western Colombia was producing more than the eastern zone, and in two of the more dynamically growing western areas (Caldas and the Cauca Valley), small to medium cultivators predominated. (See tables 1 and 4.) In these departments the dominant class extracted much of its profit from coffee through its processing and commercialization as well as from direct production. Accordingly, coffee men from western Colombia, who were increasingly influential in the Coffee Federation, had less of a stake then did their peers in Cundinamarca in the defense of large estates or of service labor systems. Throughout the period from 1910 through the 1930s, some coffee men from the West were vocal critics of latifundia and of service tenant systems. Jesús del Corral in 1914 was one such critic, as was Alejandro López in the 1920s and 1930s.[49] Significantly, when the Liberal president, Alfonso López Pumarejo, had an opportunity to choose the director of the Coffee Federation in 1935, he chose the Antioqueño Liberal, Alejandro López.

It also appears that the Coffee Federation, founded and increasingly dominated by coffee men from western Colombia, were less coercive in spirit, at least some of the time, than was the Sociedad de Agricultores, which spoke more for the *hacendados* of Cundinamarca. The occasionally softer line of the Coffee Federation probably did not reflect so much the attitudes of small growers in the west, as such folk did not reach Coffee Federation councils.[50] Nonetheless, a region that depended less on service tenantry and more on commercialization was likely to produce men eager to encourage a more competitive, and less archaic, brand of capitalism. Alluding to the diversity of modes of production and of attitudes in the coffee industry, Michael Jimenez notes that Colombia, unlike Brazil, was "not a republic of planters."[51]

One issue in which the national state was asked to play a role was the supply of labor to estates, particularly during the years of accentuated labor scarcity in the 1920s. The national government, and some departmental governments, of course, had contributed, possibly more than anyone, to creating the problem, as their public works projects attracted many rural laborers from estates. When landowners asked the national government to help them obtain laborers, the government did not respond decisively. This was in part because the interests of different sorts of landowners and of the government itself conflicted. Take, for example, the issue of the free movement of agricultural labor, raised by self-protective legislation of the Department of Boyacá. From the early years of the coffee era, in the 1870s and 1880s, coffee *hacendados* had recruited impoverished peasants in highland Boyacá; when the public works boom hit in the 1920s, the builders of railways and highways also looked to Boyacá as a source of labor. In 1926–1927, *hacendados* in highland Boyacá sought to halt the loss of their *peones* through a resolution of the departmental assembly, forbidding rural workers to leave Boyacá without the written permission of local authorities.[52] This resolution provoked an outcry from spokesmen for a modern, commercial, market economy, who viewed it as an attempt to imprison peasants on the backward estates of Boyacá. The national government in 1927 introduced a measure forbidding any barrier to the free movement of labor. Significantly, however, this measure did not actually win the approval of the Congress.[53] (Nonetheless, the argument of the commercial elite Liberals in favor of the free movement of labor, on grounds of economic utility as well as social justice, suggests at least some confirmation, in the Colombia of the 1920s, of Moore's notion that commercialized agriculture may foster democracy.)

Coffee growers, for their part, asked the national government to aid in the supply of labor to their plantations through various mechanisms—for example, by diverting some laborers from public works projects to coffee estates at harvest time or, more vaguely, by encouraging immigration. At one point the national government did offer cheap train fares to workers travelling to the coffee zones. But its efforts to aid planters to obtain workers fell far short of the concerted efforts of the government of Sao Paulo in Brazil, for example, which subsidized the ocean voyages of European immigrants to work on coffee estates there.[54]

On issues of labor discipline or control (from the point of view of estate owners) or equitable treatment of workers (from the perspective of rural laborers), it is necessary to distinguish between conflicts concerning individual peasants and those involving the collective action of groups of rural workers. In cases involving individual workers, it appears that, as in the last decades of the nineteenth century, estates in the 1920s continued to apply a certain amount of private coercion. Some accounts refer to the use of stocks and dank prisons on some large haciendas. Estates also continued to rely on the cooperation of local mayors and judges for the punishment of workers judged to be recalcitrant.

In cases where peasants organized, expressing their grievances in collective action, neither private nor municipal forces were likely to be able to contain and control the conflict. In such cases, departmental or national agencies almost necessarily came into play. As already indicated, departmental officials generally supported landowner interests. How did national authorities respond to collective action by rural workers? Four cases particularly attracted attention at the time and have been closely studied by historians: the strike against United Fruit in the banana zone near Santa Marta in 1928, the "Bolshevik" insurrection in el Libano, Tolima, in 1929, and the collective actions of peasants in the Tequendama region and in nearby Sumapaz, extending from the late 1920s through the early 1930s.

National government response in these four cases varied. In the case of both the United Fruit strike and the "Bolshevik" insurrection in el Líbano, units of the national army were sent in to repress the collective actions and authorities engaged in quite harsh repression, whereas in the Tequendama and in Sumapaz the national government pursued a more conciliatory policy. Specific features of each of these conflicts may help to explain the different government responses. In the case of United Fruit, rural workers were striking against a foreign enterprise; the Conservative government in 1928 may have been particularly disposed to an intransigent defense of United Fruit precisely because it wanted to demonstrate to the American corporation its determination to provide a climate of order and labor discipline congenial to foreign investment. In the case of the "Bolshevik" insurrection in El Líbano, the fact that the insurrectionaries employed a rhetoric of political revolution against the existing order rather than of specific economic grievance may have had something to do with the forceful reaction of national authorities. Although Socialist influence was evident in both the Tequendama and in Sumapaz, collective action tended to focus more on specific economic arrangements.

Another factor differentiating the United Fruit and el Líbano conflicts from those in the Cundinamarca coffee zones was that of political competition within a changing political climate. From the middle of the 1880s until the time of World War I, Colombia had been ruled by an increasingly dominant Conservative hegemony. Liberals several times had attempted to regain power through rebellion, but their hopes had been resoundingly crushed by defeat in the War of a Thousand Days (1899–1902). After World War I, however, a new political force emerged in Colombia. In a context of economic growth, relative labor scarcity, and rising prices, Colombian labor unions began to form, among skilled workers in the larger cities, and particularly among port workers on the Magdalena River, railroad workers, and in the foreign banana and oil enclaves. Although economic conditions after World War I were conducive to labor organization, the movement was further stimulated by the encouragement of a new political force in Colombia, a Marxist or Socialist Left. In 1919 a Colombian labor congress gave birth to a Socialist Party, with labor unions heavily represented among its affiliate organizations. By 1921 Socialist influence already was such that Socialists won control of the municipal government of the river port of Girardot as well as of some smaller towns along the Magdalena River.

The two parties that had dominated Colombian politics through most of the republican era reacted to this force on the Left in quite different ways. Conservatives were inclined to repress any sign of Marxist revolution. Some in a newer generation of urban Liberals, however, responded more positively, in some cases, or at least with greater subtlety in others. Some Liberals were attracted by Marxist ideas, and a few evolved into leaders of Colombia's Communist Party. Others saw the Socialists as a new competitor on the Left. They sought to co-opt the Socialists by enlisting them in political alliance against the Conservatives. At the same time they tried to compete with the Socialists for influence over, and clientelistic control of, rural and urban workers. The younger generation of Liberals in the 1920s were, in effect, engaged in a double competition—seeking electoral alliance with the Socialists to defeat the Conservatives in the early 1920s but also seeking to steal the political thunder of Marxism among urban and rural workers. In the process a number of young Liberals moved from the doctrinaire individualism of nineteenth-century liberalism toward more socially democratic stances.[55]

The first act of this drama of political competition had as its focus the United Fruit strike. In December of 1928, the military commander in charge of repressing the strike conducted an unprovoked massacre of strikers. Young Liberals and leftists of various degrees then competed in denouncing the Conservative government in efforts to extract political advantage from this event. The massacre of the United Fruit strikers played at least a part in the downfall of the Conservative government in 1930—though a Conservative split between two candidates was undoubtedly the most important factor in the victory of the Liberal presidential candidate.

The second act of the drama of political competition, at least as it played out in the countryside, occurred in the coffee areas of southwestern Cundinamarca during the 1930s. Here younger Liberal elites attempted to compete with leftists of various flavors to establish political bases among rural workers in the coffee zones. The desire of young national elite Liberals to compete with the Left for the allegiance of the coffee workers conditioned the relatively modulated responses of the Liberal national government to the collective peasant actions in the Tequendama and Sumapaz regions. In both areas collective action by peasants led, through national government mediation, to checks on arbitrary estate demands on workers and ultimately to the division of some coffee haciendas among the peasantry (parceliza-tion).

It should be noted here, however, that political competition between Liberals and the Left was not the only element making possible a relatively peaceful resolution to some of the conflicts in southwestern Cundinamarca. The division of hacienda lands among peasants in the region was facilitated by the fact that the Depression threatened to ruin many coffee *hacendados* who were deeply in debt. The division and sale of land to rural laborers enabled a number of estate owners to escape economic disaster.

During the 1930s, through a combination of Depression-era economic pressures on large landowners, government-sponsored parcelization, and further squatter colonization in frontier zones, the numbers of small coffee growers grew dramatically in the conflictive, hacienda-dominated coffee zones of Cundinamarca and Tolima. In Cundinamarca, between 1932 and 1939 the number of small farms cultivating fewer than 5,000 trees (two hectares or less in coffee) doubled, and those with 5,000 to 20,000 trees (about two to eight hectares), which were more viable economically, more than quadrupled. In Tolima the number of coffee growers in both categories roughly doubled in the same period. During the same years in these departments there occurred a somewhat slower growth in the number of medium-sized coffee farms (20,000 to 60,000 trees, or eight to twenty-four hectares), while the numbers of larger growers (more than 60,000 trees or twenty-four hectares) remained almost static.[56]

Given the development of conciliatory mediation by the national government and the dramatic growth in the number of small independent coffeegrowers, one might conclude that Colombia in the 1930s demonstrates a reciprocal of the Moore thesis. Commerical agriculture (specifically, coffee) in some ways may have fostered some socially democratic tendencies—in the sense that, between 1880 and 1930, coffee culture permitted a relatively servile highland peasantry to evolve toward independent enterprise in Cundinamarca, and much less servile folk to do the same in western Colombia. But events of the early 1930s also suggest, however, that political competition even in a limited democracy may tend to constrain coercive modes of production in agriculture.

The responsiveness to peasant interests in the early 1930s proved temporary, however. The enactment of Law 200 of 1936, which was intended to resolve the most rancorous issues between large landowners and *colonos* and service tenants, in fact seems in some way to have aggravated the situation of many of the rural poor. Law 200 has been a much controverted measure, both at the time and in later historical interpretation. For a considerable time, most interpreters of Law 200 viewed it as legislation that was progressive in intent but that had some unintended negative consequences. The law was considered progressive in that it proclaimed the principle of the social function of property. In particular, it sought to increase productivity by giving title to land to those who put it to economic use. Article 1 of the law made it easier for both small squatters and large landowners to claim public lands provided they were being put to economic use. The law particularly aided peasants to obtain title to land they already had occupied in areas then under conflict, as in the Tequendama and Sumapaz areas. With regard to the relations between landowners and tenants working for them, the law required full compensation for improvements tenants had made on hacienda lands. And it provided that squatters who for five years had occupied and cultivated privately owned lands could receive title to them.[57]

Some of the destructive consequences of Law 200 became evident rather quickly. Large landowners, fearing (or claiming) they would lose land under cultivation by tenants or *colonos*, hastened to expel many of them, turning instead to wage labor. Law 200 had backfired by making the tenants' position even more insecure than before. Many of the expelled *colonos* either sought new land farther out on the frontier or migrated to the cities. These events had the further undesirable effect of reducing food production. Whereas coffee estates once had contained food plots cultivated by tenants, many estate owners, fearing the food plots would serve as bases for claims to land, eliminated the tenant cultivation of basic foods. This raised food costs on the estates, thereby increasing coffee production costs. It also appears to have reduced total food production in the country. And, of course, many expelled *colonos* were unable to feed themselves and had to resort to various kinds of theft to sustain their families.

Whereas most earlier interpretations of Law 200 of 1936 viewed its regressive consequences as having been accidental, some recent interpretations have tended to take a more negative view of the law. Francine Cronshaw credits President López and his collaborators with socially meliorative intent but finds that the law was undermined in its execution. In particular, newly created land judges, who were supposed to settle land disputes on the ground, proved too weak an instrument to deal with the power of local landowners. Worse, some of those appointed were unsympathetic to the peasants presumed to be beneficiaries of the law.[58]

Some other scholars have reached still harsher judgments of Law 200. Gonzalo Sánchez is seconded by Catherine LeGrand in asserting that President López and his closet colleagues intended the law to be conservative in effect. LeGrand argues that a draft of a land law in 1933, under the moderate Liberal Olaya Herrera government, was much more favorable to the interests of small cultivators and that Law 200 of 1936 in fact represented a capitulation by the López government to pressure from large landowners. In the Sánchez-LeGrand interpretation, long-term peasant interests were undermined both by desertion on the left and by organized pressure from the right. Law 200 co-opted the organized peasantry of the Tequendama region by satisfying their demands, while at the same time making more difficult the claims of other peasants who in the future might become involved in similar conflicts. Other sources of pressure from the Left were removed early in 1935 when Jorge Eliécer Gaitán abandoned his agitation for the peasants in Sumapaz and incorporated himself into the Liberal Party, and shortly afterward the Communist Party, in a Popular Front spirit, also aligned itself with the López government. From this time, López as well as Gaitán focused more on urban constituencies. At the same time, President López was responding to the pressures of large landowners represented by the Sociedad de Agricultores, the Federación de Cafeteros, and the newly formed Employers' National Economic Association (Asociación Patronal Económica Nacional—APEN).

Thus the López administration enacted a law that would make it easier for large operators, as well as poor *colonos*, to claim title to public lands. Indeed, President López, in discussing the law at the time, explicitly reassured large landowners that the most important effect of the law would be to validate their shaky titles.[59] In a more general commentary on the law, Gonzalo Sánchez and Donny Meertens have noted that one of the "historical functions" of Law 200 was "to define a new order of legitimacy for large agrarian properties, since the peasant movement had demonstrated clearly the fragility of the existing" agrarian regime.[60]

While interpretations of Law 200 vary considerably, there is general agreement that from 1936 onward there was a general trend to more conservative, and even regressive, policies affecting the peasantry. As the expulsion of *colonos* from large estates increased rural theft, large landowners appealed to the government for increasingly repressive measures. The land law of 1936 (Law 200) was accompanied by a vagrancy law (Law 48), which facilitated the removal of expelled *colonos*. Some large landowners called for the creation of a national rural mounted police, a measure never actually implemented.[61]

A further effort to bring order to rural society occurred with the enactment of Law 100 of 1944. This law is often described, correctly, as an effort to reestablish service tenancy. But, viewed more benevolently, it may also be considered an attempt to rectify the unintended disasters wrought by Law 200 of 1936. To reassure large landowners that harboring service tenants need not mean the loss of land, the law extended the time allowed to landowners to establish a claim to land through use. To provide further reassurance, the law called for the clearer specification of terms between landowner and tenant in written contracts. To encourage the cultivation of food on large estates, tenants specifically were granted the right to grow food crops, without endangering a landowner's title to the land.[62] Law 100 may be more important as an expression of Colombian elite intent than because of its actual impact. It apparently failed in its aim to resurrect service tenancy. Wage labor had become, and remained, the dominant mode.[63]

The years from the 1920s to 1945 witnessed substantial, though sporadic and localized, agrarian conflict. But during these years the dominance of large-scale coffee growers receded as the numbers of small independent cultivators multiplied. As of 1955 Colombia's 577 largest coffee farms (more than 50 hectares) accounted for only 6.5 percent of national production. Nearly 124,000 small, family-sized farms (1.1 to 10 hectares) produced about 58 percent of Colombia's coffee. More than 11,000 larger, but not latifundiary, farms (10 to 50 hectares) added another 30 percent of national production. Government-sponsored parcelization of some large estates in the 1930s played a role in the development of coffee smallholdings. But so too did relatively low international coffee prices between 1925 and 1945, which reduced incentives for large landowners to monopolize the land. In a context of relatively low prices, large landowners were more willing to accept parcelization and perhaps somewhat less likely to contest land on the coffee frontier.[64]

The growth in numbers of small to medium-sized coffee farms (particularly in the range of from eight to fifty hectares) and the relative decline in importance of large coffee estates may be considered a triumph from the perspective of improved social equity. On the other hand, as of 1955 more than a third of Colombia's coffee farms were of less than one hectare, *minifundia* that were not economically viable. And, as Charles Bergquist emphasizes, their owners, because of their poverty and insecurity, became the principal victims (and actors) in Colombia's Violencia of circa 1948 to 1965.[65]

It is necessary to say something about the Violencia in an essay on the Moore thesis, because it was played out primarily in rural areas and because it involved the use of state-sponsored violence and dramatically affected rural property relations. Possibly two hundred thousand people, mostly peasants, are believed to have been killed and perhaps four times that many were driven from their homes. The Violencia was a complex and multifaceted phenomena. Affecting most parts of the country to one degree or another, it had many regional variations. Partly because of these regional differences, partly because of the differing perspectives of analysts of the Violencia, it has been explained in many different terms. Most interpretations have seen the Violencia as having originated in competition between the Conservative and Liberal parties to establish political hegemony; this phase was particularly characteristic of the years from 1948 to 1954. But the Violencia became more than a political conflict. It became, in many regions, various kinds of economic war, a protection racket, a way of doing business, a social pathology. It is in these extra- or para-political areas that interpretations tend to vary.

Paul Oquist, in a general synthesis, provides a perceptive explanation of the political origins of the Violencia. Oquist argues that the increasing penetration of the national state into local affairs, as well as into the regulation of economic life, during the twentieth century meant that by the 1940s the party controlling the government enjoyed hegemonic power. Because of the extension of state power into localities, control of the government now affected not merely the national capital but also what happened in the departments and localities. The increased stakes of politics were reflected in the war between Conservatives and Liberals that broke out in 1948. Political violence between the Conservative and Liberal parties, largely for the political control of localities, brought the collapse of state authority.[66]

Then, in essentially anarchic conditions, many kinds of warfare broke out. In some areas, as in the eastern plains or Tolima, Conservative police or army, Liberal guerrillas, and Conservative counterguerrillas came into play. In some regions, such as the Sumapaz and southern Tolima, national armed forces were deployed against left-influenced settler communities. In many other places the contenders were mostly local. In some cases neighboring villages carried out vendettas over long-standing disputes and traditional rivalries. Particularly in frontier areas, large landowners and poor *colonos* fought for the control of the land, probably without regard to political affiliation. In many places economically motivated violence with a political face forced medium as well as small cultivators to sell their land at emergency prices, permitting others to take their lands at slight expense. In such cases the struggle was not necessarily an interclass struggle between large landowners and small cultivators. Many of those who took advantage of the situation to accumulate land did not begin the period as large landowners: often their principal capital, initially, was their political affiliation.[67] As Bergquist points out, very small coffee growers in particular were likely to become involved. Because of their economic insecurity, they tended to depend on clientelist relations, many of them political, for survival. And those clientelist relations, the small farmers' vulnerabilities, and the economic opportunities presented by the violence all brought them into the vortex. Finally, in the later stages of the Violencia, rural gangs seized coffee crops or took protection money from large coffee growers by threatening to kill their work force at harvest time. In sum, while the Violencia had an initial common denominator in the political struggle between Conservatives and Liberals, it soon developed the multiple regional variations that are so characteristic of other aspects of Colombian history.

As is perhaps obvious, the Violencia, like other periods in Colombian history, seems to fit the Moore model only partially. In the first place, while a strongly authoritarian streak was notable in some of the Conservative leaders at the time, the violence began in a context of political competition; it was not executed by a settled authoritarian regime. Second, in some cases, such as the Sumapaz region and southern Tolima state, power was used against peasants and on behalf of large landowners. But these cases were not the general rule. Third, much of the violence was locally generated rather than state sponsored. And while some of this local violence was employed by large landowners against peasants, much of it did not correspond to class divisions but rather to political clan identities and local clientelistic relations.

Conclusion

For the most part, the Moore model does not apply very clearly to Colombia in the early republican era. In the nineteenth century various sorts of coercion may have been used by landowners with rural workers, but these were essentially private modes of coercion. The national state was not authoritarian in structure; it might best be called an oligarchic republic. In any event, the state was too weak really to affect power realities at the local level. The national government before 1880 might best be thought of as an essentially formal structure that was only remotely connected to local economic and social realities.

In the period of export expansion, and particularly after World War I, the national government did become stronger and its agents during the 1920s and 1930s began increasingly to intervene in the relations between landlord and rural labor. As a burgeoning commercial agriculture, with coffee as its principal motor, provided the financial basis for a more effective state, Moorean predictions about the relationship of the state to agrarian structures become more relevant.

But in the twentieth century, Colombia presents a very mixed picture. Some western coffee zones, particularly Caldas and el Valle, were dominated by small and medium coffee producers, and large landowners were exceptional. The issue of state use, or tolerance, of the coercion of peasants on behalf of *hacendados* did not come so much into play. The eastern coffee regions, particularly in Cundinamarca and Tolima, were characterized by large landholdings, the employment of service tenants, and, in time of need, the use of coercion, generally by local or departmental authorities, against peasants. But even within the eastern regions the picture was very mixed. Many service tenants in Cundinamarca by the 1920s had become small entrepreneurs, exemplars of petty capitalism. And even in the eastern zones dominated by latifundia in the 1920s there were already many small and medium independent cultivators. Finally, in the eastern zone some of the larger estate owners, as a matter of policy, used wage labor rather than service tenants.

Presumably because of the differences in dominant modes of production between western and eastern zones, as well as differences of opinion within the eastern zone, spokesmen for the interests of landowners were not always united. Some large coffee growers in the eastern zone, as well as in the west, were fervent believers in liberal capitalism, not only in international exchange but also in modes of production. Thus, coffee *hacendados* did not always speak with one voice. As a consequence, while landowners could depend upon support from local and departmental authorities, national government policies were more mixed.

The record on state coercion of peasants on behalf of landowner interests is also mixed. As indicated, landowners could depend on the support of local and departmental authorities. But policies of the national government changed over time. In the late 1920s the national government was willing to use the national army to repress peasant movements, most dramatically in the case of the United Fruit strike in 1928, but also in some other cases. But during the early 1930s the national government moved away from repression and toward conciliation and negotiation. In the early 1930s, in an environment of economic depression, social crisis, and political competition, some Liberals in the national government moved toward a greater recognition of peasant interests. Partly through government-sponsored parcelizations in the 1930s, smaller farms multiplied in the eastern coffee zones formerly more dominated by large estates. And on large estates, despite efforts to resuscitate service tenantry in the 1940s, wage labor became increasingly dominant.

During the Violencia of 1948–1965, conditions remained regionally diverse. In some cases government forces were employed against peasants on behalf of large landowners. In many other instances peasants were doing battle with each other rather than against *hacendados*.

Given these mixed conditions, it is perhaps appropriate, from a Moorean perspective, that the Colombian government itself did not fit easily into a simple category of democratic or dictatorial or authoritarian. Democratic in form, the government was aristocratic in spirit. In a country in which spokesmen for agrarian interests essentially spoke for large landowners (of varying views), national policies affecting rural areas were also shaped by a governing urban elite, some of whom developed social democratic tendencies by the 1930s. These tendencies became muted in the 1940s and 1950s, but nonetheless found mild expression in the agrarian reform of the 1960s.

The agrarian reform of 1961, including the preliminary discussions and its later outcome, was typical of Colombian ambiguities. The agrarian reform of 1961 was a top-down reform, motivated in part by the fear of massive peasant migrations to the cities; peasant voices were not heard in the discussions preceding the legislation. The reform was pushed through by urban Liberals over the opposition of Conservatives; but the plan had to be greatly modified to meet Conservative and organized landowner objections. The agrarian reform legislation of 1961 was quite moderate, and its ultimate effect was to place great reliance on the colonization of regions that were not accessible to markets. One critic pointed out that a substantial agrarian reform would not occur until organized peasant pressure groups made it happen. But such organized peasant groups were something that not even the urban liberals who favored agrarian reform wanted to see.[68] On the other hand, as Bergquist emphasizes, much of the Colombian peasantry already has been co-opted through the possession of *minifundia*.

In all of this there are elements that can be crammed into a modified version of the Moore framework; but the total picture is so mixed as to defy easy and categorical generalization.

NOTES

1. On the role of the Sociedad Nacional de Agricultura in Chile (founded 1869), see Thomas C. Wright, "The Sociedad Nacional de Agricultura in Chilean Politics, 1869–1938" (Ph.D. diss., University of California, Berkeley, 1971); and, more accessibly, "Origins of the Politics of Inflation in Chile, 1888–1918," *Hispanic American Historical Review* 53, no. 2 (May 1973): 239–59; and *Landowners and Reform in Chile: The Sociedad Nacional de Agricultura, 1919–1940* (Champagne: University of Illinois Press, 1982).

2. Friedrich Katz, "Labor Conditions on Haciendas in Porfirian Mexico: Some Trends and Tendencies," *Hispanic American Historical Review* 54, no. 1 (February 1974): 1–47.

3. Paul Oquist, *Violence, Conflict, and Politics in Colombia* (New York: Academic, 1980), 13.

4. Marco Palacios, *Coffee in Colombia, 1850–1970: An Economic, Social and Political History* (Cambridge: Cambridge University Press, 1980), 29–33, 39, 42–43.

5. Michael F. Jimenez, "Traveling Far in Grandfather's Car: The Life Cycle of Central Colombian Coffee Estates. The Case of Viotá, Cundinamarca (1900–30)," *Hispanic American Historical Review* 69, no. 2 (May 1989): 186, 193.

6. Luis Eduardo Nieto Arteta, *El café en la sociedad colombiana* (Bogotá: Ediciones Soga al Cuello, 1971), 15.

7. Anthony McFarlane, "El mercantilismo borbónico y la economía americana: La Nueva Granada en la época del comercio libre, 1778–1795," *Anuario de Estudios Americanos*, 47 (1990): 326–27, 338–52.

8. Frank Safford, *The Ideal of the Practical: Colombia's Struggle to Form a Technical Elite* (Austin: University of Texas Press, 1976), 43–44.

9. Frank Safford, "Race, Integration, and Progress: Elite Attitudes and the Indian in Colombia, 1750–1870," *Hispanic American Historical Review* 71, no. 1 (February 1991): 20.

10. *Jeografía física i política de las provincias de la Nueva Granada por la Comisión Corográfica bajo la dirección de Agustín Codazzi*, 4 vols. (1856; reprint, 4 vols., Bogotá: Banco de la República, Archivo de la Economía Nacional, 1957–1959). Vol. 22, *Provincias de Tunja y Tundama*, 28, 65, 226–27, 305; vol. 23, *Provincias de Soto, Santander, Pamplona, Ocaña, Antioquia, y Medellín*, 87,111.

11. *Jeografía física i política*, 23: 223, 243.

12. Frank Safford, "Significación de los antioqueños en el desarrollo económ-

ico colombiano: Un exámen crítico de las tesis de Everett Hagen," *Anuario Colombiano de Historia Social y de la Cultura* 2, no. 3 (1965): 49–69.

13. E.g., the junta of notable merchants and *hacendados* in Bogotá, January 1833 (Frank Safford, "The Emergence of Economic Liberalism in Colombia," in *Guiding the Invisible Hand: Economic Liberalism and the State in Latin American History*, ed. Joseph Love and Nils Jacobsen [New York: Praeger, 1988], 47; and "Commercial Crisis and Economic Ideology in New Granada, 1825–1850," in *América Latina en la época de Simón Bolívar: La formación de las economías nacionales y los intereses económicos Europeos 1800–1850*, ed. Reinhard Liehr [Berlin: Colloquium Verlag, 1989], 197–98).

14. Malcolm Deas, "The Fiscal Problems of Nineteenth-Century Colombia," *Journal of Latin American Studies* 14, no. 2 (November 1982): 287–328, treats various aspects of Colombia's fiscal stringencies.

15. On the limitations of private wealth among the Colombian upper classes, see Safford, *Ideal of the Practical*, 35–38.

16. Safford, "Race, Integration, and Progress," 8–20.

17. Catherine LeGrand, *Frontier Expansion and Peasant Protest in Colombia, 1810–1936* (Albuquerque: University of New Mexico Press, 1986), 11–13, *passim*.

18. See the brief, occasionally quite specific, but rather cursory treatment in Orlando Fals Borda, *Historia de la cuestión agraria en Colombia* (Bogotá: Publicaciones de la Rosca, 1975), 103–11, written for popular consumption. Hermes Tovar, *El movimiento campesino en Colombia durante los siglos xix y xx* (Bogotá: Ediciones Libres, 1975), despite its title, says virtually nothing about relations of production from 1810 to 1880.

19. Robert Carlyle Beyer, "Transportation and the Coffee Industry in Colombia," *Inter-American Economic Affairs* 2, no. 3 (1948): 17–30.

20. Orlando Fals Borda, *Campesinos de los Andes: Estudio Sociológico de Saucío* (Bogotá: Editorial Iqueima, 1961), 66–67, 96–98, 136–37, 140–61.

21. Orlando Fals Borda, *El hombre y la tierra en Boyacá: Bases socio-históricas para una reforma agraria* (Bogotá: Ediciones Documentos Colombianos, 1957), 110–111.

22. Orlando Fals Borda, *Historia de la cuestión agraria*, 132–33.

23. Catherine LeGrand, "Colombian Transformations: Peasants and Wage-Labourers in the Santa Marta Banana Zone," *Journal of Peasant Studies* 11, no. 4 (July 1984): 178–200.

24. Diego Monsalve, *Colombia cafetera* (Barcelona: Artes Gráficas, S.A., 1927), 237–84, 391–426.

25. Palacios, *Coffee in Colombia*, 80–82.

26. Michael Francis Jimenez, "The Limits of Export Capitalism: Economic Structure, Class, and Politics in a Colombian Coffee Municipality, 1900–1930" (Ph.D. diss., Harvard University, 1986), 173, 204–05, 356–58, 361–62.

27. Palacios, *Coffee in Colombia*, 80–82.

28. Charles Bergquist, in his chapter on Colombia, in *Labor in Latin America: Comparative Essays on Chile, Argentina, Venezuela, and Colombia* (Stanford: Standford University Press, 1986), has particularly highlighted the theme of familial self-exploitation in coffee.

29. Malcolm Deas, "A Colombian Coffee Estate: Santa Barbara, Cundinamarca, 1870–1912," in *Land and Labour in Latin America: Essays on the Development*

of Agrarian Capitalism in the Nineteenth and Twentieth Centuries, ed. Kenneth Duncan and Ian Rutledge (Cambridge: Cambridge University Press, 1977), 269–98.

30. Jimenez, "Limits of Export Capitalism," 355–63.

31. *Ibid.,* 20–29, 192–203, 368–69, 405–19.

32. Deas, "Colombian Coffee Estate," 269–98.

33. Jimenez, "Limits of Export Capitalism," 202–07.

34. Gonzalo Sánchez G., quoting government officials of the 1930s. See his *Los "Bolcheviques" del Líbano* (Bogotá: Ediciones El Mohan, 1976), 22–23; and *Las ligas campesinas en Colombia* (Bogotá: Ediciones Tiempo Presente, 1977), 51.

35. Palacios, *Coffee in Colombia,* 113.

36. Jimenez, "Limits of Export Capitalism," 368–70.

37. Judith White, *Historia de una ignominia: La United Fruit Co. en Colombia* (Bogotá: Editorial Presencia, 1978), 25.

38. J. Fred Rippy, *The Capitalists and Colombia* (New York: Vanguard, 1931), 130–36, 152, 154, 156–59, 172, 176.

39. Deas, "Colombian Coffee Estate," 275.

40. Sánchez, *Las ligas campesinas,* 37–38.

41. Sánchez, *Los "Bolcheviques,"* 22–23.

42. C.f. letter from Tequendama coffee *hacendados* to the minister of industry and labor, May 1933, as quoted in Miguel Urrutia, *The Development of the Colombian Labor Movement* (New Haven: Yale University Press, 1969), 131.

43. See LeGrand, *Frontier Expansion,* chaps. 5 and 6 and *passim.*

44. See Darío Fajardo M., "La violencia y las estructuras agrarias en tres municipios cafeteros del Tolima: 1936–1970," in *El agro en el desarrollo histórico colombiano: Ensayos de economía política* (Bogotá: Punta de Lanza, 1977), 265–94; Medófilo Medina, "La resistencia campesina en el sur del Tolima," in *Pasado y presencia de la Violencia en Colombia,* ed. Gonzalo Sánchez and Ricardo Peñaranda, (Bogotá: Fondo Editorial CEREC, 1986), 223–44.

45. Francine Barbara Cronshaw, "Landowners and Politics in Colombia, 1923–1948," (Ph.D. diss., University of New Mexico, 1986), 290.

46. LeGrand, *Frontier Expansion,* 120; Cronshaw, "Landowners and Politics," 100–05.

47. LeGrand, *Frontier Expansion,* 99–102.

48. Ibid., 132.

49. Jimenez, "Limits of Export Capitalism," 324, 375–79.

50. Bennett Eugene Koffman, "The National Federation of Coffee-growers of Colombia," (Ph.D. diss., University of Virginia, 1969), 92, 164, 167–76, 189–95.

51. Jimenez, "Limits of Export Capitalism," 422–45. Quotation from p. 445.

52. Salomón Kalmanovitz, "Evolución de la estructura agraria," in *La agricultura colombiana en el siglo xx,* ed. Mario Arrubla (Bogotá: Instituto Colombiano de Cultura, 1976), 152.

53. Jesús Antonio Bejarano, "Orígenes del problema agrario," in *La agricultura colombiana en el siglo xx,* ed. Mario Arrubla (Bogotá: Instituto Colombiano de Cultura, 1976), 70–71.

54. Thomas H. Holloway, *Immigrants on the Land: Coffee and Society in São Paulo* (Chapel Hill: University of North Carolina Press, 1980), 44–69.

55. Urrutia, *Colombian Labor Movement*, 72–83.

56. Cundinamarca: fewer than 5,000 trees—in 1932, 12,474 farms, in 1939, 25,826; 5,000 to 20,000 trees—in 1932, 922 farms, in 1939, 3,874. Tolima: fewer than 5,000 trees—in 1932, 9,610 farms, in 1939, 22,555; 5,000 to 20,000 trees—in 1932, 2670, in 1939, 5021 (Bergquist, Labor, 300).

57. Albert Hirschman, *Journeys Toward Progress: Studies of Economic Policy-Making in Latin America* (New York: Twentieth Century Fund, 1963), 107–13.

58. Cronshaw, "Landowners and Politics," 128–29, 233–35.

59. Sanchez, *Las ligas campesinas*, 124–47; LeGrand, *Frontier Expansion*, 141–53.

60. Gonzalo Sánchez and Donny Meertens, *Bandoleros, gamonales y campesinos: El caso de la Violencia en Colombia* (Bogotá: El Ancora Editores, 1983), 31.

61. Cronshaw, "Landowners and Politics," 279–89.

62. Ibid., 246.

63. Absalón Machado C., "Incidencias de la economía cafetera en el desarrollo rural," in *El agro en el desarrollo histórico colombiano: Ensayos de economía politica* (Bogotá: Punta de Lanza, 1977), 214–15.

64. Bergquist, *Labor*, 301–03 and *passim*. Statistics adapted from p. 302.

65. Ibid., 359–68.

66. Oquist, *Violence, Conflict, and Politics*, 16–19.

67. This was the case in the Quindío, according to the most thorough study of the Violencia in that region. See Carlos Miguel Ortiz Sarmiento, *Estado y subversión en Colombia: La Violencia en el Quindío años 50* (Bogotá: Fondo Editorial CEREC, 1985), 311–19.

68. Ernest A. Duff, *Agrarian Reform in Colombia* (New York: Praeger, 1968).

Lord and Peasant in the Making of Modern Central America

Lowell Gudmundson

It may be particularly appropriate to examine Barrington Moore's ideas on the link between agrarian structures and political development in the case of Central America. Without citing Moore very often, to be sure, this framework and variations of it have been employed over the past fifteen or twenty years, most notably in the classic works of Torres-Rivas and Cardoso and Pérez in the 1970s, and more recently by Baloyra, Williams, Paige, and Winson.[1] Moreover, the specific case of Costa Rica has long been presented by social scientists and historians as an example of a peculiar or distinctive agrarian structure leading, more or less directly, to democratic political processes and traditions. The general frameworks developed by Lenin and by Moore have enjoyed such wide currency in Central America that the Costa Rican sociologist José Luis Vega Carballo went a step further and gave public lectures in the mid-1980s in which the comparative historical development of Guatemala/El Salvador and Costa Rica since the mid-nineteenth century was contrasted in neo-Bismarkian and neo-Victorian terms.

While the application of Moore's ideas to the whole of Central America is considerably beyond my own talents (and the available historiographic evidence, in any case), I discuss in this chapter two sets of issues: what we currently know regarding Costa Rica's too often presumed demonstration of the validity of much of Moore's framework, and some of the hypotheses put forward regarding the link between agrarian structures and modern political development in other areas of Central America. My discussion of this latter subject is necessarily far more sketchy, and I attempt to err on the side of hypothesis and interrogatory rather than circumspection, in light of the exploratory nature of our enterprise.

Costa Rican Confirmations?

The peculiar development of democratic politics in Costa Rica has usually been explained on the basis of two related aspects: 1) the foresight and talents of the leadership of the winning side (the later National Liberation Party or PLN) in the 1948 Civil War, and 2) the widespread distribution of landed property in the nation's coffee economy. The first of these would-be explanations suffered considerable attack and revision in works of the mid to late 1970s, particularly by Schifter, while the second was the subject of substantial research and criticism during the 1970s in works by Stone, Vega Carballo, Cardoso, Hall, and Seligson.[2] My own critique of a simple egalitarian-based explanation has concentrated on the weakness of such a view for the nineteenth-century transitional period, and the more or less static features associated with this hypothesis, traceable to the work of Rodrigo Facio from the 1940s.[3]

The reinterpretation of the events of 1948 and their legacies for democratic politics has not progressed as rapidly as one might have hoped ten years ago. This is no doubt a reflection of the relative weakness of research in areas traditionally defined as political history in Costa Rica, when compared to socially and economically oriented research over the past decade. The less partisan and more comparative framework sketched out by Schifter and others is only now leading to further empirical work that attempts to probe more deeply into the precise timing and linkages of changes far too often ascribed to the PLN's foresight in the earlier literature. Thus, much of what I have to say about the more narrowly political side of the issue in Costa Rica I include in the next section on unanswered (or only partly answered) questions.

Where recent research has progressed most, in both its empirical findings and revised views of historical processes, is in the areas of social and economic structure. While many general and even organizational questions of politics are addressed in this literature, its focus has been primarily socioeconomic. This has dealt with the nineteenth-century transition of coffee culture, the evolution of producers and processors, and their interrelations during the century-long period of coffee monoculture (1850–1950).[4]

During the period of 1830–1860 Costa Rica and its economy was virtually reducible to the Central Valley and an emerging coffee culture.[5] The interests of the elite in areas outside of the Central Valley were limited to cattle ranches on the Pacific plain to the west and northwest, which (in any case) were of little economic or political importance compared to coffee. These estates produced relatively little monetary wealth and controlled only a tiny resident population that exercised virtually no influence in the national government, save to reinforce the position of the coffee economy. Similarly, the late nineteenth- and early twentieth-century development of banana exports from the Atlantic coast region was so remote and isolated from the coffee area that its influence on local society prior to World War I did not go beyond political intrigue at the highest levels and some additional tax and loan revenue for the central government.

In other words, unlike other nations, (perhaps Colombia in particular), there were no serious regional rivalries and elite interests in Costa Rica to block the full development of coffee and its associated interests. Within the Central Valley the eastern area around Cartago participated less fully and later in coffee's rewards, but even its rancher and merchant elite would eventually commit to the coffee regime after a brief and ineffective period of opposition and obstruction from the 1820s to the 1840s.

Coffee essentially drove forward a process of transition from a municipal or public lands cultivation system that relied heavily on ambulatory, sporadic cultivation of breaks or clearings, combined with much more reduced *ejidos* and pastures, to a privatized system of permanent coffee groves. Although the first to grow coffee were the wealthy, very early on the majority of coffee produced came from nonmerchant, nonprocessor growers. While the political system did not admit much in the way of direct popular participation, elite factions struggled far more for control of the export trade and credit than to restrict popular migration and access to public lands.

To be sure, efforts were made in this direction, led in particular by the larger colonial landowners of Cartago. However, the most serious and violent elite conflict within the coffee economy concentrated on the issues of the control of processing, export, and credit, rather than on policies that might allow any group to monopolize land resources or "fix" peasant laborer-producer populations. When, for example, the Mora and Montealegre clans violently disputed power at midcentury, both owed their wealth to commercial control rather than land monopolization, both sought out independent peasant suppliers of coffee to process and export, and neither advocated any policy to limit colonization or the movement of laborers.

In effect, the early national state in Costa Rica had no firm colonial traditions by which to limit peasant colonization in an open, contiguous area substantially larger than that occupied by the end of the colonial period. Merchant processors openly competed with each other for new crop supplies, stimulating the sort of homesteading institutionalized by the Law of Heads of Household of 1862. But, in fact, oligopoly at the processing and finance level meant that much of the risk was being farmed out to family-based producers, with much of the profit guaranteed, in advance, to the exporting and financial elite. Thus, no violent conflicts broke out over labor mobility or colonization, but when commercial oligopoly was challenged, as in 1859 by the president and leading exporter Juan Rafael Mora and his Argentine financial adviser Crisanto Medina, opposing factions of the very same merchant elite had him deposed and eventually shot. Elite strategies both helped create and responded to the existence of numerous midsized producers, not so much a middle class yet as the remnants of the colonial peasantry undergoing a rapid process of differentiation. Within this context, eviction or restrictions on mobility would be very costly and of dubious efficacy. Retaining control of oligopolistic profits from restricted trade and processing of the noble grain was worth a fight at elite levels and offered the best hope of maximizing both profits and power.

Only somewhat later and in areas removed from the mid-nineteenth century Central Valley coffee zones did the weight of large estate production vastly increase, particularly in the Turrialba Valley region to the east.[6] Here, both Cartago elite landholding patterns and railroad construction interests (Minor Keith and his associates) conspired to develop a large estate system quite unlike the pattern that had emerged earlier to the west. However, even there labor scarcity led to highly paternalistic labor recruitment and treatment within haciendas. While in the older coffee zones hacienda workers were a privileged but small minority, in Turrialba land ownership was highly concentrated and most peasants worked for others. Prior to the 1950s, sharecropping of one sort or another predominated rather than wage labor, to "bribe peasants in their ignorance," as one critic claimed, or to coddle them with a "communistic" scheme, according to another. In any case, Arce inadvertently demonstrated that peasants' incomes remained much higher and working conditions superior to what would follow with full-scale modernization based on eviction and "gang" wage labor in the late 1950s.[7]

Research on the processor elite of the older coffee zones has led to a number of important new findings. Peters has shown how, as late as the 1930s, the major processor-exporter firms still relied on independent suppliers for the bulk of the coffee processed, with their landholdings only accounting for about one-third of their output.[8] Earlier studies had shown how the number of processing plants and interests declined markedly over time, with even larger and fewer *beneficios* by the early to mid-twentieth century. This process of concentration was paralleled by a marked differentiation among producers, as we discuss below. However, despite such concentration, the most basic pattern, established in the beginning of coffee culture locally, of merchant-processor versus direct producer relations, remained the norm a century later, with vastly different power relations and antagonisms, to be sure.

Further research from the late 1970s and early 1980s, by Cazanga, Winson, and Raventós, helps clarify just what became of the processor elite and its relations with producers after the 1948 Civil War.[9] Put simply, the coffee producers' cooperative movement, which emerged as part of PLN policy during the 1950s, was able to build its own processing plants and use preferential state bank financing to modernize its operations and circumvent the much-hated processor monopoly or oligopoly. As a consequence of these policies, productivity in coffee cultivation increased dramatically over the following three decades, setting world standards by the late 1970s. At the same time, the former processor elite was forced to diversify its operations and often began coffee cultivation on lands far removed from the traditional coffee zones of the Central Valley region in order to make use of existing plant capacity no longer supplied by newly cooperativized producers.

Research on the peasant *cum* farmer population that produced the coffee has also made significant advances. We now have data that does not so much confirm the assertion of the earlier literature, that widespread distribution of land in coffee culture "led" to democracy, but provides both documentary evidence (never the strong suit of coffee equals democracy advocates) and contradictory processes. Coffee culture led to a process of differentiation among direct producers, with the eventual outcome of a society of independent farmers (wealthy but nonprocessor producers) alongside both semiproletarian and full proletarian households (often ex-smallholder groups) in village society. The bulk of peasant society prior to coffee culture had paid only the most minuscule rents and taxes. With the rapid privatization of outlying lands in the second half of the nineteenth century, a middle-class farmer group was able to consolidate its position. While the relative weakness of colonial institutions for exploiting the peasantry was important in allowing for the emergence of smallholding and wealthy farmers thereafter, it is to the latter pattern rather than to pre-coffee conditions that we must look for the rural roots of democracy in modern-day Costa Rica.

The process of coffee-based class formation varied enormously among subregions. The oldest coffee regions advanced fairly rapidly in this direction, while colonization zones with poor communications links could lag far behind. My own research on coffee producers in Santo Domingo de Heredia, and that of Mario Samper on western Alajuela colonization zones, has shown that movement was toward an essentially capitalistic differentiation process within the "peasantry," or domestic units of production.[10] Where producer households in Santo Domingo moved rather quickly in this direction, with clear lines of differentiation visible by the first two decades of the twentieth century, those of western Alajuela remained tied much longer to a mixed-crop economy in which household labor demands were more seasonally balanced and tendencies to monoculture limited until nearly mid-century.

In each case, delicate balancing mechanisms retarded the emergence of greater polarization. In the case of Santo Domingo, these included the emergence of nonpartible inheritance among the still landed (who had substantially delayed their age at marriage, earlier), and the large-scale out-migration of the early twentieth century among the land-poor. In the case of Alajuela, several factors were the virtual bottleneck of mixed cropping (sugar, basic grains, and cattle), which limited labor demands and spread them over a longer period, and the dynamic out-migration of colonizers to neighboring zones. Thus, the overall process of polarization became evident only very dimly, first as regards processor-producer antagonisms (the ideological aspects of which have been suggestively studied recently by Acuña), and only much, much later regarding village-level conflicts between owners and laborers.[11]

However, as Raventós has shown, in solving their conflicts with the private processors by creating a cooperative movement with the aid of the post-1948 state, producers also magnified their conflict with and reliance upon seasonal wage labor for ever-increasing harvests.[12] This wage labor force was initially recruitable from the ranks of marginal smallholders and laboring households under the ideological control of their village "betters," but now it increasingly appears a social pariah bereft of welfare state protection and far more rootless and migratory than in the past.

Raventós has also shown, with survey data from the early 1980s, how family farm–sized units predominated even then, reaching maximal efficiency in production and employing green revolution technology on remarkably small unit or farm sizes. In these findings, Raventós has provided a much more useful interpretation of Carolyn Hall's earlier findings on the survival of small-scale production in coffee, employed primarily for purposes of countering leftist claims of inexorable concentration in the coffee economy before. Similarly, Winson and Cazanga show how these results were obtained: by the systematic government subsidy of modernization costs for coffee cooperative members during the 1950s and 1960s.[13]

On balance, then, research on the social and economic structure of the Costa Rican coffee economy would appear to confirm much of the Moore thesis. A commercially based processor group constitutes what amounts to a primarily nonlanded elite, a working bourgeoisie for practical purposes; and the development of petit bourgeois groups in the countryside, both allies and adversaries in political and economic terms, leads eventually to competitive electoral regimes. Labor recruitment is left largely in the hands of smallholders themselves, with the few permanent estate laborers offered extremely favorable conditions unavailable to the one- or two-month harvest laborers picking both hacienda and family farm harvest on a piece-rate basis. The classical confrontations of the commercial agrarian versus the traditional villager, or the Junker modernizer versus the coerced tenant and wage laborer, do not appear with sufficient clarity in the Costa Rican countryside. For the *minifundista* harvest laborer, wages and working conditions appear both beyond individual landlord control and embedded in a kin network of which he or she forms part. For the wealthier smallholder recruiting his poorer brethren for harvest labor, they are only seasonal help for a family enterprise that appears largely self-sufficient the remaining ten or eleven months of the year.

However, there are a number of caveats in order here. It need be noted that, while very favorable, pre-coffee conditions did not lead directly or mechanically to such an outcome; privatized landholding and the precise distribution of land resources were not given by preexisting conditions. Elite political conflicts (or the lack of same) had a great deal to do with what ultimately emerged. Similarly, the greatest formal political participation on the part of smallholder producers awaited the results of differentiation, by which their numbers were vastly reduced and the survivors' wealth level increased. Moreover, the survivors clearly owed their existence not only to good luck and sociodemographic behavior modifications (inheritance, age at marriage, migration, etc.) but to systematic state intervention in their favor. Each of these caveats ought to lead one to research questions in the political sphere, and it is precisely here where too few questions have been posed in the recent past.

Costa Rica: Unanswered Questions

While social and economic research may suggest the utility of much of Moore's approach in explaining the Costa Rican experience, many difficulties arise when one attempts to deal with the precise timing and significance of key political changes themselves. What few works have recently appeared dealing with political history, such as those of Salazar and Salazar, have mainly limited themselves to sketching the institutional structure and its changes, along with well-worn schemes of periodization and ideological interpretation.[14] Empirical work on key moments of political change and the groups involved has only just begun to appear.

One major difficulty with any application of the Moore thesis to Costa Rican experiences lies in the simple fact, pointed out by Schifter long ago, that the winners of 1948 were neither populist nor uniquely reformist groups storming a repressive, oligarchic state.[15] In fact, without taking into account the preceding, decade-long experience of an elite-led populist movement (*calderonismo*) with militant labor union support, the real meaning of the post-1948 reforms could never be discovered. How might one interpret this curious succession of elite-led competitive reforms? Was thoroughgoing petit bourgeois reform of the kind experienced after 1948 possible only because the largest landed and merchant interests (the structural enemies of the winning reformers in 1948 while, paradoxically, their electoral and insurrectionary allies) had been both weakened and frightened into an alliance with petit bourgeois rebels? Does this odd combination of coalitions and reform impulses lessen its usefulness as a test of the Moore thesis? It would certainly seem to, at least in its most simplified form.

While no very substantial local efforts have been made in this area since the early 1980s, recent research by Fabrice Lehoucq sheds some light on the critical period of 1946–1953.[16] It seems likely that a core of urban and professional middle-class insurrectionist supporters predominated on the winning side in 1948, and that large-scale petit bourgeois support within the coffee sector was organized after the fact rather than functioning as a major factor leading to the insurrection itself. Indirect evidence of this includes the remarkably small vote gained by the Social Democratic Party in the 1948 election. More important, Winson shows quite clearly that the vast majority of both technical and institutional changes in coffee production (state subsidies and cooperatives, basically) took place after José Figueres gained election to the presidency in 1953 and not during the "junta" days of 1948–1949.[17] However, in this area we have very little concrete evidence regarding the timing and specifics of these linkages between social structure and partisan politics.

If one attempts to establish linkages even earlier, the evidence remains every bit as contradictory and incomplete. Silva has recently shown, as Stone did much earlier, how extraordinarily limited formal participation in the political process was before 1870.[18] Indeed, other Central American countries such as El Salvador had electoral codes that were at least as egalitarian as Costa Rica's until virtually 1948. However, we also know that municipal policies and land registration procedures were far more subject to influence on the part of the less wealthy or the illiterate, despite the formal limitations. Thanks to recent work by Salas we now have a very precise understanding of the formal mechanisms of land privatization, and some of the conflicts engendered by them, but as yet no very clear picture of municipal-level political participation and its relationship to land titling.[19]

Another area in which little research has been forthcoming is that of the relationship between owners and rulers. From the Guardia dictatorship of 1871–1882 forward it is increasingly clear that the top political leadership acted with some degree of independence *vis-à-vis* the coffee oligarchy whose interests it presumably safeguarded. Guardia himself was something of an outsider to the clan-based alternation of the presidency (among the Mora and Montealegre clans during the 1840–1870 period) within the coffee elite. Many of his policies can best be seen as designed to wrest political power from these narrow cliques. He exiled the former president, J. M. Montealegre, to California for life in 1872, and Liberals of modest origins formed much of the basis for his regime's support, while old money families more often felt his wrath.

Thereafter, during the early twentieth century, leading elite figures of the so-called Olympic groups (so named because they were supposedly both uniquely talented and above base partisanship) acted in ways unchar-acteristic of Liberal ideologues. Three-time president Ricardo Jiménez, as well as Cleto González Víquez, sponsored the reintroduction of proto-nationalist and protectionist ideas into what amounted locally to Liberal orthodoxy. Negative views of the role of foreign monopoly capital, the need for state intervention in planning the development of even the export sector (coffee), or tariff protection for the domestic cattle industry were all clearly non-Liberal ideas put forward by the early 1930s under Liberal intellectual sponsorship.

While Olympic positions were often abstract and gradualist, other elite politicians followed so-called traitorous policies *vis-à-vis* the coffee oligarchy's interests. President Alfredo González Flores advocated an income tax as the solution to the fiscal disruptions of World War I and paid for his progressivism with the Tinoco coup of 1917. Similarly, Rafael Angel Calderón Guardia was elected in 1940 as a member in good standing of the blue-blooded coffee aristocracy and ended up as the architect of the historic alliance with the Communist Party banana workers' union, only to be vilified and exiled by the 1948 coalition of petit bourgeois insurrectionist and terrified oligarchic forces.

While the reality of relative autonomy on the part of the political directorate of the dominant classes is undeniable, no serious work attempting to explain its origins and limits has yet appeared. Plausible sources of such relative autonomy might include the following: the emergence of a middle-class cadre within Liberal ranks, beginning in the Guardia era in the 1870s and proceeding thereafter in urban areas in terms of personnel and in rural or municipal settings electorally after the turn of the century; the growth of state revenue from the banana enclave, allowing elite politicians the use of resources not beholden to the coffee oligarchy; and the recognition on the part of a visionary faction of that same oligarchy that both external shocks (1914 and 1929) and internal challenges (particularly the banana workers' union) counseled flexibility. In order for things to remain the same, they would indeed need to change.

The paucity of hard data in the area of traditional political history can also be seen in the much–commented upon but as yet little-studied electoral reforms of 1909–1913 and 1925. In the first instance, President Ricardo Jiménez extended considerable power to the municipal-level authorities for the first time. In the second case, the vote was made secret rather than public, although, as we see below, this did little in the short run to break the hold of elite, personalistic political machines.

References in the existing literature to the municipal reforms jokingly call the legislative assemblies of those years the ones of the *Hermenegildos*, in reference to the increase in blacklander, rustic candidates for deputy.[20] This intriguing term and the issue it raised were noted by Stone but have not been seriously pursued by researchers, despite the fact that electoral lists exist for certain districts and could be compared with census and probate data to ascertain the class basis and degree of participation under these reforms. It seems clear that many of these rustics were in fact either heads of locally wealthy families who produced but did not process coffee, or their political servants. In any event, the beginning of rural middle-class political action, evident since 1948, can be seen quite clearly in what has thus far been presented only negatively in the Costa Rican literature as rustic invasion and vulgarity, bossism (*gamonalismo*) in the first two decades of the twentieth century, or mass participation in fraudulent elections thereafter.

Popular participation in a fraud-ridden political system during the 1920s and 1930s has been examined from the perspective of social history in an article by Mario Samper.[21] He finds that, while the Reformist Party of Jorge Volio (studied earlier in some detail by his daughter, Marina Volio)[22] did indeed win substantial support during the 1920s in some smallholder districts in Alajuela, the movement's strongest support came from urban artisanal groups. More important, he shows that smallholder and agricultural laborer support was likely stronger for the dominant political figure of the 1930s, León Cortés, and that clientelistic arrangements delivered limited but real benefits in terms of road building and depression-related relief.

However, lest too linear a connection be made here between popular participation and electoral perfection, Samper is quick to point out that a peculiar sort of patterned and competitive fraud was standard practice in all of the elections of the period: candidates would generously inflate their victory margins in districts they controlled, expecting their rivals to do the same in their own areas of strength (a practice no doubt familiar to most Chicagoans). Rather than a pattern of fraud designed to exclude the poor, or to herd them to elections to vote for landlord candidates, fraud in Costa Rica involved the beginning of broader participation as each candidate was expected to cultivate popularity as a native son at all social levels within the district. Suspiciously homogeneous bloc voting was standard practice, even though roughly half of propertyless laborers were registered to vote by the 1920s and virtually no workplace "choke-point" could be used to insure the coercion of a "correct" vote even before the secret ballot of 1925.[23]

Two additional areas in which it is difficult to reconcile a simplified version of the Moore thesis with Costa Rican experience are the questions of the army and educational reform. Recent works by Fischel and Quesada Camacho on the growth of public education in late-nineteenth- and early-twentieth-century Costa Rica have rejoined the debate over the intent and achievements of Liberal reformers.[24] However, neither work examines the internal conflicts within the elite that approved and carried out the reforms nor measures their impact with empirical data beyond that used a decade or more ago.

While it might be plausible to see the drive for mass primary education as something of a concession on the part of the legislative elite to petit bourgeois allies in the countryside, there are problems with such an interpretation. The educational reforms were undertaken between 1885 and 1889, long before the municipal-level concession of 1909–1913 and by an extraordinarily elitist group of officials. Moreover, in both education and political participation dramatic changes were forthcoming, which affected not only the propertied in village society. By 1927 nearly half of self-declared "laborers" claimed to be registered to vote, and educational achievement for both propertied and propertyless men and women had notably improved. It seems likely that it was a process undertaken by a visionary segment of the economic elite's political class, the consequences of which would extend well beyond the political concessions wrung from the system in 1909–1913 (or in 1948 for that matter). Literacy remained a qualification for the vote throughout the first half of the century, but far larger numbers could meet that test by the 1920s and 1930s. This was also the case for women, who were not able to vote in any case until 1949, with the promulgation of a new constitution.

In the earlier interpretation of the events of 1948 the abolition of the army was often seen as the crowning achievement of the winners. While this was no doubt a very foresightful policy, particularly on the part of "rulers" unable to poll more than 5 percent in the preceding election, such an interpretation vastly overstates the military exploits of the insurrectionists and the importance of the decree itself in the decline of military influence in politics. In a recent work Muñoz has argued that the military lost its once substantial influence in Costa Rican politics as a consequence of both the widespread hatred of the Tinoco dictatorship of 1917–1919 and the open intimidation of the local armed forces by the United States in forcing an end to the border war with Panama in 1923, moreso than owing to events of the late 1940s.[25] It would appear that the United States inadvertently sided with democratic forces in Costa Rica, in 1917–1919, 1923, and 1948. In this case intervention produced results diametrically opposed to similar actions in Nicaragua and Panama, perhaps in large part owing to the fact that troops were never actually landed and thereby did not discredit local elites and fan the flames of a wounded nationalism. In any event, imperialism may also have played a key role in the political development of Costa Rica and not just in its more unfortunate neighbors.

The abolition of the army by the authors of the 1949 Constitution has often been misrepresented by partisans as both dramatic and unique. Muñoz is quite right to challenge this self-congratulatory view. However, long before 1919–1923 professional military forces were few in number and of little influence as a separate interest group. Most military figures leading coups in the past—against Mora in 1850, by Guardia in 1871, or by the Tinoco brothers in 1917—did so at the behest of civilian forces against unpopular regimes. They acted merely as barracks commanders within a civilian elite political contest with few troops and little in the way of a military institutional interest to defend.

Clearly, much remains to be demonstrated as regards the role of the military. However, any process of demilitarization of politics in which 1948 plays a minor role would not only substantially adjust local thinking on the matter but might also require adjustment in the application of the Moore thesis to the case at hand. Rarely has it been thought that imperialist intimidation could stand in for both popular insurrection and bourgeois revolution in solving the problem of arms and politics.

While the unanswered questions referred to above have been dealt with in terms of timing and linkages, their importance goes well beyond mere periodization. Preexisting social and economic structures did not lead, by themselves, to the peculiar coffee culture to be found in Costa Rica. Policy decisions clearly made a difference at key moments. To cite but two examples we might point to the long-standing refusal on the part of elite factions with largely merchant interests to sponsor policies restricting access to public lands. Today, with their power vastly increased thanks to export trade growth since the 1960s, cattlemen's associations take precisely the position that Robert Williams would have predicted for them: they make the most reactionary and alarmist claims of communist conspiracy behind both popular movements and state policies.[26] Similar voices were heard in the debates of the early twentieth century but they were rejected by relatively autonomous political elites concerned more with the virtues of buying and selling than with land rents or police power *vis-à-vis* labor.

The second example is perhaps a clearer case of public policy making a difference that the market, left to itself, would have neither made nor sanctioned. Any analysis of the modernization of coffee cultivation and the improvement of yields undertaken at midcentury would have clearly shown that the largest farms were leading the way in both categories. Following the logic of "the market knows best," no one could have seriously believed that three decades later Costa Rica would be characterized by maximal efficiency and technological advances on medium, family-sized coffee farms. In other words, preexisting economic patterns may have been reconcilable with petit bourgeois reformism and the cooperative movement it sponsored, but they did not point unequivocally in this direction. Key policy decisions made the difference here, and while we know much about their implementation and outcomes, we know little about their genesis. Herein lies the greatest contribution of Winson's recent study. Leadership on the National Liberation Party (PLN) side made a difference, a very large difference indeed, in terms of the subsequent evolution of the coffee economy.

On balance there can be little doubt as to the success of petit bourgeois reform in coffee culture in Costa Rica. While resolving earlier contradictions and creating new ones, this model remains an important ingredient in the electoral and generally conservative bent of modern Costa Rican politics. For precisely this reason Winson's description of the process is without peer, but his characterization of this experience as one of "landlord capitalism" seems doubly inappropriate: First, because the expression suggests precisely the experience of northern Central America discussed below, and second, because Winson himself has effectively demonstrated the victory of cooperativized producers over processors, the only group that could possibly be the "landlords."[27] Far more useful are the terms *farmer* or *classical*, within the Leninist tradition, in suggesting the remarkable lack of extra-economic coercion in the development of coffee culture locally. Of the two, *farmer* and *farm* enjoy substantially greater currency in Costa Rica, as a useful anglicism preferable to the modern equivalent, capitalized domestic units of production.

While the role of petit bourgeois reform is clear, the role of Moore's "commercial agrarians," or the bourgeoisie of processors and merchant exporters, is largely the opposite of any triumphant democracy scenario. As an economic class they did produce a political leadership or class, which at critical junctures pursued more democratic policies than the commercial agrarians themselves wanted to see pursued. But, as actors in key moments of political conflict and violence, in 1917 and again in 1948, they opposed both democratic forms and reforms.

As Jeffrey Paige points out, the "bearers" of democratic reform in Central America have ranged from small farmers and petty professionals in Costa Rica, to insurrectionary peasants in El Salvador and backward ranching elites in Nicaragua.[28] But the dominant commercial agrarians have rarely been found tolerating, much less supporting, democratic reform. Any essentialist reading of the bourgeoisie, or Moore's depiction of it, as inherently democratic is incompatible with the broad outlines of Costa Rican and Central American agrarian history. Even in Costa Rica, the historical bourgeoisie generated a fairly autonomous political directorate, found its shared proprietorship with smallholders more compelling than antagonistic commercial relations when faced with challenges from labor, and had no ultrareactionary or military allies to turn to in the crisis of 1948.

Paradoxically, what may have saved the Costa Rican bourgeoisie from its own reactionary instincts was the overwhelming societywide commitment to export agriculture and coffee culture. Had their opponents in 1914–1917 or in 1948 been groups seeking to turn back the clock or to defend regional and sectoral interests antithetical to those of coffee production, rather than the petit bourgeois forces within the coffee economy, the behavior of the bourgeoisie might well have been far less gracious in what amounted to defeat. As in few other cases in Latin America—Argentina or

Uruguay before 1930, perhaps—exports and their interests ruled state policy, popularly and apparently naturally, regardless of which faction held power. Violent conflicts over the division of the spoils could develop, but virtually no one questioned coffee's right to reign supreme prior to the Communist Party banana workers' union of the 1940s. Faced with its first such mortal enemy, the coffee processor bourgeoisie found the demands of its junior partners among the growers far less threatening than in the past.

Central American Comparisons

Virtually all recent studies of Central American development and its modern-day crisis have assumed that its agrarian structure is profoundly tied to its political difficulties. Whether in masterful studies such as those of Browning and Martínez Peláez, in more popularized versions such as the recent works by Weeks and Brockett, or in the comparative study of cotton and cattle in our own time by Williams, the underlying message has been one of agrarian structure blocking more modern, democratic political regimes from emerging.[29]

Unfortunately, few studies have reminded us, as Baloyra did, that political outcomes are very rarely mechanically "given" by underlying structures, whatever their limitations.[30] In this sense, Williams was particularly effective in showing the diverse outcomes possible with the same export activity, a conclusion that even a summary study of coffee in the nineteenth century should have prepared us for already. Indeed, the same author's study of coffee in Central America returns to this point by means of a "path analysis" of the political consequences of choices made early in the export development cycle.[31] However, these were tendencies or paths neither narrowly defined nor set in cement and immune from subsequent political and economic decisions. Moreover, the tendency to deal with essentially only Guatemala and El Salvador under the heading of Central America has been both notable and lamentable, obscuring elements of similarity and difference in the southern half of the isthmus. In the brief comments that follow I suggest some of these major differences, as well as a number of questions regarding the experience of northern Central America.

Absent Oligarchies and Development in the South
The enormous differences in the national histories of Nicaragua, Costa Rica, and Panama, especially since the mid-nineteenth century, have tended to exaggerate each country's distinctiveness. And yet, each has been characterized by an elite structure drawing its strength from control over trade and government rather than landed property. Throughout the region (with a few important exceptions in Pacific-coast Nicaragua, to be sure), the basis

of the colonial and pre-coffee economy was in open-range cattle herding with only the most tenuous control over rural labor or peasant production.

Unlike northern Central America, the estates of the south rarely had either Indian villages or peasant cultivators as hostage labor sources. Colonial demographic disasters, isolation, or the distractions of the transit trade in Panama led to the unique situation of an elite unable (or lacking the interest, in the case of Panama) to directly dominate its commoner population economically. This led elite factions to struggle endlessly for largely political and relatively ineffective means to dominance. The end results could either be recurrent instability and political infighting, or the rapid transformation of such weak colonial structures by export agriculture, as in the case of nineteenth-century Costa Rica, but the underlying fact of an absent landed oligarchy remains a constant.

While the historiography of modern Panama and Nicaragua has borrowed liberally, of necessity, from the work of the other social sciences, this fact cannot hide the enormous gaps in our knowledge, certainly compared to the work discussed above for Costa Rica. Nevertheless, much of the best recent work probes the full implications of this situation of a weakened elite and its still subsistence-based peasantry. In the works of Castillero Calvo, Soler, Gudeman, Jaén, Howe, and Weeks and Zimbalist the most basic of Panama's historical processes are quite convincingly tied to the nature of the merchant class of Panama City and its ineffective hold on the often ignored hinterland.[32] Perhaps only in Honduras, another case of at least partially southern development, would Gudeman's claim that privatized land ownership and its attendant "mental mapping" of the environment are a mid-twentieth century innovation ring true.[33] While the U.S. role in the creation and frustration of Panama as a neonation is central to understanding the historical context, the weakness of specifically landed interests in the evolution and politics of a local elite is both legendary and, especially today with the U.S. invasion and reimposition of yet another *rabiblanco* regime, nightmarish.

In Nicaragua, as well, the difficulty in identifying any successful agrarian oligarchy able to impose its own peace before the Somoza era is a constant of local historiography. Works by Wheelock, Lanuza, and Vázquez all point out the very slight structural differences among elite interests during the nineteenth century, hypothesized as grain- and cattle-producing interests versus tropical (cacao, indigo) export producers, or simple city-state rivalries masquerading as class or sectoral conflicts.[34] Similarly, these authors see little substantial difference in Conservative or Liberal policies prior to the Zelaya regime at century's end, when most of the land-privatizing agenda of Liberals in the isthmus remained to be undertaken in Nicaragua.

What requires an explanation in Nicaragua is coffee's inability to revolutionize local politics in the early twentieth century. We now know that coffee exports did increase dramatically, and the strong suspicion is that most production was carried out by smallholders who sold to merchant exporters. Why this did not lead to the consolidation of a coffee export coalition within the elite remains a key question, which several different researchers are currently addressing, at least in part.[35] While no very substantial evidence has been presented yet, most assume that the debacle of the Walker affair discredited elite liberalism for decades, and the U.S. intervention in the early twentieth century frustrated whatever belated steps were being taken in the direction of a modernization program based on coffee's interests rather than the traditional elites of the coastal plains.

The role played by the U.S. intervention and civil war may well have been key, as in Panama, but the long-term consequences are clear. The landed elite of the Somoza era, described firsthand by Gould, was even then anything but a solid oligarchic force by northern Central American standards.[36] They proved incapable of resisting virtual extortion from an (in a bourgeois sense) irresponsible Somocista state and were caught in a situation in which private ownership of land itself remained subject to doubt.

The very juridical basis of bourgeois society was reduced to a series of political plums in vulgarized political free-for-all of National Guard officers, Somocista cronies, and Conservative old-line families. Gould's descriptions of the sordid careers of National Guard commanders such as Juan Angel López or the labor activist turned Somicista influence-peddler Irma Guerrero, "La Irma," would either bemuse or enrage any self-respecting northern oligarch. This clearly is not the stuff of which orderly oligarchic regimes are made.

The Weight of the Past: Junker and Classical Paths in the North?
While some interpreters of Central America, on the basis of knowing only Guatemala or El Salvador, have been guilty of overselling their expertise, the more justifiable reason for such simplifications can be found in the clearly visible weight of past history in those two societies. Unlike their southern neighbors, where both the historiographic record and social relations were often reinvented after new commercial or export ventures finally solidified a dominant group (itself only one generation removed from the hammock and sandals in many cases), Guatemala and El Salvador appear to have followed models of development more clearly tied to the past. Winson refers to this as an experience based on the retention of colonial forms of labor exploitation, as opposed to the more thoroughgoing development of market, capitalistic relations in agriculture in southern Brazil and Argentina.[37] Similarly, Martínez Peláez argued long ago that "feudalism" survived in Guatemala until the 1944 revolution, a position that Cardoso

criticized (in terms Winson also employs) as mistaking the retention of precapitalist elements and institutions in the transition to capitalist agriculture with the survival of feudalism as a system.[38] Whatever the emphasis or the semantic choices involved, there has been considerable agreement on the resiliency and relevance of colonial forms of social organization in the north.

Baloyra is perhaps only the most recent, and systematic, of authors to argue that coercive labor systems in agriculture are at the heart of a regime type seen most clearly in Guatemala and El Salvador.[39] While "reactionary despotism" required, in effect, labor coercion in agriculture and extreme wealth concentration, these were necessary but not sufficient conditions for the emergence of such a regime. Of critical importance was the creation of a praetorian army called upon first to repress at any cost the enemies of oligarchic exporting interests. This same army would eventually turn on elements of its very patron class as the military leadership came to dominate not only politics but increasingly the economy after the mid-twentieth century. Moreover, the growth of a state-employed, dependent middle class, supportive of neofascist politics, added to the military basis of power for the ever less simple oligarchic regime. The key dates for the consolidation of reactionary despotism would be 1932 and 1979 for El Salvador and 1954 for Guatemala, although in the latter case the role of the army was indeed great from the very beginnings of coffee oligarchic rule in the 1870s.

Beyond this most basic similarity of regime types, however, historians have always recognized major differences in the evolution of agricultural labor systems. Of greatest importance was the presumed emphasis upon the forced migration of Indian labor to the largely unpopulated coffee regions of the Pacific piedmont in Guatemala, versus the more or less classical enclosure process in El Salvador. Cardoso was perhaps the first to systematically put forward such a model for Central America, building upon the work of Browning for El Salvador and a number of different authors for Guatemala.[40] Within this framework, neither case could be neatly assigned to *Junker* or classical models, since in both cases the political outcomes were decidedly reactionary and even in El Salvador the role of former estate owners (would-be *Junkers*) was assumed to be very great indeed. Nevertheless, the influence of models borrowed from Lenin and Moore was quite apparent.

While our understanding of the origins and dynamics of these models has advanced in the past decade, some important elements are being reconsidered in the most recent literature. Chief among these issues are the social bases of the Liberal revolutions of the 1870s and 1880s, the importance and mechanics of land privatization during this time period, the evolution of forced and market-driven labor systems in Guatemala, and the appropriateness of class-based versus ethnicity-based policies during the Guatemalan revolution and thereafter. My discussion of these issues simply highlights the questions of direct relevance to any application of the Moore thesis to the cases at hand.

Both Liberal recruitment and land privatization issues are at the heart of any understanding of modern Guatemalan and Salvadoran politics. Remarkably, there is as yet little empirical work on which to base sound judgments. The earlier literature, of which Martínez Peláez and Castellanos Cambranes are good examples, presumed great elite continuity, recognizing only "progressive fractions" of the dominant class (whether considered feudal or not) as distinguishing themselves in the move toward the Liberal export regime based on coffee.[41] Likewise, McCreery's ground-breaking studies tended to emphasize both extraordinarily direct control of the state by leading economic interests and their continuity before and after coffee's revolution.[42]

And yet, there were those, such as Villamar Contreras, who saw 1871 and Barrios as a petit bourgeois revolution rather than as merely elite reorientation with the slightest of additions of new blood.[43] This was perhaps the implicit argument Cardoso advanced against Martínez Peláez and the feudalism-until-1944 model. Pérez later echoed this position when he explained much of the Liberal political elite's repressiveness and insecurity on the basis of its having created itself as an economic class at the same time as it seized state power.[44] The differences here are clearly more than those of emphasis, and they will not be clarified until we have the sort of detailed study of the participants in the so-called coffee growers' revolutions that Palma Murga has done for late-colonial merchants and Wagner for late-nineteenth-century German investors.[45]

The land privatization policies pursued by Liberals once in power have also come under new scrutiny. Where we once believed that theirs was a draconian policy implemented by dictatorial regimes in a matter of months, we now see that the process was more complex. Castellanos Cambranes has shown how earlier, Conservative regimes in Guatemala had sanctioned forced, perpetual leases of village lands to coffee growers, leases that the Liberals under Barrios simply deeded over in many cases.[46] Thus, 1871 might well be seen more as capstone than cornerstone of the Liberal Revolution in Guatemala. He also shows that, contrary to earlier emphasis on the Pacific slope area, enclosure-privatization was of considerable importance in other areas of Guatemala, not to mention the *sui generis* regime of German planters and Indian villages in the Alta Verapaz region. My own research, as well as that by Robert Williams, suggests that the beginnings of the forced rental policy can be found in the cochineal industry in the 1830s around Antigua and Amatitlán, where land tenure arrangements and outcomes were far more like Costa Rican parcelization than the land grabbing characteristic of the western regions of Guatemala under Liberal developers in the 1870s.[47]

For El Salvador, Lindo-Fuentes revises downward very substantially the earlier estimates by Browning and Menjívar of common lands seized in the 1880s.[48] He argues that ever since the 1850s the corrosive effects of the market and the California trade, under ostensibly Conservative but coffee-growing leaders such as Dueñas and Gallardo, had done much of the work for which Liberals would later claim credit (and be blamed for by twentieth-century historians). Once again, as with Guatemala, our understanding of the evolution of Salvadoran politics and agrarian structure will depend upon the reinitiation of empirical research on the nineteenth and early twentieth centuries, pioneered by authors such as Colindres, Guidos Vejár, and Richter but largely abandoned during the lost decade or more of Salvadoran civil war.[49]

Happily, such empirical work has begun to emerge, in two recent doctoral dissertations by non-Salvadorans long dedicated to work in and on that country's history. José Antonio Fernández has shown how widespread small producers of indigo were early in the nineteenth century, while Aldo Lauria has challenged the idea of an estate-dominated agriculture in El Salvador between 1840 and 1930.[50] In both cases, the vision of a simple and dramatic resolution to the labor problem *via* Liberal enclosure in the 1880s is rejected in favor of a far more nuanced treatment of peasant production within and on the margins of commercialized agriculture.

The issues of labor forms and their evolution, as well as the ethnic versus class bases of conflicts coming out of the coffee era, are also at the center of any model of lord and peasant in the making of modern Guatemala or El Salvador. Where we have traditionally seen an emphasis on the hated *mandamiento* system in coercing Indian labor to work in coffee in Guatemala until 1944, further research by McCreery reveals a lively debate among employers and elite politicians over the virtues and practicality of its replacement by wage or contract labor as early as the 1920s.[51] This was so despite the author's larger argument that the Guatemalan elite both owned and ruled in a virtually direct relationship of control over the state prior to 1944.

Whatever the precise timing of the demise of overt state coercion, there can be little doubt, based on Carol Smith's work, that ethnicity remains a key, perhaps *the* key to understanding labor exploitation in modern Guatemala.[52] The apparent triumph of market-driven labor recruitment cannot hide the even more basic fact of a segmented economy and labor market throughout Guatemala. Smith has pursued the implications of this fact back into the nineteenth century, while the differing views of Handy and Wasserstrom on the effectiveness of class-based versus ethnicity-based programs of land reform under Arbenz represent only the most recent of the long-standing debates on the Indian and national question in Guatemala, stretching back through the exchanges between Guzmán Bockler and Houper and Martínez Peláez, to the nineteenth-century Liberal theorists and their adversaries.[53]

Unlike Guatemalans, Salvadoran Indians ceased to exist, superficially, as a consequence of the 1932 massacre. However, questions remain as to how great a process of proletarianization and *ladinización* they may have experienced before or after the critical events of 1932. Works by Kincaid and Pérez would lead us to question any scenario in which proletarianization had substituted a class basis for community, ethnic, or colonial identities, regardless of the defense mechanisms of shedding Indian garb and language after the repression.[54] Pérez, in particular, suggests that the actions of the would-be insurgents of 1932, while clearly based temporally and geographically on the coffee economy and its crises, betray a clearer relation to election fervor and colonial Indian rebellion tactics (as described by Taylor for Mexico) than proletarian revolution (as described by Zamosc).[55]

The disappearance or submergence of Indian identity as part of *mestizo* or *ladino* nation-state formation (1880–1920) was a process common to much of Central America, as Jeff Gould's recent work on the myth of the *Nicaragua mestiza* has brilliantly shown.[56] However effective the myth, it also generated its own opposition to the extent that it marked a difference justifying dispossession and coercion. Thus, the Salvadoran case, just as in Nicaragua, may well prove more ethnically complex than we have been prepared to recognize.

These issues of Liberal origins and policies, as well as the ethnic component of class relations, remain at the heart of any understanding of northern Central American history. Discovering the immediate historical causes of the rise of reactionary despotism in the north requires more than just establishing a reactionary oligarchic context with labor-repressive elements in agriculture. In such an ethnically divided society, petit bourgeois insecurities at key moments of change, whether within civilian or military ranks, may have played a major role in generating one of the most nightmarish political histories in modern times. Indeed, it would seem ironic that all studies of European fascism assign a central role to the middle classes in this process, while arguing over the direct or indirect role of the landed and industrial elites, whereas Central American analysts have given little attention to a class that has far too often been protrayed as inherently and eternally progressive or reformist.

The study of Central American agrarian history provides a wealth of materials for exploring the Moore thesis, both in terms of expected outcomes and insuperable obstacles. Despite the frequent use of terms such as *Junker*, yeoman, farmer, etcetera, in the literature, to suggest a loose comparison, we remain limited to a study in contrasts: neo-Bismarkian versus neo-Victorian paths, reactionary despotism in pure form in the north and progressively diluted as one moves south versus electoral democracy in the far south in Costa Rica. While daunting problems for research outside of Guatemala and Costa Rica are all too evident, a truly comparative framework based on the Moore thesis will surely find more than one variety of lord and peasant, as well as radically divergent political outcomes, not only in north and south but within each region. Central American diversity belies the all too common notion of city-state or mini-state simplicity and backwardness. Indeed, such diversity offers a unique laboratory for studying the historical links between agrarian structure and political power.

NOTES

1. Edelberto Torres-Rivas, *Interpretación del desarrollo social centroamericano* (San José: EDUCA, 1971); Ciro Cardoso and Héctor Pérez, *Centroamérica y la economía occidental, 1520–1930* (San José: Universidad de Costa Rica, 1977); Enrique Baloyra, "Reactionary Despotism in Central America," *Journal of Latin American Studies* 15, no. 2 (1983); 295–319; Robert Williams, *Export Agriculture and the Crisis in Central America* (Chapel Hill: University of North Carolina Press 1986); Jeffery M. Paige, "The Social Origins of Dictatorship, Democracy and Socialist Revolution in Central America" (Ann Arbor: University of Michigan, CSST Working Paper #35, September 1989); Anthony Winson, *Coffee and Democracy in Modern Costa Rica* (London: Macmillan, 1989).

2. Jacobo Schifter, *La fase oculta de la guerra civil en Costa Rica* (San José: EDUCA, 1979); Mitchell Seligson, *Peasants of Costa Rica and the Development of Agrarian Capitalism* (Madison: University of Wisconsin Press, 1980); Carolyn Hall, *El café y el desarrollo histórico-geográfico de Costa Rica* (San José: Editorial Costa Rica, 1976); Samuel Stone, *Le dinastía de los conquistadores* (San José: EDUCA, 1975); Ciro Cardoso, "The Formation of the Coffee Estate in Nineteenth-Century Costa Rica," in *Land and Labour in Latin America*, ed. Kenneth Duncan and Ian Rutledge (London: Cambridge University Press, 1977); José Luis Vega Carballo, *Hacia una interpretación del desarrollo costarricense: Ensayo sociológico* (San José: Editorial Costa Rica, 1983); and *Orden y progreso: La formación del Estado Nacional en Costa Rica* (San José: ICAP, 1981). For a discussion of several of the anticonsensus works, see Lowell Gudmundson, "Costa Rica and 1948: Rethinking the Social Democratic Paradigm," *Latin American Research Review* 19, no. 2 (1984): 235–42.

3. Gudmundson, *Costa Rica Before Coffee* (Baton Rouge: University of Louisiana Press, 1986); Rodrigo Facio, *Estudio sobre economía costarricense* (Jan José: Editorial Zurco, 1942).

4. Much of this work is summarized and discussed in Victor Hugo Acuña and Iván Molina, *Historia económica y social de Costa Rica (1750–1950)* (San José: Editorial Porvenir, 1991). See also the review articles on agrarian historical research in the *Revista de Historia* (Heredia, Costa Rica) 19 (1989), by José Antonio Salas, Mario Samper, and Jorge Mora.

5. The following pages are based on Gudmundson, *Costa Rica Before Coffee;* and "Peasant, Farmer, Proletarian: Class Formation and Inheritance in a

Smallholder Coffee Economy, 1850–1950," *Hispanic American Historical Review* 69, no. 2 (1989): 221–57.

6. For descriptions of the Turrialba region see Hall, *El café*; and José Antonio Salas Víquez, "La distribución y apropiación privada de la tierra en Turialba, 1821–1900," in *Cuadernos de Historia* (Heredia, Costa Rica, 1986).

7. Antonio Manuel Arce, "Rational Introduction of Technology on a Costa Rican Coffee Hacienda: Sociological Implications" (Ph.D. diss., Michigan State University, 1959).

8. Gertrud Peters Solórzano, "La formación territorial de las grandes fincas de café en la Meseta Central: Estudio de la firma Tournon (1877–1955)," *Revista de Historia* 9–10 (1980): 81–167.

9. Winson, *Coffee and Democracy*; José Cazanga, *Las cooperativas de caficultores en Costa Rica* (San José: Ediciones Alma Mater, 1987); Ciska Raventós, "Desarrollo económico, estructura y contradicciones sociales en la producción de café," *Revista de Historia* 14 (1986): 179–98.

10. Gudmundson, "Peasant, Farmer, Proletarian"; Mario Samper, *Generations of Settlers* (Boulder, Colo.: Westview, 1990).

11. Victor Hugo Acuña, "La ideología de los pequeños y medianos productores cafetaleros costarricenses (1900–1961)," *Revista de Historia* 16 (1987): 137–59; and "Patrones de conflicto social en la economía cafetalera costarricense (1800–1948)," *Revista de Ciencias Sociales* (Universidad de Costa Rica) 31 (1986): 113–22.

12. Raventós, "Desarrollo económico."

13. Winson, *Coffee and Democracy*; and Cazanga, *Las cooperativas de caficultores*; see also Carolyn Hall, *Costa Rica: A Geographical Interpretation in Historical Perspective* (Boulder, Colo.: Westview, 1985).

14. Jorge Mario Salazar, *Política y reforma en Costa Rica, 1914–1958* (San José: Editorial Provenir, 1982); Jorge Mario and Orlando Salazar, *Legislación electoral, partidos políticos y elecciones en Costa Rica, 1889–1987* (San José: Editorial Porvenir, 1989); and Orlanda Salazar, *El apogeo de la República Liberal (1870–1914)* (San José: Universidad de Costa Rica, 1990).

15. Schifter, *La fase oculta*.

16. Fabrice Lehoucq, "Class Conflict, Political Crisis, and the Breakdown of Democratic Practices in Costa Rica: Reassessing the Origins of the 1948 Civil War," *Journal of Latin American Studies* 23, no. 1 (1991): 37–60; and "The Origins of Democracy in Costa Rica" (Ph.D. diss., Duke University, 1992).

17. Winson, *Coffee and Democracy*.

18. Stone, *La dinastía*; Margarita Silva, "La estructura jurídico-institucional del sistema electoral en Costa Rica, 1821–1870" (paper presented to the Latin American Studies Association Meetings, Miami, Fla., 1989).

19. José Antonio Salas Víquez, "La privatización de los baldíos nacionales en Costa Rica durante el siglo XIX: Legislación y procedimientos utilizados para su adjudicación," *Revista de Historia* 15 (1987): 63–122. To gauge what might be done with these sources, see Margarita Rojas H., "Los campesinos de San Rafael de Heredia, 1830–1930: De usufructuarios comunales a propietarios privados" (Licenciatura thesis, Universidad Nacional, Heredia, C.R., 1991).

20. Stone, *La dinastía*, 106–07, 222–23.

21. Mario Samper, "Fuerzas sociopolíticas y procesos electorales en Costa Rica, 1921–1936," *Revista de Historia* Número especial (1988): 157–222.

22. Marina Volio, *Jorge Volio y el Partido Reformista* (San José: Editorial Costa Rica, 1972).

23. Figures on voter registration and educational attainment as declared in the 1927 census come from Gudmundson, "Peasant, Farmer, Proletarian," 245–46.

24. Astrid Fischel Volio, *Consenso y represión: Una interpretación sociopolítica de la educación costarricense* (San José: Editorial Costa Rica, 1987); Juan Rafael Quesada Camacho, "Democracia y educación en Costa Rica" (paper presented to the Latin American Studies Association Meetings, Miami, Fla., 1989).

25. Mercedes Muñoz Guillén, *El Estado y la abolición del ejercito, 1914–1949* (San José: Editorial Porvenir, 1990).

26. Williams, *Export Agriculture and the Crisis.*

27. Winson, *Coffee and Democracy.*

28. Paige, "The Social Origins."

29. Severo Martínez Peláez, *La patria del criollo* (San José: EDUCA, 1973); David Browning, *El Salvador: Landscape and Society* (Oxford: Clarendon Press, 1971); John Weeks, "An Interpretation of the Central American Crisis," *Latin American Research Review* 21, no. 3 (1986): 31–54; Charles D. Brockett, *Land, Power, and Poverty: Agrarian Transformation and Political Conflict in Central America* (Boston: Unwyn Hyman, 1988); Williams, *Export Agriculture and the Crisis.*

30. Baloyra, "Reactionary Despotism."

31. Robert Williams, *States and Social Evolution: Coffee and the Rise of National Governments in Central America* (Chapel Hill: University of North Carolina Press, 1994).

32. Alfredo Castillero Calvo, "Transitismo y dependencia: El caso del Istmo de Panamá," *Estudios sociales centroamericanos* 5 (1973): 65–114; Stephen Gudeman, *The Demise of a Rural Economy: From Subsistence to Capitalism in a Latin American Village* (London: Routledge and Kegan Paul, 1978): James Howe, *The Kuna Gathering: Contemporary Village Politics in Panama* (Austin: University of Texas Press, 1986); Omar Jaén Suárez, *La población del Istmo de Panamá del siglo XVI al siglo XX* (Panama: Impresora de la Nación 1978); Ricuarte Soler, *Formas ideológicas de la nación panameña* (San José: EDUCA, 1972); and ed., *Panamá: Dependencia y liberación* (Panama: Ediciones Tareas, 1982); Andrew Zimbalist and John Weeks, *Panama at the Crossroads* (Berkeley: University of California Press, 1991).

33. Gudeman, *Demise.* For a discussion of the Honduran case within this framework, see Darío Euraque, "La 'Reforma Liberal' en Honduras y la hipótesis de la 'Oligarquía Ausente,' 1870–1930," *Revista de Historia* 23 (1991): 7–58. For synthetic works that develop a north/south dichotomy for Central America, see Richard Adams, "The Conquest Tradition of Mesoamerica," *The Americas* 46, no. 2 (1989): 119–36; and Samuel Stone, *The Heritage of the Conquistadores: Ruling Classes in Central America from the Conquest to the Sandinistas* (Lincoln: University of Nebraska Press, 1990).

34. Alberto Lanuza Matamoros, "La formación del Estado Nacional en Nicaragua: Las bases económicas, comerciales y financieras entre 1821 y 1873," in *Economía y sociedad en la construcción del Estado en Nicaragua,* ed. Alberto Lanuza, Juan Luis Vázquez, Amaru Barahona, and Amalia Chamorro (San José: ICAP 1983): 7–138; Juan Luis Váquez, "Luchas políticas y Estado oligárquico," in *Economía y sociedad,* 139–206; Jaime Wheelock Román, *Nicaragua: Imperialismo*

y dictadura (Mexico: Siglo XXI 1975); and *Raíces indígenas de la lucha anticolonialista en Nicaragua* (Mexico: Siglo XXI, 1986).

35. Elizabeth Dore, "Coffee, Land and Class Relations in Nicaragua, 1870–1920" (paper presented to the American Historical Association Meetings, Chicago, 1991). Soon to be presented doctoral research on the Carazo region of Nicaragua by Julie Charlip of the University of California at Los Angeles, and ongoing work by Jeff Gould on Matagalpa and the Segovias, will undoubtably help clarify these issues further.

36. Jeffrey Gould, *To Lead as Equals: Rural Protest and Political Consciousness in Chinandega, Nicaragua, 1912–1979* (Chapel Hill: University of North Carolina Press, 1990).

37. Anthony Winson, "The Formation of Capitalist Agriculture in Latin America and Its Relationship to Political Power and the State," *Comparative Studies in Society and History* 25, no. 1 (1983): 83–104.

38. Martínez Peláez, *La patria del criollo;* Ciro Cardoso, "Severo Martínez Peláez y el caracter del régimen colonial," *Estudios sociales centroamericanos* 1 (1972): 87–115.

39. Baloyra, "Reactionary Despotism"; this is essentially the argument developed by Weeks, as well, but with less caution as to whether this alone determines regime outcomes.

40. Ciro Cardoso, "Historia económica del café en Centroamérica (siglo XIX): Estudio comparativo," *Estudios sociales centroamericanos* 10 (1975): 3–57.

41. Martínez Peláez, *La patria del criollo;* Julio Castellanos Cambranes, *Coffee and Peasants in Guatemala: The Origins of the Modern Plantation Economy in Guatemala, 1853–1897* (Stockholm: Institute of Latin American Studies, 1985).

42. David McCreery, "Coffee and Class: The Structure of Development in Liberal Guatemala," *Hispanic American Historical Review* 56, no. 3. (1976): 438–60; and "Debt Servitude in Rural Guatemala, 1876–1936," *Hispanic American Historical Review* 63, no. 4 (1983): 735–59; and "An Odious Feudalism: *Mandamiento* Labor and Commercial Agriculture in Guatemala, 1858–1920," *Latin American Perspectives* 13, no. 1 (1986): 99–177; and *Rural Guatemala, 1760–1940* (Stanford: Stanford University Press, 1994).

43. Marco A. Villamar Contreras, *Apuntes sobre la Reforma Liberal* (Guatemala: Universidad de San Carlos, 1979). See also José Luis Arriola, "Evolución y revolución en el movimiento liberal de 1871: Breve esquema de una revolución pequeño-burguesa," *Anales de la Academia de Geografía e Historia* (Guatemala) 49 (1976): 99–121; and Jorge M. García Laguardia, *La Reforma Liberal en Guatemala: Vida política y orden constitucional* (Guatemala: Editorial Universitaria, 1972).

44. Héctor Pérez, *A Brief History of Central America* (Berkeley: University of California, 1989), 94.

45. Gustavo Palma Murga, "Núcleos de poder local y relaciones familiares en la ciudad de Guatemala a finales de siglo XVIII," *Mesoamérica* 12 (1986): 241–308; Regina Wagner, "Actividades empresariales de los alemanes en Guatemala, 1870–1920," *Mesoamérica* 13 (1987): 87–124. The Guatemalan historian Arturo Taracena called attention to this obvious if neglected fact when noting that the triumphant Liberal army under Barrios in 1871 was not even referred to as "Liberal" but rather as the Army of the West (Ejercito de Occidente), suggesting that the leadership of the region of Los Altos may well have played a larger role than any group of Liberal party ideologues from the capital.

46. Castellanos Cambranes, *Coffee and Peasants*.

47. Some very preliminary findings are reported in Gudmundson and Héctor Lindo-Fuentes, *Central America, 1821–1871: Liberalism Before Liberal Reform* (Tuscaloosa: University of Alabama Press, 1995); Williams, *States and Social Evolution*.

48. Héctor Lindo-Fuentes, *Weak Foundations: The Economy of El Salvador in the Nineteenth Century, 1821–1898* (Berkeley: University of California Press, 1990); Browning, *El Salvador;* Rafael Menjívar, *Acumulación originaria y el desarrollo del capitalismo en El Salvador* (San José: EDUCA, 1980).

49. Eduardo Colindres, *Fundamentos económicos de la burguesía salvadoreña* (San Salvador: VCA Editores, 1977); Rafael Guidos Véjar, *El ascenso del militarismo en El Salvador* (San Salvador: VCA Editores, 1980); Ernesto Richter, "Proceso de acumulación y dominación en la formación sociopolítica salvadoreña," *Informes de Investigación* (San José: CSUCA, 1976): 16.

50. José Antonio Fernández, "To Colour the World Blue," (Ph.D. diss., University of Texas at Austin, 1992); Aldo Lauria, "An Agrarian Republic: Production, Politics, and the Peasantry in El Salvador, 1740–1920," (Ph.D. diss., University of Chicago, 1992).

51. David McCreery, "Wage Labor, Free Labor, and Vagrancy Laws: The Transition to Capitalism in Guatemala, 1920–1945," in *Coffee, Society, and Power in Latin America*, ed. William Roseberry, Lowell Gudmundson, and Mario Samper (Baltimore: Johns Hopkins University Press, 1995), 206–231.

52. Carol Smith, ed., *Guatemalan Indians and the State, 1540–1988* (Austin: University of Texas Press, 1990); and "Culture and Community: The Language of Class in Guatemala," in *The Year Left 2: An American Socialist Yearbook*, ed. Mike Davis et al. (London: Verso, 1987), 197–217; and "Ideologías de la historia social," *Mesoamérica* 14 (1987): 355–66, and "Local History in Global Context: Social and Economic Transitions in Western Guatemala," *Comparative Studies in Society and History* 26, no. 2 (1984): 193–228.

53. Jim Handy, "National Policy, Agrarian Reform, and the Corporate Community During the Guatemalan Revolution, 1944–1954," *Comparative Studies in Society and History* 30, no. 4 (1988): 698–724; as well as Handy's book-length study of the agrarian reform experience under Arbenz, *Revolution in the Countryside: Rural Conflict and Agrarian Reform in Guatemala, 1944–1954* (Chapel Hill: University of North Carolina Press, 1994); Robert Wasserstrom, "Revolution in Guatemala: Peasants and Politics Under the Arbenz Government," *Comparative Studies in Society and History* 17, no. 4 (1975): 443–78; Carlos Guzmán Bockler and Jean-Loup Herbert, *Guatemala: Una interpretación histórico-social* (Mexico: Siglo XXI, 1970); Martínez Peláez, *La patria del criollo*. For excellent analyses of these debates, and of the late-nineteenth-century Liberals and their discussion of the ethnic and national questions, see Carol Smith, "Ideologías;" and "The Origins of the National Question in Guatemala: An Hypothesis," in *Guatemalan Indians*, ed. Carol Smith; Steven Palmer, "A Liberal Discipline: Investing Nations in Guatemala and Costa Rica, 1870–1900," (Ph.D. diss., Columbia University, 1990).

54. A. Douglas Kincaid, "Peasants into Rebels: Community and Class in Rural El Salvador," *Comparative Studies in Society and History* 29, no. 3 (1987): 466–94; Héctor Pérez, "Indians, Communists, and Peasants: The Rebellion of 1932 in El Salvador," in *Coffee, Society, and Power in Latin America*, ed. William

Roseberry, Lowell Gudmundson, and Mario Samper (Baltimore: Johns Hopkins University Press, 1995), 232–61.

55. William Taylor, *Drinking, Homicide, and Rebellion in Colonial Mexico* (Stanford: Stanford University Press, 1979); León Zamosc, "Class Conflict in an Export Economy: The Social Roots of the Salvadoran Insurrection of 1932," in *Sociology of "Developing Societies": Central America*, ed. Edelberto Torres-Rivas (New York: Monthly Review Press, 1988), 56–75.

56. Jeffrey Gould, "'Vana Ilusión:' The Highlands Indians and the Myth of Nicaragua Mestiza, 1879–1924," *Hispanic American Historical Review* 73, no. 3 (August 1993): 393–429.

Applying Moore's Model to Latin America

Some Historians' Observations

Frank Safford

The historians involved in the conference that produced this book tended to adopt an attitude of skepticism toward a general application of the analysis of Barrington Moore to Latin America. This was true of most of the historians whose essays analyze country case studies, as well as of many of those participating in the conference discussion. Even in cases where there does seem to be some correspondence between estate dominance and the coercion of rural labor, on the one hand, and authoritarian tendencies, on the other, the participating historians tended to find important ways in which the Moore model does not apply or applies unevenly. This essay brings together some of the salient skeptical observations embodied in the essays and attempts to bring into play some of the interesting observations made by participants in the conference.

The historians' skepticism runs through all of the essays, though unevenly. Tulio Halperín Donghi's chapter represents in some respects a radical critique of the Moore thesis, in the sense that he, in effect, tries to turn Moore upside down. Argentina would appear to be one of those Latin American countries where landowners most controlled the state, at least until well into the twentieth century. This has been the conventional way of understanding Argentine political history. Yet Halperín insists that landowners, while conceded to be important to the economy, lacked effective political power. Indeed, Halperín suggests, landowners often viewed the state as a predator rather than as an ally or an instrument acting for their interests. Further, he contends that landowners, while generally conceded to be the most powerful economic interest in Argentina before 1930, had difficulty acting as a conscious political class. As Halperín added in conference discussion, Argentine landowners enjoyed a *"natural* hegemony" rather than a *"class* hegemony."

While Halperín seems to seek to overturn the Moorean assumptions altogether, other contributors see their particular cases in a more checkered and variegated way. In the last case study in this volume, for example,

Lowell Gudmundson writing on Central America notes some very *general* correspondences to the Moorean patterns but on closer examination finds particular divergences. In Costa Rica a commercial elite, rather than large landowners, dominated the economy, and democracy emerged triumphant. By contrast, in Guatemala and El Salvador large landowners were powerful and used authoritarian government, in different ways, as an instrument of labor control. Yet Gudmundson's Central American cases diverge from Moore's analysis in many ways. As in other cases in this volume (Halperín on Argentina, Bauer on Chile, and Safford on Colombia), Gudmundson finds the Costa Rican political elite has been relatively independent even from dominant economic interests. And he notes that leadership in Costa Rican democratization came from sources that do not conform to the Moorean model—more from small farmers and the dependent professionals than from the commercial bourgeoisie. More strikingly, Nicaragua and Panama appear to be radically at odds with Moore's predictions. In both countries merchants have been a more important force than landowners. Yet both have had substantially authoritarian political solutions. In this connection Gudmundson notes the impact of a factor that does not come into Moore's cases, the role of United States intervention—which reinforced the military as a repressive force in Nicaragua and Panama while contributing to its weakening in Costa Rica.

Some of the analytical points made in these chapters are of such general importance that they merit underlining. Several of these points have to do with the problem of categories of analysis. Arnold Bauer's essay makes at least two such important observations. First, Moore in his discussion of European and Asian cases treats them as if each country had established an enduring political identity, whether democratic, authoritarian, or (as in the case of India) completely *sui generis*. Bauer reminds us, however, that in the case of post-Independence Latin America it is not always possible to specify a consistent political identity. Chile from the perspective of the 1960s looked historically democratic but during the experience of 1973 to 1990 much more authoritarian. Another such reversal might be found in Venezuela, authoritarian in mode through the first half of the twentieth century and more democratic since 1958. In many Latin American cases it is difficult, over time, to determine a clear political identity, democratic or authoritarian.

In the conference discussion Paul Gootenberg and Tulio Halperín offered a variation on this point. Gootenberg and Halperín observed that in Moore's analysis of his European and Asian cases, he "knew" the outcome. He was dealing with cases that he could treat, or at any rate did treat, at least heuristically, as complete. In Latin America, however, Halperín noted, we "don't know the outcome"; that is, we don't know the historical direction in which the political systems are moving. "Knowing the future,"

Halperín added, "enables us to structure our understanding." Not knowing the future, he concluded, may lead us to an abstract precision that is in reality quite vague.

Bauer's chapter raises another important question regarding categories of analysis, a question that recurs implicitly in other chapters. Moore's scheme implies that there are clearly identifiable archetypical social groups—landowners, merchants, bourgeoisie, and so on. Yet in Latin America the boundaries between landowner and merchant often tend to dissolve. In Buenos Aires province in the immediate post-Independence period many of the largest landowners were merchants. And a similar diffuseness of function may be found in more recent times in Colombia and Central America. In the conference discussion several participants emphasized the need to use "contextual" rather than "essentialist" definitions of social groups and institutions.

Another obstacle to generalizations about the relationship of rural structures to political systems lies in the variety of agrarian patterns within a given country. As my essay notes in the case of Colombia, there has been considerable variation in agricultural modes of production across regions and even within localities—depending in various degrees on wages, rent arrangements, and coercive relations. Given such various modes of production, how does one identify the dominant agrarian structure that is presumed to determine, or at least to shape, the character of the political system? This may be a problem that is particularly acute for the analysis of the larger, more complex countries of Latin America, such as Mexico, Colombia, or Brazil. But it is probable that, on closer examination, it affects most countries.

Moving beyond the question of categories of analysis, many of the authors in this volume seem to deny the capacity of landowners, or of other dominant economic groups, actually to control the state. The essays of Halperín on Argentina, Gudmundson on Costa Rica, and mine on Colombia depict disjunctures between landowner power and the political elite. All three seem to see the political elite as operating more or less autonomously. Paul Gootenberg in the conference discussion suggested that the expansion of Latin America's export economies after 1880, by increasing the financial resources of national governments, actually increased the autonomy of national states.

But while a number of the participants affirmed the relative independence of the political elite, and thus the state, from landowner control, they at the same time asserted what may be a reciprocal—that in Latin America the more or less autonomous state has had little capacity to affect what really happens in the regions or localities that the state supposedly governs. My essay on Colombia particularly emphasizes that the government has been able only marginally to affect what actually happens with regard to structures of dominance in the rural locality. John Coatsworth in his remarks at the conference noted that because landowners had difficulty getting the state to intervene effectively in their behalf, they ordinarily had to turn to their own private goon squads. With regard to the relative absence of the national state in rural localities, Mark Szuchman added that, in order to understand the effective structures of power, we need to look at reciprocity among groups at the regional rather than the national level.

Both in some of the essays and in the conference discussion several historians questioned Moore's identification of landowners with authoritarian politics. Several of the case studies—particularly those of Argentina and Chile—note that landowners at some points proved a force for democratization, at least in the sense of sponsoring the extension of the suffrage to their rural minions. Admittedly they did this for tactical reasons; their motive was to strengthen their own power vis-à-vis urban voters and the political elites who controlled the state. Indeed, as Halperín and Bauer aver, in Argentina and Chile, landowners after 1880 appear not to have been concerned about controlling rural labor; rural workers were firmly under their control. Rather, from the landowners' point of view, the real danger lay in the emerging urban groups.

Coatsworth also urged the need to be more precise about various modes of rural repression and to be clear about which of them were politically important. Coatsworth asserted that repression *within* units of production has not been "politically important." State repression *outside* units of production—in the repression of peasant movements and land invasions, for example—has been more important politically. Landlords did not need the help of the state to repress resident laborers or *peones*. It has been against independent peasants who have invaded estate land that landowners have most appealed for the use of state coercion. In general, Coatsworth contended, state repression has come into play over control of the land more than over labor relations within the estate. It may be observed here that the local cases discussed in my essay on Colombia suggest that it is not always easy to distinguish between labor relations and land issues. Furthermore, as Evelyne Huber indicates in her introduction, it is possible that contests between estate owners and peasants over land may represent, at least in part, an attempt by landowners to close off economic alternatives to people that the landlords viewed as their labor force. In that sense conflicts over land might well aim at labor control as much as aggrandizement of land for its own sake.

The organizers of the conference chose to focus upon the relationship between agrarian structures and the nature of the political system between roughly 1880 and 1930. We chose that period as a focus of analysis in part because in that period export expansion increased the value and importance of land and thus increased the stakes in its mode of exploitation. At the same time, increased exports brought more revenues to the national states and thus enhanced their capacity, presumably, to govern and act at the local level. Given the emphasis in the conference on the era of export expansion, it came as something of a surprise that John Coatsworth found a remarkable lack of reference in the conference essays to external factors in the political evolution of the countries they discuss. In this regard, it should be said that the role of the external economy is embedded in almost all of the chapters. Further, Gudmundson particularly emphasizes the critical, but quite variable, role of U.S. political intervention in Central America. In the cases of the larger South American countries discussed, the role of external political intervention may be said to have been much less significant.

Conclusion

Agrarian Structure and Political Power in Comparative Perspective

Evelyne Huber and John D. Stephens

In this concluding chapter we review the evidence contained in the case studies in this volume and present additional evidence from other cases in Latin America, Europe, the British settler colonies, and Japan, in order to attempt a more general evaluation of the explanatory power of Moore's hypotheses concerning the relationship between agrarian structures and political outcomes. We proceed primarily by examining the relationship between agrarian structures and authoritarian political trajectories and asking which of the elements characteristic of these trajectories were weak or missing in the democratic ones, and secondarily by identifying the relationship between agrarian structures and democratic trajectories and asking which of their characteristics were weak or missing in the authoritarian ones.

Two brief reminders are in order here. First, we are using the conceptualization of democracy laid out in the introductory chapter, namely a formal institutional one. A political system is democratic if it has responsible government, protected civil rights, and high levels of institutionalized contestation and political inclusion. Political inclusion refers to enfranchisement and nonproscription of political parties. Depending on the extent of the franchise, we can speak of full or restricted democracies, the former being characterized by universal suffrage. The presence even of full formal democracy per se does not necessarily imply substantive inclusion of the popular sectors in terms of equality of political influence or in social and economic terms.[1] These are interesting and important questions, but one has to keep them separate analytically from the question of formal democracy.

Second, the time period that is relevant for Moore's hypotheses is from the onset of rapid modernization to the attempted entry of the masses into the political system. Of course, the need to understand the patterns of production, class, and class-state relations prevalent at the onset of rapid modernization requires that the analysis reach further back into history,

beginning with the emergence and consolidation of such traditional patterns.

Our comparative analysis focuses on structure as well as on agency.
Keeping in mind that Moore attributes the central role in the antidemocratic
alliance that leads the way to modern authoritarianism to large landlords
engaged in labor-repressive agriculture, who in the process of modernization attempt to intensify the pressures on rural labor, we pose the following
specific questions.

At the structural level: (1a) Was the pattern of landholding dominated
by large estates at least to the degree of making the owners of these estates
the most economically powerful agrarian class at the national level? Posing
the question in this way makes it possible to overcome the simple dichotomy
of largeholding versus smallholding countries; in particular, it makes it
possible to accommodate regional variations in landholding patterns within
a country, a problem emphasized by Safford in the last chapter. (1b) Was
the availability of a large supply of cheap labor crucial for the operation of
these large estates? Were labor relations characterized by politically backed
coercion?

At the level of agency: (2a) Did large landlords resort to attempts to
restrict the rights of the rural population in order to ensure themselves of
what they perceived to be the necessary supply of cheap labor? This
formulation encompasses such attempts both within and outside units of
production. In particular, it encompasses attempts to deny the rural population access to any alternatives to estate labor and the right to unionization.
(2b) Did large landlords engage in attempts to prevent or reverse democratization?

As to the political outcomes: (3) What were the effects of (2a) and (2b) on
a country's political trajectory; specifically, did they obstruct the transition to
and consolidation of democracy? To repeat a point made in the introduction,
given the frequency of political change in Latin America, or—as Safford
puts it—the lack of a clear political identity, we are using the notion of
political trajectory, conceptualized as the predominance of authoritarian
versus democratic forms of rule. Answering this last question, of course,
requires an examination of the power of the large landlords relative to other
segments of the economically dominant class, and the relationship of these
different segments to each other, to the state, and to subordinate classes.
We handle the problem of multiple holdings, that is, the problem of
landowners being also merchants and financiers, by classifying segments of
the dominant class according to their primary source of income.

In addition to these questions about the links between agrarian structures and political trajectories we also reflect on the dimension of modernization from above, which is central to Moore's path to fascism. As Jonathan
M. Wiener points out, Moore's identification of the "reactionary coalition"

is an important contribution to the analysis of politics in developing countries, but there are clearly wide variations in attempts at "reform from above." Similarly (and relatedly), there are wide variations in forms of modern authoritarianism, and fascism is a rare form.[2]

South American Countries and Mexico in this Volume

In analyzing the relationship between agrarian structures and democratic or authoritarian political trajectories in Latin America, our main focus is on the period of significant export expansion after 1880. The relationship between state and society began to change in two fundamental respects in this period. Before this period the central state was generally too weak to establish a centralized authoritarian system and provide landowners with effective, centrally controlled coercive force. In many cases, state power was not really consolidated in the sense that the central government had not yet succeeded in establishing an effective monopoly on organized force. Authoritarianism before this period consisted of a combination of unconstitutional transfers of power at the center and decentralized domination through local notables. Export expansion in response to growing external demand provided the resources for state expansion and for greater state penetration of society. The stakes for control of the central state and its coercive apparatus were raised; it became a potentially important instrument for both pro- and anti-democratic forces.

Society itself became more complex due to the economic growth induced by export expansion. Urbanization, transport expansion, and industrialization linked to the export sector created new sectors of middle and working classes. These new social forces began to exert pressures for their inclusion in the political system. Before this period, democracy was not really on the agenda in any of the Latin American countries. One reason was that, as just mentioned, state power was in many cases not really consolidated, and there could be no institutionalization of contestation before state power was consolidated. Another reason was that pressures from nonelite sectors for political inclusion were too weak at the national level, even though there were some instances of strong popular movements at the local level. Despite the trappings of republican constitutions, the most "democratic" systems that were established before the period of export expansion were constitutional oligarchies. Thus, it was not until after 1880 that landlords had to confront the possibility that democratization might bring a substantial widening of political inclusion and might undermine their control of rural labor. This threat, of course, emerged at the very same time as the increase in external demand for export products heightened the demand for rural labor. Accordingly, the landlords' relationship to the central state assumed a new importance in defending their access to cheap labor. The growing importance of state action also provided the stimulus for landowners to organize themselves in order to pursue their interests more effectively.

Argentina

Halperín's essay on Argentina confirms that the country was characterized by a largeholding pattern. Yet, with the exception of some areas of the interior, labor relations at the onset of export expansion were not of the traditional type, where a resident labor force was kept on the estates through legally backed coercion. There was no traditional peasantry from which to recruit estate labor and the dominant activity was ranching, which had lower labor requirements than crop production. Under Rosas (1829–1852), in the context of conflicts between seminomadic gauchos and expanding estates over access to wild cattle and common usage lands in the pampas, antivagrancy laws had been enforced to impose law and order in the countryside, provide a labor pool for expanding estates, and produce conscripts for the army.[3] However, the last decade of the Rosas regime saw a shift from cattle to sheep ranching, for which Irish, Basque, and Galician immigrants provided labor. The period of peace and security between 1848 and 1850 particularly encouraged immigration and improved the labor supply.[4] There was high labor mobility and also a significant use of temporary labor, especially for more specialized tasks. Before fencing came to be used on a large scale, many large estates used tenancy arrangements for stock raising. Wheat production, which became very important toward the end of the nineteenth century, was also predominantly done by tenants. According to Allub, tenancy arrangements were dominant for other types of crop production as well, and there was a high turnover among tenants, as landlords alternated between crop production and grazing.[5]

The combination of comparatively low labor requirements in ranching, particularly after the introduction of large-scale fencing, and the great prosperity of the agrarian export economy in Argentina made the securing of cheap labor less of a problem for Argentine landlords than it was for their counterparts in other Latin American countries. Nevertheless, as Halperín points out, the landed elites attempted again to have antivagrancy laws written into the provincial code of 1884. He does not explain why these attempts failed, but one may speculate that the reasons were related to a lack of unity and determination on the part of landlords to muster all their economic and political resources to get these laws incorporated into the code. Had the prosperity of the landlords been significantly affected by them, one might have expected stronger efforts and a different outcome. Similarly, there was no landlord unity in opposition to democratization. Though many landlords opposed the electoral reforms of 1912, others supported them and assumed leadership positions in the Radical Party, the main promoter and beneficiary of these reforms.

There was another reason for the comparatively moderate landlord opposition to democratization in Argentina. Halperín emphasizes very strongly that the landlords never controlled the state directly but that their interests were protected due to the hegemony of the agrarian export model. Though the relationship between the state and the landed classes had been an ambiguous one for most of the nineteenth century, often troubled by competing demands for manpower and money for internal and regional wars, the universal commitment to the agrarian export economy meant that the landlords did not need to establish a direct presence in the state apparatus and to forge alliances with other social groups to gain control over the state. In addition, the comparatively low labor requirements of ranching and the great prosperity of meat and grain exports meant that markets were sufficient to serve the interests of large landowners, so that the landowners did not need direct state intervention on their behalf. The Radicals showed no signs whatsoever of attempting to attack the agrarian export model, either. Thus, landlords had little a priori reason to change their traditional political position vis-à-vis the state in order to mobilize against democratization and prevent the Radical government from taking power.[6]

Under the new democratic arrangements, though, the social consequences of the pattern of rural labor relations came to haunt the landlords. The poorly integrated nature of rural society, particularly the absence of traditional estate populations, translated into a lack of social hegemony of the landlords and consequently the lack of a strong electoral base for the Conservatives. Thus, when landlords experienced their growing marginalization from political power along with the great escalation of state demands for material resources under the Radical governments, they turned against democracy. Again, the reason for this turn had nothing to do with control over rural labor; the issues were access to political power and perceived abuses of political power and squandering of resources by the Radical government. The onset of the depression aggravated the struggle for scarce resources and served as a catalyst for the formation of an authoritarian coalition to restore a Conservative government.[7] In the case of Argentina, then, landlords were not a strong obstacle to initial democratization in the 1910s, and neither was the problem of labor control a decisive factor in the landlords' later opposition to democracy. This is consistent with Moore's arguments about the importance of rural labor relations for the landlords' role in the formation of a reactionary coalition.

Mexico and Peru

In both Mexico and Peru, large landholdings were dominant and the availability of a large cheap labor force for the estates was important. As

Mallon's chapter makes clear, large landlords in both countries attempted to impose severe restrictions on the rights of the rural population, particularly on access to land and water, which served to ensure an adequate labor force for the large estates. Mallon makes the point that in Morelos the strength of the popular movement and its demands for the decentralization of power and local autonomy were crucial for the use of repression by the state, rather than the landowners' need to underwrite coerced labor. However, local autonomy for the popular movement precisely meant more leverage for the commercialized village economy (and thus more alternatives for rural labor) against the large landowners who were supported by Conservative as well as Liberal central state elites. Mallon also points out that the landowners maintained troops on the estates, private ones in Peru and rural guards in Mexico. This obviously gave the landlords the means not only to enforce their claims on property against claims from the rural population but also to enforce peasant compliance with their obligations vis-à-vis the estates.

In the main periods under consideration in Mallon's essay, democracy was not on the agenda in either Mexico or Peru, as state consolidation had been achieved in neither. However, when state consolidation was achieved, it did by no means set the stage for democratization; rather, it was accompanied by a reconstruction of authoritarianism, of a centralized variety in Mexico and a decentralized one in Peru. These patterns corresponded to the difference in the capacity of the two states to penetrate local areas; this capacity was much more limited in Peru. In the absence of an effective central state, capable of exercising coercion at the local level, landowners resorted to the use of their own private repressive forces.

In Mexico Díaz followed the centralizing authoritarian pattern set by earlier Conservative and Liberal rulers. He rapidly distanced himself from the agrarian social movements that had helped him gain power and relied on support from large landowners and domestic and foreign capitalist interests. Support from landowners was based precisely on his denial of rights to the rural population. One could see in Díaz's regime the incarnation of Moore's reactionary coalition. However, as Coatsworth emphasizes, in contrast to Moore's cases foreign capital was an essential partner in the dominant coalition in Mexico.[8] Moreover, there was great heterogeneity among domestic landed and capitalist elites. Mineral exports were more important than agricultural ones, and agriculture was highly diversified. Finally, Díaz had to construct a strong centralized state apparatus while holding the reactionary coalition together. The recent process of centralization of the state apparatus made it vulnerable to tensions and corruptions internal to the state. The dependence of the state on domestic and foreign elite support added to its vulnerability, as divisions among different sectors of domestic elites and competition among foreign interests put it under severe strain. Such tensions eventually led to the breakdown of the reactionary coalition and opened the way for the eruption of revolutionary movements.

Large landlords in Mexico, then, were neither a hegemonic force capable of allying in a dominant position with the bourgeoisie, nor did they have the option of allying with a well-consolidated state to impose stable authoritarian rule. Traditional landlords as a class were eliminated by the revolution, and thus they had no decisive influence on the postrevolutionary political outcome. After the revolution, centralizing elites whose power base was military more than economic rebuilt an authoritarian state apparatus. As Mallon emphasizes, the strength of popular agrarian movements, which had their roots in the historically shaped strength of peasant communities and village economies and which had played an important role in the revolution, forced the elites to construct an inclusive form of authoritarianism.

In Peru Piérola and his successors collaborated with the large landowners in reconstructing the decentralized and privatized authoritarianism that had been in operation before the War of the Pacific. The Peruvian state remained a minimalist state until the 1960s, pursuing economic laissez-faire policies and leaving landlords in control of local politics. Though one can see the governments up to 1962 as essentially representing a reactionary coalition of landlords, a dependent bourgeoisie, and the state (i.e., the military, which was the only strong part of the state apparatus), there are three important differences from Moore's model. First, this coalition also included foreign capital as an essential partner; second, the modernizing landlords in the coastal areas who used largely wage labor were much more important members of the coalition than the traditional landlords in the mountains who still used a resident labor force; third, the coalition had by no means a project of modernization from above, pursuing instead, as just noted, policies of economic liberalism. Furthermore, the coalition's hold on political power was not secure, but rather challenged repeatedly by Apra, the political party that managed to construct an alliance among sectors of the middle and working classes and initially put forward a radical anti-imperialist and anti-oligarchic program. Still, the coalition was truly reactionary and maintained sufficient cohesion and repressive capacity to reassert its control over the state and put down popular movements when radical demands challenged the prerogatives of its urban or rural members. In the more accessible areas, repression was effected by the security forces of the central state, whereas in the more remote areas the use of private repressive force continued, abetted by the state. In the mountain areas, the struggle was mainly over access to land and by the 1960s began to include the elimination of gratuitous services, whereas on coastal plantations the struggle centered around rights to organize and demands for better wages and working conditions. In either case, Peruvian landlords could count on state backing in their resistance to these demands, and the political outcome was an essentially authoritarian trajectory.[9]

Chile

The Chilean landholding structure was also dominated by large estates and these estates required a large labor force, mainly provided by resident laborers. As Bauer makes clear, recruiting and keeping a resident labor force was no problem because of the lack of alternatives for the rural population. Land monopolization in the Central Valley was extensive, and access to land in the southern frontier region was denied to the local rural population. Thus, while landlords had no need to enlist state support for direct labor coercion, they did need to protect their monopolization of access to land and to prevent labor organization from spreading to rural areas. Due to early state consolidation and export prosperity, landlords were able to establish relatively stable constitutional rule in the second half of the nineteenth century, and they even widened inclusion to nonelite sectors. However, when effective political participation of nonelite sectors threatened to escape their control in the early twentieth century, the municipal Committees of the Largest Taxpayers, which were in charge of the administration of suffrage, simply reduced the number of registered voters.[10] In other words, they clearly imposed limitations on the rights of the lower classes, which at that time were still largely rural.

Nevertheless, no typical Moorean reactionary coalition emerged in the early twentieth century in Chile, for several reasons. Though landowners themselves invested in urban commercial and financial activities and thus personified the landlord-bourgeoisie alliance, they could not count on the undivided loyalty of the military. When the representatives of landowning and bourgeois interests blocked all reform attempts of the first president elected as the candidate of a middle-class party, the military staged a coup in 1924, and a period of political instability followed in which a sector of the military even proclaimed a short-lived socialist republic.[11] Furthermore, the main export was minerals, and the mines were all foreign owned, which meant that foreign capital was an important factor and that there was a revenue base for the state independent of the landed bourgeois class.

After 1932 the landowners in Chile did allow for effective participation of middle- and working-class parties, but their electoral strength, based on their hegemony in rural areas, allowed them to ward off any challenges to their property and keep unionization out of the rural sector until the 1960s. When rural mobilization and the Unidad Popular government directly threatened their economic and political positions, the landed bourgeois class turned decidedly against democracy. Yet, as in other cases of emerging bureaucratic authoritarian regimes, the landlords-bourgeoisie benefitted from the policies of the new regime but did not get to participate in the actual exercise of governmental power, as the military imposed itself as a largely autonomous set of rulers.

Colombia

Colombia differs from the other South American cases in that large estates coexisted with a very significant sector of small and medium holdings, which had their origins in the existence of an agricultural frontier. In the nineteenth century, farmers from Antioquia moved to the uncultivated slopes of the central cordillera to the south, where they first engaged in subsistence production and later in coffee production.[12] With the expansion of coffee production after 1880 an intense struggle began for the appropriation of public lands between large landowners and squatters. Though most public lands were awarded in large blocs to wealthy individuals and conflicts between large landowners and squatters were generally decided in favor of the former, large numbers of smallholdings survived and many more were newly established.[13] In the first half of the twentieth century, small family-owned and -operated farms became the most important producers of coffee.[14] These small family farms, however, were far from prosperous; elites appropriated much of their potential profits through control over credit and over the processing and commercialization of coffee. Moreover, large landowners who were frequently also processors, merchants, and bankers exercised strong social and political domination at the local level.

As Safford emphasizes, labor relations on large coffee estates in Colombia varied by region and even within regions. In the older coffee areas, large estates typically operated with a resident labor force that was granted the use of a plot of land in exchange for a certain amount of work on the owner's estate. By the 1920s, their labor was mostly remunerated at rates below those for nonresident labor.[15] In addition, seasonal labor was procured through labor recruiters in other areas, often with less than benign methods. A contract system was also in use, under which an agricultural worker opened up a plot of land, used it for subsistence and the planting of coffee trees, and after a stipulated period sold the trees to the large landowner and renounced all claims on the land. In the newer coffee zones, large estates were more typically worked by renters and sharecroppers, and independent small and medium farms were more common. However, many of these small farms could not support a family, and thus some of its members were forced to work for others and attempt to rent additional land.

Before the 1920s the main restrictions that large landowners attempted to put on the rights of rural labor concerned access to land. The lack of meaningful employment alternatives outside of agriculture ensured the availability of a cheap labor force as long as the rural population did not have access to independent subsistence agriculture. Though national policy, particularly legislation regarding the appropriation of public lands, was potentially important for landlords in this endeavor, control of the local state apparatus, particularly of judicial and police authorities and thus of the implementation of policy, was generally sufficient to protect landowners' interests. As Safford's essay makes clear, the central state in Colombia was extremely weak in the nineteenth century, and even though the expansion of the coffee economy brought the state much needed resources to strengthen its functions and authority, it still did not manage to enforce its rules in many areas of the country. Thus, the national state was for the most part neither a necessary nor an effective ally of large landowners in their efforts to control rural labor. Moreover, there was no elite consensus at the national level, which could have formed the basis for a stable landlord-state-bourgeoisie alliance. Though there were no clear socioeconomic cleavages as members of the dominant class had diversified holdings in commerce, finance, land, and later manufacturing, historical divisions between the two traditional parties, the Liberals and Conservatives, ran deep.[16]

The strength and historical enmity of these parties is a crucial element for understanding the political development of Colombia. What began as a struggle for power between elite political groupings with different views on a desirable social and political order, particularly the role of the Catholic Church, became a struggle between two crossclass camps divided by memories of death and destruction in repeated civil wars for which landlords mobilized their dependent workers. Internally, the camps were tied together by a combination of social domination and patronage and the need for mutual assistance against the opposing camp. Over the years political alignments became hereditary, and partisan political networks were the main avenue for smallholders to attempt to secure and improve their position vis-à-vis landowners and smallholders from the opposing camp. Civil wars added to geographical fragmentation to keep the economy sluggish and the state weak until the turn of the century. It was only after the War of the Thousand Days had ended in 1902 that bipartisan reformers succeeded in instituting peaceful competition for political power among elite factions at the national level. Over the following decades, political order and economic growth, with its concomitant social changes, for the first time put the issue of democracy on the agenda.

Safford makes clear that the rapid economic growth of the 1920s, driven by coffee production and large inflows of foreign capital, both as loans and direct foreign investment, led to a competition for labor between agriculture and other sectors with higher wages, notably construction, transport, and manufacturing. In this situation, labor organization and agitation spilled over into the coffee economy, particularly in Cundinamarca and Tolima.[17]

Coffee workers organized and fought to gain control of land, reduce their labor obligations, and improve their remuneration. Large coffee growers, particularly in the older areas with more traditional labor relations, fought back both at the local and national levels, using paid thugs to fight workers with privately organized violence, calling for troops to restore order, and organizing pressure groups to influence government policy. The Conservative government in the late 1920s countered labor mobilization with repression, but increasingly influential factions in both parties advocated a reformist strategy to deal with urban and rural militancy.

The Liberals won the 1930 election in Colombia and proceeded to implement a number of reforms to institutionalize the labor movement, regularize the awarding of titles to public lands, and promote a parcelization program. Moreover, the government formally democratized the political system by instituting universal male suffrage. This reformist Liberal government was also dominated by elites with diversified holdings in commerce, finance, land, and manufacturing; it was a government brought to power by and representing neither an emerging autonomous manufacturing bourgeoisie nor the subordinate classes. Nor could it be considered a government controlled by large landowners, as such, because agricultural production on large estates was not a crucial economic basis for most members of the dominant class; as pointed out above, control over the processing and commercialization of coffee was a major mechanism for the extraction of profits from coffee production. Thus, significant sectors of the elite could accept the idea of leaving coffee production in the hands of smallholders.

Safford argues that the political elite, and thus the state, in Colombia operated to a considerable extent autonomously from the economically dominant class. The political divisions in this class certainly meant that they did not control and use state power as a unitary class actor. However, members of the economically dominant class were very powerful in both parties. Even if they did not exercise political power directly, they set the parameters within which the incumbents in political offices could rule. These parameters could be wider; that is, they could allow for more reformist legislation at the national level, precisely where the power of the central state was insufficient to guarantee implementation at the local level. And there is little doubt that at the local level in rural areas, where legislation affecting land ownership or the rights of rural subordinate classes had to be implemented, large landowners were the effective political power holders. Thus, the impact of the reformist and democratic national state of the 1930s remained limited in many local areas. For instance, Safford points to the essentially conservative effect of the legislation on the appropriation of public lands. Traditional strongmen continued to control elections and the local state through a combination of patronage and intimidation.[18]

Moreover, much of the progress that was made in this period was reversed between 1944 and 1946, when the Liberals were badly split and the Conservatives were in ascendancy.[19] Due to the growing inability of Liberal and Conservative leaders to compromise at the national level, state authority at all levels broke down and in 1948 the country descended into the period known as La Violencia. National and local political issues as well as personal interests and vendettas became the subjects of armed conflict. Large landowners fought each other as well as smallholders, as did the smallholders themselves. The entire social fabric of Colombia was threatened by this violence, which finally brought contending elite factions together in the attempt to forge a new accommodation. Under the political pact of 1958 they agreed to share state power in a formally democratic context. Nevertheless, violence continued to be a severe problem for at least another decade. In the 1970s, some progress was made in the direction of genuine democratization by opening up the political process to parties other than the Liberals and Conservatives, but in the 1980s the drug trade brought another wave of violence and another fundamental challenge to state power.

In sum, then, Colombia's trajectory has been predominantly authoritarian in essence, despite the at times formal democratic shell. The form of authoritarianism resembles the Peruvian one of privatized, localized authoritarianism more than, for instance, the Mexican form of centralized authoritarianism resting on a strong state. Landowners were an obstacle to democratization, but not by forming a reactionary alliance with the central state. As noted above, they were not a clearly hegemonic faction of the dominant class, and it would be difficult to apportion responsibility for the problems of democracy to landowners as opposed to other factions or other problems, such as the tradition of Liberal-Conservative rivalry. Still, it is clear that the landowners' use of violence to challenge the central state and to strengthen their domination over the local agricultural population obstructed the consolidation of state power and the ability of the state to enforce even minimal democratic rights of the subordinate classes.

Other South American Countries

In turning to the South American cases that are not treated in this volume, we can group them into two categories: countries with agrarian export economies and countries with mineral export economies. The former group comprises Brazil, Uruguay, Paraguay, and Ecuador; the latter, Venezuela and Bolivia. Brazil, Uruguay, Ecuador, and, to a lesser extent, Paraguay are largeholding countries where landlords were the economically most powerful class during the period of modernization. In Brazil and Ecuador, traditional rural labor relations with large estate populations were very widespread, though there was considerable regional variation. Plantation

agriculture with wage labor and a variety of smallholding, squatting, share-cropping, and tenancy arrangements were characteristic of many areas in these two countries. For traditional estates as well as for plantations, the availability of cheap labor was crucial, and, accordingly, landlords attempted to restrict the rights of the rural population not only in access to land but in rights to organize.[20] Similarly, landlords in both cases opposed democratization in the sense of political inclusion, as opposed to institutionalization of (oligarchic) political competition.[21] What varied was the wider economic and social context, and thus the effect of landlord opposition on the installation and consolidation of democracy.

Paraguay

Paraguay developed in a rather unique way. The dictator Francia (1814–1840) destroyed the colonial aristocracy and expropriated large tracts of land owned by the church and by Spanish and Creole elites. About half of the land in the fertile central region was cultivated directly by the state in the form of large farms, and much land was subdivided and leased to small and medium famers.[22] Due to the severe disruption of external trade in this period, the state pursued a deliberate and successful policy of agricultural diversification.[23] Though large private landholding became more important again and external trade increased in the second half of the nineteenth century, Paraguay continued to deviate from the modal Latin American pattern. There emerged neither a hacienda system of production nor specialized export agriculture with plantations, and Paraguay did not participate in significant export expansion and prosperity. Large estates were mostly devoted to cattle ranching and forestry and coexisted with smallholdings where owners, tenants, and squatters grew a variety of crops.[24] By the early 1950s, forest products accounted for 40 to 50 percent of all exports, and foreign capital owned a significant share of this export production.[25] Given this social structure, elites based their power and patronage networks on the control of trade and credit rather than land.

In 1870 electoral legislation established universal male suffrage, which led to the formation of the Colorado and Liberal parties in 1887 and their rapid expansion and consolidation into political machines based on patronage. Though patronage was primarily anchored in the private realm, some significant overlap of political and economic clientelism emerged.[26] Over time, some form of institutionalized intraparty competition emerged, but not a single peaceful transfer of power between these two parties took place.[27] The victory of Paraguay over Bolivia in the Chaco War greatly increased the power, prestige, and sense of national mission of the military establishment. At the same time, the war experience politicized the middle classes and intensified the political struggle, though the lower classes did not acquire any autonomous mobilization capacity until the 1980s. The

Colorado and Liberal parties and the military competed with each other for control of the state. An attempt to impose a purely military government failed because the parties were too strongly entrenched.[28] The result was another period of political instability ending in the Stroessner dictatorship, which lasted from 1954 to 1989. Thus, the problems of democracy were a result of the inability of elites to come to an arrangement of power sharing among themselves combined with the weakness of pressures from subordinate classes. The low level of economic development and the particular rural social structure of Paraguay obstructed the emergence of popular organizations, and what little there was of it was ruthlessly repressed by Stroessner.

Since Stroessner's overthrow in 1989 the question of democratic rights for the urban and rural lower classes in Paraguay has assumed great saliency.[29] Though there are large areas of relatively recent colonization in the east, where small and medium holdings are dominant, population pressures on the land are high in the traditional areas with large landholdings. Peasant movements had organized themselves in the early eighties to fight for land and for higher wages and had met with severe repression on Stroessner's part. Repression alternated with concessions under Rodríguez.[30] While it is too early to detect clear political realignments, the formation of a coalition among rural and urban propertied classes, overcoming traditional party divisions, and a more professionalized military, in support of some form of restricted democracy to keep peasant and worker movements weak, is a distinct possibility.

Brazil

In Brazil there was great regional variation in the production of agricultural exports and in rural labor relations. Coffee production on plantations with immigrant labor in Sao Paulo and sugar production on plantations with wage labor in the northeast contrasted with crop production on traditional large estates with resident laborers and sharecroppers and with ranching in these and other areas. Regional and product diversity led to rivalries among different groups of landlords that, however, could be contained through the political arrangements of the Old Republic, which included a high degree of autonomy for the states and mutual accommodation among regional oligarchies at the national level. Agricultural producers and exporters dominated the national Congress and held key decision-making positions within the administration.[31] The onset of the depression resulted in the breakdown of this arrangement and triggered the political crisis that brought this period of undisputed landlord political control to an end through the coup of 1930.[32] Nevertheless, landlords continued to play a very important political role under Vargas and during the period of restricted democracy from 1945 to 1964, helping to keep Brazil on an authoritarian trajectory.[33]

The coup of 1930 has often been interpreted as a coup against the old oligarchy, particularly the Sao Paulo coffee elite. The overthrown president was a Paulista himself and handpicked by his Paulista predecessor, and the Commercial Association of Rio, an umbrella organization representing the interests of merchants, landowners, and industrialists, gave him strong support.[34] Furthermore, the Paulista revolt of 1932 was backed by old oligarchs in Sao Paulo, Rio Grande do Sul, and Minas Gerais.[35] However, as Skidmore argues convincingly, the coup coalition of 1930 was very heterogeneous, and its "nonrevolutionary" segment included dissident members of the coffee elite, of old political elites (mostly tied to landowners), and of the military leadership. The "revolutionary" segment included junior officers (the *tenente* movement) and liberal constitutionalists with a base in the still small urban middle classes. The lower classes had no political weight at the time as the urban labor movement was very small and politically divided, and rural labor was entirely unmobilized.[36] Even the "revolutionary" segment of the coup coalition did not push for an entry of the masses into politics. The *tenentes* were suspicious of elections on the grounds that they would just restore traditional elites to power, and the liberal constitutionalists wanted the literacy requirement enforced in order to keep rural oligarchs from manipulating the votes of their clienteles.[37] The constituent assembly, which transformed itself into the first Congress under the constitution of 1934, took a clearly repressive stance vis-à-vis the increase in popular mobilization in the mid-1930s. It voted for a National Security Law in 1935 and later voted various times for declaring a state of siege, which gave the federal government strong repressive powers.[38] On the other hand, sectors of landowning elites with state-based political power went into opposition to Vargas over the issue of the centralization of power. The military command, in contrast, backed such centralization because it wanted a monopolization of military power at the center.

Thus, there was not really a united reactionary coalition ruling Brazil, but such unity was not necessary because the rural sector remained entirely unmobilized. The lack of any rural organization until the late 1950s meant that landlords were left in the position of ultimate authority on their estates and mostly also controlled local politics. Since rural states were overrepresented in the national government, representatives of landlord interests were in a position to prevent, until 1963, any central initiatives that might have extended effective rights to organize to the rural population, not to speak of land redistribution. In view of this situation, neither Vargas nor his successors Dutra and Kubitschek in the 1945–1960 period ever raised the issue of changes in land tenure patterns.[39]

In the late 1950s pressures from below for political and economic change in Brazil began to mount. Up to that point, state paternalism and intervention in civil society had kept pressures for democratization from the emerging middle and working classes weak. However, with increasing urbanization and industrialization the control potential of corporatist institutions eroded, and unions resorted to increasingly autonomous and militant action.[40] Peasant leagues began to form illegally and put forward demands for land and for higher wages for seasonal labor. Despite repressive state responses to these leagues, a national Peasants' Congress was held in November 1961, and in its aftermath rural violence increased in Minas Gerais, Rio de Janeiro, and several northeastern states. These events were perceived as an acute threat by economic and political elites because many national politicians owed their existence to the backward political systems in areas still manipulated by landowners.[41] After the passage of a law in 1963 that authorized the formation of rural syndicates, rural organization efforts intensified, as did threat perception among elites. Goulart's mild land reform bill met with fierce congressional opposition from an interparty alliance of deputies.[42] When he threatened to override congressional opposition by decree on the land reform and other issues, he cemented an opposition of established economic and political elites who appealed with growing insistence for military intervention.

Since 1945 the military had played a moderator role in politics, responding to calls from civilian elites for intervention to remove governments that had lost their ability and willingness to protect elite interests. As Stepan shows, the successful performance of a coup correlated with the prior denial of legitimacy to the incumbent government by civilian elites and with calls for military intervention in major newspapers representing established interests.[43] Before the coup of 1964, attacks on Goulart and appeals to the military were strong. The military itself abhorred Goulart's encouragement of growing popular mobilization and feared in particular a spillover of mobilization to sergeants and enlisted men.[44] This community of interests and support for authoritarianism among the landlords, the bourgeoisie, and the state bears a strong resemblance to Moore's reactionary coalition. Landlords and the bourgeoisie did not actually participate in ruling the country, though, since the military and its technocratic civilian allies monopolized political power after the coup. Still, the government's policies responded to their interests through the ruthless repression of peasant leagues and militant labor unions.

The return to meaningful electoral politics in the 1980s in Brazil allowed large landowners to regain politically powerful positions in the more backward states. The antidemocratic posture of many of them became manifest again when they managed to defeat any meaningful land reform proposals in the constituent assembly and hired armed guards to defend their properties. Yet, the progress of industrialization had clearly removed them from the position of the economically most powerful class, and it had increased pressures from below for democratization, with the result that formal democracy was established.[45]

Ecuador

In Ecuador there were also deep divisions between different sectors of landlords, mainly along the lines of traditional highland landowners versus modernizing, export-oriented coastal landowners closely linked to commercial and financial interests. The main political representatives of these two sectors were the Conservative and Liberal parties, respectively, though the sector-party alignment was far from perfect.[46] Access to cheap labor was very important for both sectors. The coastal elites abolished the Indian tribute and imprisonment for debt, in order to mobilize labor for the coastal plantations. However, semifeudal labor relations, in the form of a piece of land being given in usufruct in return for labor obligations on the land and in the household of the landowner, existed in both highland and coastal areas.[47] Pressures from below for democratization remained comparatively weak because of the absence of any significant industrialization before the 1960s, but when popular protests and strikes did emerge, Conservative as well as Liberal governments resorted to repression, as both coastal and highland landowners were opposed to the extension of democratic rights to the lower classes.[48] A period of oligarchic constitutional rule with Liberal dominance facilitated by the cacao boom gave way in 1925 to a period of high political instability in which the military played an important role. There was no reactionary coalition in Moore's sense and no stable authoritarian rule, though the political trajectory of the country was clearly nondemocratic. Both sectors of landowners were antidemocratic, but they were locked in a struggle for political power in which neither one could count on the loyalty of a united military. Rather, different factions in the military became power contenders of their own, pursuing initially an authoritarian course autonomously and then in changing alliances with civilian forces.

Between 1947 and 1955 Ecuadorean banana production increased by some 800 percent, and banana plantations with capitalist labor relations became the dominant form of production on large coastal estates. However, large plantations accounted for about one-fifth of banana exports only; the rest came from small and medium banana farms, a considerable number of which emerged on land newly colonized with government support. The banana boom led to a significant migration from the highlands to the coast.[49] In 1948 Liberals, Conservatives, and the military decided to accept the results of the elections, and thirteen years of restricted democracy followed. Democracy was restricted insofar as the large illiterate proportion of the population remained disenfranchised and the military remained an important political actor. Landlords initially made no strong attempts to prevent or reverse this limited democratization, since it did not pose an immediate threat to their interests. A large proportion of rural labor was illiterate and thus disenfranchised, land reform was not an issue, the government did not attempt to interfere in rural labor relations, and popular movements promoting the rights of rural labor were very weak. Rural unionization remained confined to coastal banana plantations.

By the late 1950s social mobilization in Ecuador began to increase and the populist Velasco Ibarra won the presidential elections of 1960. In the same year he established a National Agrarian Reform Commission, which sparked a heated debate among the landowning elite. After his overthrow in 1961, his vice president, Arosemena Monroy, took power and demonstrated considerable support for domestic social reform. This prompted the traditional elite, among whom landlords remained prominent, to encourage the military to step back into power; the Conservative Party issued an official statement calling for a coup, as did a major Guayaquil newspaper.[50] Yet the military junta that took power in 1963 pursued a rather independent political project, which involved a mild land reform that eliminated traditional, semifeudal, rural labor relations.[51] Under attack from the traditional elites and without an organized popular support base, the junta withdrew from power in 1966. After a renewed populist interlude and amid renewed calls for intervention from the traditional elite, the military again took power in 1973 and remained until 1979.[52]

The availability of oil exports in the 1970s gave the Ecuadorean state greater autonomy from domestic economic elites and, combined with industrialization, it reduced the economic importance of the landowning class. These developments made the formation of a strong Moorean reactionary coalition less likely than ever, and in 1984 illiterates were allowed to vote for the first time in a presidential election. Nevertheless, landowning elites together with industrialists and merchants continued to obstruct the consolidation of democracy by calling for the removal of the elected left-wing president, and under his right-wing successor the parties representing elite interests supported extraconstitutional means to gain the upper hand in a power struggle with the congressional Left.[53]

Uruguay

Uruguay was similar in its agrarian structure to Argentina. Ranching became clearly dominant in the late nineteenth century and did not pose the problem of securing a large supply of cheap labor. The monopolization of land kept a growing rural population of *minifundistas* and immigrants underemployed, in search of land to rent, and available for work on the large estates.[54] The traditional landlords of the interior, the leaders of the Blanco Party, were more in need of labor, but they were of secondary economic importance and were militarily defeated in 1904 by the Colorados, based in the coastal middle classes. The large landowners engaged in ranching were not closely linked to either one of these traditional parties but, rather, wanted an end to the civil wars. Thus, they initially accepted that the Colorados became the dominant political force and introduced a form of restricted democracy. The position of the Blancos, who opposed democratization and endangered political stability by boycotting several elections and threatening renewed rebellions, kept the large landowners from forming a strong opposition front against the first two Colorado presidents, despite these presidents' reformist orientation.[55] Their opposition against Batlle's reformism in his first period in office (1903–1907) largely took the forms of a rhetorical battle and of efforts to strengthen the organization representing ranching interests. However, when Batlle began implementation of a series of policies affecting rural areas in his second period in office (1911–1915), most importantly taxes on land and a colonization scheme, the large landowners moved into more strident opposition.[56] Most of them began to support strongly the National Party (Blancos), and some of them supported the dissenting Colorados.

Opposition against Batlle crystallized around the issue of constitutional reform, but the alignments were heavily shaped by support for or opposition to his overall reform course.[57] The Batllista forces suffered an electoral defeat, and though the next president of Uruguay was a Colorado and initially supported by Batlle, he soon declared that a phase of consolidation was to replace the rapid reforms of the previous years.[58] In contrast to Argentina, then, the strength of the National Party, historically grounded in the rural areas, provided large landowners the option of working through a political party to protect their interests in a democratic context. The strength of the National Party together with the strength of conservative factions in the Colorado Party prevented the implementation of any reforms that would have affected landed interests in a significant way. As a result, the large landowners accepted democracy, until a combination of party factionalization and economic deterioration began to threaten their interests.

Factionalization proceeded in both parties, and a faction of the National Party came to support social reforms along with Colorado factions. In 1929 the Federación Rural was instrumental in setting up a committee representing rural and urban capitalist interests to pressure against such reforms. The perceived threat to their interests was intensified by the depression, which in 1932 sent exports down to 58 percent of their 1930 value.[59] In 1933 a Colorado faction allied with a Nationalist faction that had close connections to landowners and staged a bloodless coup to exclude other factions from executive power.[60] Policies beneficial to landowners followed, such as a reduction in the land tax, the suspension of mortgage payments on rural property, bonus payments to livestock producers, and exchange rate policies favorable to exporters. Yet the coup did not mean that a Moorean coalition of large landowners and a dependent bourgeoisie took control of a strong state to repress peasants and workers. Rather, factions of political parties, though in part inspired by landowner and urban capitalist interests, were the key players; and the military did not play a role as repression remained very mild and was carried out through the police forces under the control of the government. In accounting for the absence of such a coalition, one can point to the relative strength of the parties and the relative weakness of the state apparatus, as well as to the position of landlords. State consolidation and party consolidation took place at the same time, and after the defeat of the last attempted Blanco rebellion in 1910 the military was deliberately divided into small units and the officer corps was significantly reduced in size.[61] Thus, landowners did not have the option of bypassing politicians and allying directly with the bourgeoisie and a strong state apparatus to impose an authoritarian regime. Moreover, labor control was not a salient issue for landowners, which would have required control over coercive force. Finally, there was the precedent of 1916, when landowners, together with urban bourgeois interests, managed to influence a sufficient proportion of the parties to put an end to reformism. Accordingly, the landlord-bourgeois coalition did not establish firm control over the state apparatus and acquiesced to gradual redemocratization between 1938 and 1942.

In the 1950s Uruguay entered a period of economic stagnation that was to last until the 1970s. This stagnation engendered growing popular mobilization and intense social conflict, which sparked urban guerrilla violence. Both rural and urban elites were profoundly threatened by this growing militancy, and they sought renewed direct participation in political power.[62] They supported the curtailment of political rights under the last elected president, as well as the military coup that followed in 1973. However, under the military regime they were relegated to the role of beneficiaries of the new policy orientation, rather than being included as class actors in the exercise of political power.[63]

Venezuela
Venezuela was also dominated by large estates, and coffee became the most important export commodity in the nineteenth century, until oil took its place in the 1920s.[64] However, there were important regional differences; ranching remained important in large parts of the lowlands. There were also differences in land tenure and labor relations; in addition to very large estates with a resident, semi-bound labor force, there were medium and small holdings, and mixtures of tenancy and sharecropping arrangements and wage labor.[65] Coffee cultivation did not create a strong and cohesive landed class capable of imposing its rule. Rather, during the nineteenth

century there was a high turnover of land ownership due to unending elite struggles.[66] Regional military strongmen, mostly based in the large cattle ranches on the lowlands, remained the major power contenders, at best balanced against each other and kept in check by a strong central ruler, at worst fighting for power in civil wars. Protracted civil strife was one major impediment to agricultural export expansion and prosperity. It meant that the chronic labor shortage in many rural areas was aggravated by a demand for troops and that investments in agricultural improvements were risky. Control of the state was an important avenue to wealth, as the winners confiscated the property of opponents and awarded themselves trade monopolies. Landlords allied themselves with regional military strongmen to protect their property and advance their interests.

Given the low level of development, Venezuelan society remained relatively undifferentiated and susceptible to rule by personalistic dictatorial regimes. The last of the powerful central strongmen was Juan Vicente Gómez, who held power from 1908 until 1935. He succeeded in consolidating state power, establishing a national army with a monopoly on coercive force, and setting up a transport and communications network. Under his rule, the system of large estates was consolidated and export agriculture increased. The establishment of public order contributed to this consolidation, as did the awarding of large land grants from public lands by Gómez. Gómez himself became fabulously wealthy, as did many of his supporters, but there was also an accommodation with sectors of the traditional elites.[67]

With the consolidation of large private estates, larger sectors of the rural population, who before had pursued slash-and-burn agriculture, were brought into some sort of contractual relationships with estate owners, mostly through debt mechanisms. In the coffee areas, this process had taken place earlier. Labor control was, at least in part, politically backed. For instance, Gómez stationed troops in rural areas, particularly on his own enormous properties, to deal with peasant unrest, and estate owners and supervisors were often granted semiformal police powers.[68] Thus, authoritarian rule was stabilized and predominated at all levels of society, from the large estates to local and regional authorities and the national government. The labor requirements and methods for labor procurement used by the large landlords were one factor among many that caused landlords to support authoritarian rulers, though historically they were of less direct consequence for political outcomes than the problems of consolidating state power.

From the 1920s on, the growing importance of oil in the Venezuelan economy transformed the society and relegated large landowners to an economically as well as politically secondary position.[69] The prices and thus the total value of agricultural exports declined steeply between 1920 and 1935, though their total volume showed only a moderate decline after

1925.[70] A commercial and financial bourgeoisie had emerged in the end of the nineteenth century and it grew in importance in the oil-based economy. Urban middle and working classes grew, as well, and began to organize and press for democratization. The large landowners and the bourgeoisie for the most part supported Gómez's centralization of power because he brought stability by critically weakening the regional caudillos.[71] Gómez dealt with incipient mobilization through repression, but his successors attempted to keep pressures for democratization in check through a combination of repression and partial concessions. In the rural sector, though, they sided with large landowners and heavily obstructed unionization attempts by organizers linked to Acción Democrática (AD); despite strong efforts on the part of the latter from 1937 on, only seventy-seven peasant unions were recognized by 1945.[72]

In 1945 a faction of the military sided with AD, the main organized political force in Venezuela representing the middle and lower classes, and a coup ushered in the democratic period of 1945 to 1948. The elections with universal, including illiterate, suffrage during this period demonstrated the total lack of hegemony of landlords over the rural population. AD won between 70 and 78 percent of the vote in every election and received heavy support in rural areas.[73] AD's rapid implementation of a wide range of reform policies, particularly the promotion of labor organization in urban and rural areas and plans for an, albeit moderate, land reform, led to the emergence of very strong opposition from landlords and the bourgeoisie. However, opposition grew also from all other political parties because of their marginalization from political power, from the church because of educational reforms, and most importantly from the military because of their loss of political influence.[74] In 1948, a coup reestablished an authoritarian regime, which proceeded to halt the reform process and to destroy AD and the popular organizations it had sponsored. Landlords, of course, were highly supportive of these developments, but they were not a decisive force in bringing them about. How negligible their political clout was became clear upon redemocratization in 1958. A multipartisan commission studied the issue of land reform, and its proposal, which included provisions for the distribution of private lands, was supported by all parties, except for the communists.[75]

Bolivia

Bolivia's main agricultural areas were dominated by large estates with a traditionally semibound labor force. Up to the 1950s landowners continued to use a variety of customary practices and coercion to extract cheap labor from a resident labor force and from surrounding *minifundistas* and members of Indian communities.[76] Landowners successfully opposed the extension of any form of democratic rights to the rural population; the very definition of citizenship and thus suffrage qualifications included not only literacy but also income or property qualifications and therefore excluded the entire rural Indian population.[77] However, the large landlords as an integral part of the economically dominant class rapidly lost their hegemony at the national level after the 1920s. Agricultural production was concentrated on the high plateau and in the valleys nearby, where haciendas had encroached on virtually all the fertile land previously belonging to Indian communities. Agricultural methods remained very backward and reliant on cheap Indian labor; agriculture was stagnant and clearly secondary in importance to mining. The economic importance of mining exports provided a resource base for the state and thus for the potential autonomy of the state from landlord interests. Moreover, though the old landed and commercial segments of the economically dominant class and those linked to the mining companies were closely intertwined, there were strong rivalries and conflicts among them.[78]

In Bolivia's economic stagnation in the thirties, elite infighting intensified and gave rise to political instability. After the end of the Chaco War in 1936, the military began to play an increasingly independent political role. At the same time, the urban middle and the working classes, which had grown around the mineral export economy, began to organize in various radical groups. Military factions allied with middle-class forces to gain control of the state. Though the dominant classes still managed to obstruct any serious reforms, they were unable to forge a strong reactionary coalition with the state to prevent the success of the revolution and the subsequent political democratization and land reform.[79] The land reform then destroyed the landholdings of the old elite and at the same time state power in the countryside. Violence against landlords and among groups of Indians vying for land became widespread and, in some areas, anomic. Where strong rural organizations were present, they came under the control of local bosses who competed with each other for political power.[80] Thus, when authoritarianism was restored by the military, not only did landlords play no role but there was no strong state apparatus effectively controlling the country. Rather, the military turned against the incumbent postrevolutionary government and used an alliance with the well-organized sections of the peasantry to install itself in power.[81]

Central America

In turning our attention to Central America, the most obvious question is, what accounts for the democratic trajectory of Costa Rica, which is so deviant from the political trajectories in the rest of the region? As Gudmundson points out, the evolution of the landholding structure in Costa Rica has been the subject of debate. Even though Gudmundson rejects the idealized view of Costa Rica as a country of smallholders, his analysis suggests that the landholding structure evolved in a different way from that of other Latin American countries. It was the spread of coffee cultivation that led to a transition from a municipal, public-lands cultivation system to a system of permanent private coffee groves. The economic base of the economically dominant class was in commerce rather than land. Though the wealthy were the first ones to engage in coffee cultivation, they had no colonial tradition of limiting access to frontier lands. Thus, instead of attempting to monopolize land, they did so with the processing and export of coffee, which was produced by small and medium suppliers. Even where coffee was produced on large estates, the labor scarcity combined with the option of migration led to sharecropping arrangements and comparatively high peasant incomes. Accordingly, landlords did not attempt to enlist state support in curtailing the rights of the rural population, nor did they attempt to control the state directly. Gudmundson argues that from 1871 on, the actions of the political leadership demonstrated some autonomy from the coffee elite; this autonomy was strengthened in the early twentieth century by the revenue from the banana enclave. As in Argentina, the agrarian export model was hegemonic, and the slow move toward institutionalized contestation and responsible government, along with the increasing political participation of medium-sized farmers, did not constitute a direct threat to the interests of the coffee elite.

Gudmundson makes a further interesting argument in relation to the military. He suggests that the military lost much of its influence in the second and third decades of the twentieth century due to U.S. pressures on the Tinoco dictatorship and for an end to the border war with Panama in 1923. In sum, the basic ingredients for the formation of a Moorean reactionary coalition—large landlords dependent on state support to ensure a large supply of cheap labor, and a state with a strong coercive arm—were absent. If, in turn, we look for the forces that supported democratization in Costa Rica and were weak or absent in the cases with authoritarian trajectories, the significant classes of medium and independent small farmers that emerged with the spread of coffee cultivation stand out. Gudmundson thus corroborates a very important critique of Moore's view of the bourgeoisie as a major carrier of democracy. With very few European exceptions, the bourgeoisie promoted the institutionalization of contestation in order to gain a share of power for themselves, but they opposed universal political inclusion, particularly inclusion of the working class. True to form, the coffee elite in Costa Rica, even though thoroughly bourgeois, was at best tolerant, but not supportive, of democracy.[82] Medium and small farmers were important in the institutionalization of political contestation in the nineteenth and early twentieth centuries; pressures from the growing urban middle and working classes effected wider political inclusion in the twentieth century. The fact that the coffee elite did not control the state was important in that it allowed for the growth of labor organization and for the implementation of quite significant social reform policies in the thirties and forties. How important this was becomes clear if one compares Costa Rica to the rest of Central America.[83]

Gudmundson emphasizes the differences in the nature of the large landowners in Nicaragua and Panama on the one hand and Guatemala and El Salvador on the other. In the former cases, he argues, there was no strong landed oligarchy, but rather a factionalized, economically dominant class based on the control of trade and the state apparatus. The result was great political instability, aggravated by U.S. intervention, and little resistance against personalistic dictatorship. In contrast to Costa Rica, the spread of coffee cultivation in Nicaragua created neither a strong processing and exporting elite that could have imposed constitutional oligarchic rule nor a prosperous class of medium farmers that could have pushed for its own political inclusion and thus for at least restricted democracy.

In Guatemala and El Salvador, in contrast, the landed oligarchy was strong and colonial forms of labor extraction survived through the period of coffee expansion. In order to be able to keep the rights of rural labor restricted by force, the oligarchies built up strong repressive apparatuses. Since the coffee oligarchies were in part identical with and for the other part closely linked to the commercial and financial bourgeoisies, their building up and allying with the military against the subordinate classes created dominant coalitions closely resembling Moore's reactionary alliance. In El Salvador the violent repression of the rebellion of 1932 signaled the determination of this alliance to prevent or repress any attempts to extend even minimal rights to the rural population.[84]

Subsequently any pressures for democratization coming from the urban middle and working classes met with intransigent responses from the alliance. In Guatemala the first and only attempt at democratic rule, beginning with the election of Arévalo in 1944, crumbled under the combined opposition of the oligarchy, United Fruit, and the U.S. government. After the overthrow of Arbenz in 1954 authoritarianism was restored with a vengeance.[85] However, in Guatemala as well as in El Salvador, the reactionary alliance began to crack as the military assumed an increasingly independent political role.[86] Massive U.S. military aid facilitated the distancing of the military from domestic political forces and its assumption of a largely autonomous position.[87] On the one hand, the military continued to perform a valuable function for the oligarchy in that it repressed any attempts at popular mobilization, but on the other hand military officers started to compete with the oligarchy (and with each other) in the search for wealth. The results are political systems with authoritarian essence in the form of military impunity, at times hidden behind a formally democratic facade.[88]

Caribbean

The predominance of authoritarianism elsewhere in the Caribbean and in Central America (and, as we shall see, in the American South) makes the prevalence and stability of democracy in the English-speaking Caribbean all the more striking.[89] It would also appear to be inexplicable from the point of Moore's theory: Like most other societies in the circum-Caribbean, the British West Indies were slave plantation societies and thus obviously labor-repressive and highly authoritarian. Emancipation in 1838 was followed by other forms of labor repression, the details of which varied from colony to colony. In most colonies this included resort to the importation of inden-tured labor, primarily from India.[90] In Guyana and Trinidad, this became the primary source of labor supply until the termination of the system in 1917.[91] In other colonies, the introduction of a whole array of legal controls short of actually making migration illegal supported the new labor control system. These almost always included some method of preventing planta-tion laborers from becoming independent peasants by regulating their access to land. Beckles contends that, in Barbados, this system of labor control was so effective that "workers had little room for manoeuvre; they were given the choice of starving, working under unsatisfactory conditions, or migrating," a situation that continued until the relevant legislation was repealed in 1937.[92] Moreover, the option of migrating was made difficult by laws forbidding prospective migrants from leaving dependents behind and forbidding the encouragement of emigration. Similar systems were devel-oped in the other West Indian colonies.

Though planters were the dominant political force in all of the colonies, they did not have ultimate control of the state. It was in the hands of the colonial power. This prevented the development of Moore's authoritarian coalition. The first important instance of the British imposing legislation on the planters to which they were bitterly opposed was Emancipation itself. Throughout the rest of the nineteenth century, the Colonial Office would, on occasion, disallow some of the most repressive legislation passed in the colonies. As Britain became more industrial and democratic, the divergence of interests became more severe. By the labor rebellions that swept all of the islands between 1935 and 1938, the British government had become unwill-ing to respond with the repression that the West Indian planters, like their counterparts in Central America, wanted. Instead, Britain extended rights to labor and supported constitutional decolonization and democratization.[93]

Advanced Capitalist Countries

Five of the eight cases that Moore examines belong to the group of advanced capitalist democracies of the contemporary world. Thus, in this group of countries, we can ask whether Moore's characterization of the politics of large landlords fits the countries that he did study and whether it can be extended to cases left out of the analysis. For the purposes of this survey, it is useful to divide this group of countries into three groups: the national states of western and central Europe, the settler colonies of Britain, and the single Asian case, Japan.[94]

Western and Central Europe

Observing the correlation of the patterns of landholding and democratic development in European countries, it would appear that Moore's line of analysis would provide a powerful explanation for the contrasting political trajectories of differing countries. The small European countries (Denmark, Norway, Sweden, Belgium, Netherlands, and Switzerland), all of which were overwhelmingly smallholding and thus had no powerful landed upper class, experienced relatively smooth transitions to democracy between the mid-nineteenth and early twentieth century and suffered no reversals of democracy in the twentieth century.[95] Four of the six countries with large-holding regions and thus a powerful class of large landholders (Italy, Germany, Austria [-Hungary], and Spain) experienced difficulties on the road to democracy and suffered reversals of democracy in the twentieth century. A fifth, Portugal, never became a full democracy, and even the restricted democracy that did exist in that country in the early decades of this century later gave way to an authoritarian regime that survived until the 1970s. In this group, only Britain avoided the turn to authoritarianism in the twentieth century. France, an intermediate case with regard to landholding and landed upper-class strength, at least by the mid-nineteenth century, also avoided that fate. Moore provides explanations for these two deviations: the absence of labor-repressive agriculture in Britain and the revolutionary break with the past in the case of France.

This correlation, by itself, only suggests that Moore is correct. It still must be demonstrated (1) that large landlords in these countries were antidemocratic, (2) that the political posture of the landlords contributed to the difficulties these countries experienced in the transition to democracy, and (3) that the opposition of landlords to democracy was rooted in their repressive methods of labor control.

Before turning to the largeholding cases, a brief word is in order about the class coalitions that led to democracy in the smallholding countries.[96] In all of them, small farmers were an essential positive force in the process of democratization. They were pivotal in Norway and Switzerland, both of which became full democracies in the nineteenth century while they were still agrarian societies. In Denmark, Sweden, Belgium, and the Netherlands, it was the working class that played the key role, but small farmers along with sections of the urban middle class were essential allies in the push for democracy. Conversely, Castles's and Tilton's studies of Sweden and Tumin's analysis of the Netherlands, which explicitly apply Moore's analysis to those cases, contend that the absence of a powerful landed upper class opposed to democracy was one feature that accounts for the relatively smooth transition to stable democracy in those countries without the "revolutionary break with the past" that Moore argued was an essential feature of the democratic path.[97] The same observation could be made about the other four countries.

Nineteenth-century Italy contained significant largeholding regions in the south and in the Po Valley, and the large estates in these areas were sufficiently numerous to sustain a very significant landed class. Moreover, an alliance, or at least an accommodation, between the landed class, the bourgeoisie, and the state did develop in the period between unification and the First World War. There is no question that the politics of both the southern landlords and the Po Valley landlords in the prewar period were antidemocratic. How much of their posture was motivated by labor control is unclear simply because the system of labor control was not threatened by the prevailing political arrangements. The events of the immediate post–World War I period argue, however, that labor control was an important reason for their political posture.

In accounting for the breakdown of Italian democracy, conscious attempts by the landed upper classes to influence events in an authoritarian direction were a very important determinant of the outcome. The postwar strike wave, factory occupations, peasant organizing, and victories by the Socialists in local council elections alarmed the bourgeoisie and the Po Valley landlords. Both groups began to fund the Fascists on a massive scale as the Fascists made violent attacks on peasant organizations, trade unions, Socialist Party offices, and local councils controlled by the Left the main focus of their activity. Increasingly, the Po Valley landholders not only provided money but actually participated in the movement. As Cardoza's detailed study of the province of Bologna demonstrates, the large, commercially oriented landlords were the most pivotal group in influencing the direction of events in the Po Valley.[98] Their support for authoritarianism was clearly motivated by the threat to their control of labor represented by the tremendous thrust of union organization and socialist victories in municipal elections after the war.

Thus, it would appear that the Italian case fits Moore's argument quite well. However, while it most decidedly is true that the landlords' mode of labor control was an important source of their opposition to democracy, it is not correct to characterize the Po Valley landlords' method of labor control as labor-repressive in Moore's sense. Rural labor was formally free in the period immediately preceding the transition to democracy. Moreover, there were no effective means of limiting labor mobility, such as the crop lien system, debt peonage, and the restraints on labor recruitment enforced in the postbellum American South. On the other hand, organization of rural labor was difficult under prevailing political conditions and rural labor had no effective suffrage rights. The introduction of democracy changed the situation radically in ways that challenged the traditional mode of labor control. Rural labor now had rights to organize that were enforced by the state. In many localities, the parties representing the interests of rural labor (the Socialists and, in Italy, also the Populari) controlled local government. The local state intervened on the side of rural labor, upholding the right to organize, enforcing labor contracts, and so on. The counterreaction of landlords was strongly to support an end to the political system that brought these problems. What this example shows is that methods of labor control cannot be categorized into a simple dichotomy even when one's sole interest is predicting the posture of landlords toward various forms of political organization. There is a wide spectrum of political and organizational rights compatible with market control of labor.

Recent work on German history by Blackbourn and Eley and Calleo attacks what they see as the dominant view in current historical thinking on German political development, including that of Moore.[99] However, it is probably fair to say that they would not contest the assertion, common to the dominant view, that historically an alliance developed between the East Elbian landed upper class, the Junkers, and the Prussian state, and that the political leadership of unified Germany after 1870 depended on this alliance for its key political support. In the wake of the depression of 1873, the heavy industry segment of the bourgeoisie, particularly the coal and steel interests, joined the coalition, with the tariffs of 1879 and later the naval armaments program consolidating the coalition. Moreover, their disagreement with Moore focuses on the strength and dependence of the bourgeoisie. They do not contest the argument that the Junkers were very politically influential and their politics extremely antidemocratic and that their posture contributed to the maintenance of the authoritarian state in the imperial period and the breakdown of the democratic state in the Weimar period.

The motivation for the antidemocratic posture of the Junkers has been a point of contention. Skocpol points out that, by 1820, East Elbian agriculture was dependent on hired labor and this dependence increased throughout the century.[100] It is almost certainly true that for the period up to World War I tax exemptions and benefits, subsidized credits, and, above all, tariffs were the dominant economic concerns of the Junkers.[101] However, labor control did not disappear from the agenda. By the Imperial German period, the introduction of agricultural machinery and the intensification of agriculture had introduced a strong seasonal demand for labor. The landlords satisfied this by hiring migrant workers from Russian Poland and Austrian Galacia. Out of fear that this would strengthen the Poles in Prussia,

Bismarck expelled them and closed the border in 1886. Due to political pressure from large landlords this ban was soon lifted. As a result, the number of Polish seasonal workers entering Germany increased from seventeen thousand in 1890 to three hundred thousand in 1902 and continued to increase thereafter.[102] During the Weimar Republic, by contrast, the economic policies of the Junkers and their chosen political instrument, the Deutschnationale Volkspartei, focused almost solely on tariffs, opposition to Social Democratic social welfare policies (Sozialpolitik), and support for subsidies to indebted estates (Osthilfe). Labor control was not an important issue.

Of the other European breakdown cases, the Austrian appears to be closest to the German. Certainly, the class-state constellations in the eighteenth and nineteenth century are quite similar. The basic state alliance was also between the Crown, the army (which was very closely identified with the Habsburg monarchy), the bureaucratic elite, and the landed nobility. The ethnic divisions within the empire and later Austria-Hungary divided the nobility and often set the non-German nationalities, particularly the Magyar magnates, against the monarchy, but as Taylor emphasizes, when they had to choose between defending their class privileges and advancing claims for national autonomy, they virtually always chose the former.[103] The system of labor control in the countryside can be accurately labeled labor-repressive: though Joseph II abolished true serfdom, the Robot, or obligatory labor service, which remained in effect until 1848, was actually the more critical provision in limiting labor mobility.[104] And even in the post-Robot period, the great lords remained the predominant power in the countryside. Indeed, they gained at the expense of the minor noble landholders. There is no doubt that labor control in the Hungarian half of the Dual Monarchy was labor-repressive even in Moore's restrictive sense into the twentieth century. For instance, the Hungarian Agricultural Labor Act of 1898 "outlawed agricultural strikes, made agricultural laborers criminally liable for breaches of seasonal contracts, and further provided that fugitive laborers be returned to their place of work by the gendarmerie."[105] A similar measure was passed in Romania.

The Austrian case differs from the German in that the landed upper classes themselves played little active role in the interwar events, though what contributions they did make were supportive of authoritarian forces.[106] The reason for this is that, compared to other regions in Austria-Hungary, German Austria contained a disproportionate amount of the mountainous areas, which were predominantly smallholding. The contribution of the landed upper classes to the breakdown of Austrian democracy was primarily an indirect effect of their shaping the ideology of the predominant party of the Right, the Christian Socials. As Lipset and Rokkan argue, this party was a product of the historical alliance of the Habsburg state and the landed oligarchs with the Catholic Church.[107] It represented a fusion of the organized Catholic institutional culture with this elite alliance, with the latter group defining the class character of the Catholic camp's political ideology. It was the Christian Socials who engineered the coup of 1934. The goal was not rural labor control nor any other motive of the by now relatively weak landed upper class, but rather the exclusion of the Social Democrats from the political system.

There is no doubt that landholding in absolutist Spain was extremely concentrated: the nobility and the church held over two-thirds of the land in the country.[108] In the course of the nineteenth century, a political coalition of forces gradually assembled around the Moderado Liberal (later dynastic Conservative) Party that did resemble Moore's authoritarian coalition.[109] There is little question that landlords, both aristocratic and bourgeois, were politically conservative to reactionary. It is also arguable that in the latifundia districts their antidemocratic posture was motivated in part by their need for a large supply of cheap labor. Whether the form of labor control was labor-repressive is debatable. It certainly approached that in Andalusia and Estramadura in the first half of the nineteenth century, where the local landlords and their allies controlled municipal government, which "was central to [their] power: as municipal oligarchs they controlled wages, prices, and the letting of municipal commons in their own interests."[110]

Even more than in Italy, the immediate reaction of the upper classes in Spain to the threat represented by the political mobilization and trade union organization of the working class and landless agricultural workers was a central, if not the central, dynamic in the breakdown of the democratic regime.[111] Not only did large estates dominate the countryside more than in the other European cases discussed here, it was also a very heavily agricultural country. Thus, it is not surprising that the agrarian question was the focal point of class conflict during the Second Republic and that the landlords emerged as among the most implacable opponents of the Republic.

Unquestionably, labor control was a central issue in the conflict. Before the republican government even presented its modest land reform program, the provisional government passed legislation that radically changed the operation of local labor markets in ways that benefitted agricultural workers and tenants and incurred the hostility of the large landholders. These laws protected the rights of tenants, limited the workday to eight hours, established arbitration boards to mediate labor disputes, and forbade employers from recruiting labor outside of a given municipality before the local supply of labor was exhausted. Malefakis contends that together these laws "constituted a revolution without precedent in Spanish rural life. For the first time the balance of legal rights swung away from the landowners to the rural proletariat."[112] As in the Italian case, democracy radically changed the parameters within which labor market conflicts were carried out. It was this transition rather than one from political restrictions on labor mobility to free labor markets that was the source of landlord grievances.

The development of agrarian class relations in Portugal closely parallels that of Spain. Though the liberal regime of the 1830s had in principal freed both land and labor, remnants of the traditional system of labor control (*enfiteuse*) remained until the advent of the republic in 1910.[113] In the initial years of the Portuguese Republic, events developed as they had in Spain; wide suffrage rights incorporated a large proportion of the adult male population (literate males and all heads of households), and the institution of the right to organize was met with a wave of strikes, rural as well as urban. However, unlike Spain, the Republicans then reversed some of these reforms, by restricting the suffrage to literate males only, thus excluding virtually all peasants and many workers, and by siding with employers in labor market disputes.[114]

Despite these changes the Portuguese landed aristocracy remained "the greatest reservoir of antirepublican sentiment."[115] This sentiment was motivated by two sets of economic grievances: wheat prices and labor control. The Republican governments' periodic attempts to provide urban dwellers with cheap bread pitted them against landowners on issues such as agricultural tariffs. The threat to traditional forms of labor control was in part a product of economic modernization and the consequent opportunities for urban employment opened up for rural workers. But it also was a product of legislation and proposed legislation introduced during the Republic, moderate though this was when compared to Spain. This legislation included the rights of rural workers to organize, tenancy laws, and land reform schemes that proposed the redistribution of unutilized land to the landless, thus removing them from the supply of rural labor. Significantly, proposed land reform legislation preceded the military coup of 1917 and that of 1926 (which ended the Republic), and in both cases landowners actively supported the coups.

Moore ends his discussion of France with the French Revolution. He argues that the outcome of the French Revolution was decisive for the development of democracy in France because it destroyed the seigneurial system and the political power of the landed aristocracy.[116] He then correctly notes that the Restoration returned political power to this class, but since it did not move to share it with the upper bourgeoisie, its period in power was necessarily limited. The Revolution of 1830 then finished the work of the Great Revolution and the "old aristocracy disappeared from the political arena as a coherent and effective political group."[117]

In its broad outlines, Moore's analysis is correct, but it exaggerates the demise of the political power of the nobility in this period. It should be noted that, due to developments before the Revolution, peasant property was widespread, if insecure, before that event. The redistribution of noble land effected by the Revolution was not great; emigré nobles were expropriated and thus the total amount of French land owned by the nobility dropped from one-quarter to one-fifth.[118] One must add to this the church lands expropriated in 1790 and sold to the highest bidder. Naturally most of this land went to the wealthy bourgeoisie and not to peasants, but there is no question that many peasants did benefit from the land reform. More important for the peasantry was the guaranteeing of property rights and thus the securing of peasant property and the abolition of seigneurial rights. As late as the 1870s, Republican politicians used the threat that seigneurial rights would be reimposed as a potent political weapon to woo the peasantry.[119] The abolition of seigneurial rights also meant that landlords who wanted to make a living from the land would have to turn to commercial market agriculture. As transportation improved throughout the century, especially with the advent of railroads, this was even more emphatically so. The Revolution also dislodged the aristocracy from its privileged position in the army and bureaucracy.

The political influence of the French landed upper class declined throughout the nineteenth century, but it continued to be a significant political actor at least to the first decade of the Third Republic. Yet France did become democratic in this period. Was this in part because the landlords turned to commercialized agriculture? The fact that they continued to align themselves with the most conservative and antidemocratic forces in the political struggles of the century suggests that this was not the primary reason. One answer is that the landed upper class was too weak. It is certainly true that France in this period was an intermediate case between the small democracies of Europe and the authoritarian states, both in terms of the proportion of land controlled by large landlords and in terms of the political power of landlords. Second, the bourgeoisie and the traditional nobility were deeply divided politically, and even the bourgeoisie itself was divided on the very question of the desirability of democratic government. Third, and perhaps most important, by the end of the Orleanist monarchy, the aristocracy had lost its enclave in the army and the bureaucracy. Thus, Moore's authoritarian coalition of the state, landed upper class, and nobility did not materialize in late-nineteenth-century France.

Moore attributes the democratic trajectory of Britain in large part to the successful adaptation of the landed upper class to commercialized agriculture and to the elimination of the peasantry as a result of the turn to sheep raising. A variety of alternative interpretations of the British path to democracy have been offered by various authors and it is impossible to mediate this debate here.[120] Suffice it to say that the political representatives of the landed upper class, the Tories and then the Conservatives, were considerably less resistant to democratic reform than their counterparts elsewhere in Europe, even sponsoring a major suffrage extension in 1867, and it is at least plausible to argue that this flexible posture was facilitated by the absence of a need for coercive labor control on the part of landlords.

British Settler Colonies

Two of the four British settler colonies, Canada and New Zealand, were predominantly smallholding. They both experienced smooth transitions to democracy. In the Canadian case family farmers played an essential, and positive, role in the transition to democracy. In New Zealand, democratic forms were established virtually at the outset of colonization.

The United States and Australia, by contrast, were characterized by the existence of large estates engaged in labor-repressive agriculture. The labor control systems were clearly labor-repressive in Moore's sense. Until the 1840s, Australian sheep ranches and runs relied on assigned convict labor.[121] The defeat of the American South marked only a temporary hiatus in the labor-repressive system. It was reestablished in the form of debt peonage and the crop lien system.[122] In both cases, the landlords were opposed to democracy and there is no doubt that this was motivated in large part by their desire to defend the system of labor control. Yet democracy was apparently established in both countries over their opposition. In both countries, the inability of the landlords to control the central state is the key to the landlords' political failure. In Australia, the colonial state sided with the landlords' opponents, ending the system of convict transportation and assignment and establishing parliamentary government with relatively wide suffrage.

In the United States, the victory of democracy was more apparent than real. It was not victorious in the South. When the development of populism, which initially was multiracial, began to threaten the new system of labor control, southern state governments moved to exclude Blacks, who formed the bulk of the rural labor force, from the political system. This process was completed by the first decade of the twentieth century and this political system was not dismantled until the 1960s, by which time agricultural modernization had greatly reduced the labor needs of southern landlords.[123] The U.S. case shows once more that landlords need not control the national state in order to operate a system of repressive labor control. Control of the local state coupled with noninterference from the national state is sufficient.

Japan

All five of the cases of modern capitalist authoritarianism examined in this section fit Moore's analysis insofar as all five of them did have a significant and politically influential class of large landlords into the modern era. Ironically, Japan, the one case discussed extensively by Moore, does not fit this characterization.[124] A powerful bureaucratic and military state, created in part in response to outside threats, not a powerful landed upper class, is the root of Japanese authoritarianism.[125] This state directed industrialization from above and created a bourgeoisie dependent on the state for its very existence. The military retained tremendous formal governmental power even during the period of Taisho democracy in the twenties, and when the political agenda of the bourgeois politicians threatened the military's own project, it moved to eliminate party government.

Dore and Ouchi ask the more modest question of why the army's drive to internal power and external expansion was not resisted by other elites, including the landlords.[126] Landlords not only did not resist the army's power grab but on balance were supportive of it. However, the landlords' support for the army did not arise out of their needs for labor control. More recent scholarship[127] does not support Moore's view that agrarian class relations in Japan after the Meiji Restoration were labor-repressive.[128] In the initial years after the Restoration, landlords relied on traditional paternalism to control their tenants, but this system eroded as industrialization created more options for rural labor in urban employment and for landlords in industrial investment. By the twenties, landlords were eager to get out of agriculture. In 1927, a group of landlords in the House of Peers, acting with the support of the Japan Landlord's Association, issued three proposals for land reform, all of which called for the state to purchase at least all tenanted farm land at current market prices.[129] To the extent that there was an economic basis for landlord support of authoritarianism in the 1930s, it was due to the army's support of the landlords' demand for curtailing rice imports. The army desired self-sufficiency, and the landlords, higher rice prices.

As mentioned at the outset of this section, political developments in eastern Europe in the interwar period were heavily influenced by the crumbling of three empires at the close of World War I. Alapuro's analysis of Finland and comparison with elsewhere in eastern Europe underlines the importance of the state's sudden loss of the means of coercion at the time of the Russian Revolution for the subsequent development of these countries.[130] At the same time, he also confirms the importance of agrarian class relations for the different outcomes in different countries. The existence of a powerful landed upper class was a barrier to the introduction of democracy in Poland, Hungary, Latvia, and Estonia.

Conclusion

In surveying the evidence from the Latin American cases we can say that Moore was correct in seeing traditional large landowners as basically antidemocratic. In all cases they attempted to restrict the rights of the rural population in various ways, attempts that are clearly incompatible with democracy as a system of rule with equal rights for all. The problem of labor control was important but not precisely in the sense indicated by Moore. Landlords who were dependent on a large labor force were more resolutely authoritarian than landlords who were not. Large landowners in Uruguay and Argentina who were ranchers, and the Costa Rican coffee elite whose main profits came from processing and trade, were less intransigent to the installation of democracy than their counterparts in other countries. However, among the landlords who did need a large labor force, the use of actual restrictions on labor mobility, the classical case of politically backed labor coercion in Moore's sense, was not very widespread. In many cases rural labor was governed by a labor market, but under conditions highly unfavorable for labor. The key to keeping rural labor abundant and cheap was the closing off of alternatives to estate labor, most prominently access to land and water, and the prevention of rural organization.

Political action on the part of large landlords was shaped by the perceived immediacy of the threat to their control of land and access to labor. In part, this threat depended on the historical stength of peasant communities and their impact on the strength of rural social movements, in part it depended on the degree of industrialization reached and the spillover of mobilization from the urban to the rural sector, and in part it depended on concrete actions of governments. The stronger these threats, the more likely landlords were to seek to influence and ultimately control the central state and enlist its support in the repression of social movements and the solidification of the landlord control of land. A few examples illustrate this point well. Mexican landlords in Morelos were unambiguous in their search for assistance from a strong central authoritarian state in the nineteenth century. Peruvian landlords, in contrast, relied primarily on their own coercive resources until rural mobilization intensified in the 1960s. Chilean landlords tolerated restricted democracy from the 1930s to the early 1970s, but when they began to feel acutely threatened by rural mobilization and the actions of the Unidad Popular government, they called for state repression. Landlords in Brazil did not have to forge a reactionary coalition at the national level before the late 1950s, given the weakness of pressures from below.

The political outcomes of landlord attempts to enlist the support of the state in keeping rural labor in a disadvantaged position also differed in important ways from Moore's path to modern authoritarianism. The composition of the reactionary coalition was different from the one in Moore's cases. The nature of the bourgeoisie and of the state itself was different, and foreign capital was an important coalition partner, albeit an informal one. In most cases, landlords were closely linked to the financial and commercial bourgeoisie, and in many cases even to the emerging industrial bourgeoisie. They either diversified their own holdings to participate in these other sectors, or they had family ties to other sectors. To the extent that an industrial bourgeoisie emerged independent of the landed class, it tended to do so late and to be weak. In Moore's scenario, the question of the strength of the bourgeoisie is problematic, but he indicates that it had to be of intermediate strength in order to be a worthwhile ally for the landed classes and the state. Whereas foreign capital could substitute for a domestic bourgeoisie, to some extent, in strengthening the commercial impulse (an important indicator of the strength of the bourgeoisie for Moore), it could not do so as a domestic political actor.

In Moore's cases, the state is a monarchical, well-consolidated state. In many Latin American cases, state power was not consolidated before the period of export expansion. To some extent, of course, the two processes were interactive, in that the delayed consolidation of state power made it more difficult for landlords to take advantage of expanding world market opportunities, and export expansion made resources available that facilitated the consolidation of state power. The state needed to provide the infrastructure for expanding trade, particularly in transport, which was difficult to do as long as armed challenges called for a diversion of resources to the building of a strong central army. Without adequate transport facilities and faced with the threat of damages to their lands from armed confrontations, landlords were unwilling to make the investments necessary to respond to growing world market demand. On the other hand, in some cases export expansion did take place before the consolidation of state power and then provided the state with revenues to achieve consolidation. This occurred, for instance, in areas with a natural transportation advantage, such as the coastal areas of Uruguay, or in areas that were less affected by the struggles for power at the center, such as the north and south of Mexico. In Uruguay, export expansion took place in the last two decades of the nineteenth century, despite the continuation of civil wars until the first decade of the twentieth century. In Mexico, export expansion in the north and south began before Díaz consolidated political power and greatly reduced armed challenges to the state in central Mexico. In Venezuela and Peru, in contrast, significant export expansion did not begin until the political instability resulting from strong intra-elite rivalries and involvement in wars was brought to an end. Where state power was not consolidated, the state could not function as a strong and reliable ally for the landed class.

One case that appears to come close to Moore's scenario is the alliance between the state and landowners in Brazil under the Old Republic. However, even here there are two important and interrelated differences; state power was highly decentralized and the state elite did not have a project of modernization from above. Other cases that suggest parallels to Moore are the bureaucratic authoritarian regimes.[131] Certainly landlords, along with the rest of the economically dominant classes, supported the coups that ushered in the bureaucratic authoritarian regimes. However, landlords as a class were not important partners in the bureaucratic authoritarian coalition. To the extent that the bureaucratic authoritarian regimes were based on a coalition with economically dominant classes, their base was the internationalized section of the bourgeoisie. Foreign capital was an important economic partner, but for obvious reasons not part of a governing coalition. The main base of the bureaucratic authoritarian regimes was in the military as an institution, and they received strong support from higher-level technocratic state personnel. The military had acquired a high degree of autonomy from domestic social classes, at least in part due to external support and training. Thus, when the military established the bureaucratic authoritarian regimes in Brazil, Argentina, Chile, and Uruguay, it ruled largely without formally consulting organized interests, even those of the economically dominant classes. This was particularly true in the early periods of consolidation of the bureaucratic authoritarian regimes, when the initial support coalitions disintegrated under the effects of orthodox economic stabilization policies imposed by the regimes in close collaboration with international financial institutions.[132] Bureaucratic authoritarianism, then, is a distinctively modern regime form characteristic of countries in a dependent position in the world economy and the world system of states. Moore made it very clear that he was not interested in countries whose political dynamics were shaped in essential ways by foreign influences.

Corresponding to the differences in the nature of the state and the alliance possibilities for forming a reactionary coalition, the forms of authoritarianism that resulted were different from those in Moore's cases. Latin American authoritarian regimes established by some form of reactionary coalition of landlords, the bourgeoisie, and the state tended to be weaker; they controlled their societies to a lesser extent, and their hold on power was less secure. Only in the Mexican case under Díaz did the coalition have a project of modernization from above.[133] Also, the element of mass mobilization "to make reaction popular" was completely absent. In many cases, particularly in the mineral export economies where radical mass parties managed to mobilize sectors of the middle and working classes into an alliance demanding democratic rights for the majority, authoritarian regimes dominated by reactionary coalitions alternated with more open regimes dominated by representatives of the middle and sometimes even working classes.[134] The vulnerability of authoritarian regimes and the frequency of political changes confirm that it is more useful to conceptualize the political consequences of agrarian class relations in Latin America as more authoritarian versus more democratic political trajectories, rather than as specific regime forms.

The question of the landed upper class's relation to the state also proved pivotal in the historical experience of the countries outside of Latin

America reviewed here. In the post-Emancipation period in the English-speaking Caribbean, the economically dominant planter class was dependent on a large supply of cheap labor and did rely on political methods, though short of actually binding labor to the land, to assure itself of this essential factor of production. However, the colonial power and not the local planters ultimately held the reins of state power. Thus, in the 1930s, when the British government became unwilling to support repression, the path toward democratic development opened up.

The political development of advanced capitalist countries also provides support for Moore's thesis on the role of large landholders in the development of modern authoritarianism. All of the countries that lacked a powerful landed upper class experienced a relatively smooth transition to democracy. Conversely, in every country, save one, with a powerful landed upper class in the nineteenth century, that class adopted a strongly anti-democratic posture. In Britain, the one exception, the landed upper class supported a party that sponsored a major suffrage reform. Moore's contention that the British landlords were able to do this because they did not depend on a large supply of cheap labor and repressive methods of labor control is certainly a very plausible explanation for this exception.

The development of the remaining five European countries would appear to conform to Moore's expectations. (1) The landed upper class was an essential element of the political coalition underpinning the traditional monarchical authoritarian regime of the nineteenth century; (2) the landed upper class relied on political methods to assure itself of a supply of cheap labor, which arguably was one reason for its opposition to democracy; and (3) after a more or less democratic hiatus in the early twentieth century, democracy gave way to a modern form of authoritarianism. However, labor control was not an issue in the democratic breakdown in two of the countries, Germany and Austria, and in Austria the landed upper class made only an indirect contribution to the breakdown. Moreover, though rural labor control was central to the dynamics of democratic collapse in Spain, Italy, and, to a lesser extent, Portugal, the system of rural labor control prior to the democratic period was not clearly labor-repressive in Moore's sense. However, it is correct to say that democracy, along with the rights of rural workers and tenants to unionize and organize politically, was a threat to that system of labor control, and thus labor control was a source of landlords' aggressive antidemocratic posture.

The two British settler colonies that did have very significant landed upper classes, the United States and Australia, again demonstrate the importance of the landlord-state relationship. Developments in Australia closely parallel events in the West Indies one hundred years later. The colonial power aligned with other social forces in the colony against the landlords' attempt to continue the labor-repressive system and thus brought about its demise. Moore's analysis of the United States is flawed by his treatment of the American state as being essentially analogous to the centralized national states of Europe. The decentralization of the American state allowed the reimposition of a labor-repressive system and authoritarian politics in the South after a brief hiatus. As in some of the Latin American cases, the control of local coercive power was sufficient to buttress the system of labor control.

Finally, we argued that the development of modern authoritarianism in Japan does not conform to Moore's authoritarian path, which is ironic given that it is one example of that path discussed at length in the book. Though Japanese landlords were antidemocratic, labor control was not a central issue in their political grievances, and the landlords' importance for the installation of Japanese fascism was, in any case, at best secondary.

To conclude, our analysis has demonstrated that landlords were important actors in the political development of their countries and that the nature of labor relations was an important factor shaping their political behavior. Where access to cheap labor was important, which was the case for most kinds of large-scale agricultural production, landlords played a predominantly antidemocratic role. Our analysis has also shown, though, that regime forms are the result of complex interactions between sectors of economically dominant classes, the state, and subordinate classes. Class and class-state constellations in turn are heavily shaped by a country's position in the world economic and political system and thus are necessarily different in Latin America from the way they were during comparable stages of development in advanced industrial countries.

Among the Latin American countries, we have found different forms of authoritarian rule and different paths to modern authoritarianism. One form of authoritarian trajectory consisted of a combination of political instability and personalistic dictatorship and was the result of an intense struggle for control of the state among different factions of economic elites that appealed for military support. This form was typical of countries where economic elites were very heterogeneous and not very prosperous (e.g., Venezuela). Another form consisted of a combination of severely restricted democracy at the center with de facto authoritarianism at the local level under landlord domination and was the result of an alliance between the hegemonic faction of the economic elites, the military, and in some cases the middle classes. This type emerged in countries where landed elites were prosperous either because they controlled the crucial export sector (e.g., Brazil) or because they had diversified their holdings into other sectors (e.g., Chile). A third form of authoritarianism, bureaucratic authoritarianism, consisted of rule by the military as an institution and was the result of the growing autonomy of the military from domestic social forces in the context of intensifying social conflict and external support for the military. In these cases, landlords contributed to the installation of authoritarianism by calling for military intervention to keep popular mobilization in check, but they did not participate in the exercise of political power. This last form conforms most clearly to Moore's notion of modern authoritarianism, in the sense that it was a reaction to the attempted entry of the masses into politics. However, the other two forms also persisted into the stage of popular mobilization; the first dealt with such mobilization by generalized repression and the second primarily by the repression of rural mobilization.

Our analysis, then, agrees with Skocpol's critique of Moore's work concerning the need to conceptualize more precisely the potentially autonomous role of the state and the impact of a country's position in the international economic and political system in explaining the trajectories toward democracy or authoritarianism.[135] However, it also underlines the great value of Moore's work, which lies in drawing our attention to the importance of agrarian class relations and of the relationship between landed elites, the bourgeoisie, and the state in the process of modernization for an understanding of political outcomes. In our search for a general theoretical understanding of the chances for democracy to develop and be consolidated, his work teaches us to remain sensitive to historical contingencies and multiple paths to the same outcome.

NOTES

1. Certainly, in Latin America we can find authoritarian populist systems that were more including in economic and social terms than formal democracies. However, we are prepared to argue that in the long run the existence of formal democracy is a precondition for economic and social inclusion of popular sectors.

2. Jonathan M. Wiener, "Review of Social Origins of Dictatorship and Democracy," *History and Theory* 15, no. 2 (1976): 146–75.

3. John Lynch, *Argentine Dictator: Juan Manuel de Rosas, 1829–1852* (Oxford: Clarendon, 1981), 104–05.

4. Ibid., 309, 296.

5. Leopoldo Allub, "Las clases altas terratenientes y el desarrollo del capitalismo en el campo argentino," *Orígenes del autoritarismo en America Latina*, ed. Leopoldo Allub (Mexico, D.F.: Editorial Katun, 1983), 83.

6. One could read Halperín as saying that Argentine landlords might have wanted to exercise a more organic control over the countryside but could never achieve that, though they were recognized as the most prominent social group. This was certainly the case in the 1920s, when the electoral weakness of the Conservatives became obvious. However, one still has to explain why the landlords did not muster all their resources to mount resistance at the national level against the introduction of democracy. The point is that democratization posed less of a threat to them than to their counterparts in other countries, where cheap agricultural labor was a crucial precondition for economic prosperity.

7. David Rock, *Politics in Argentina 1890–1930: The Rise and Fall of Radicalism* (Cambridge: Cambridge University Press, 1975); and Peter Smith, "The Breakdown of Democracy in Argentina 1916–1930," in *The Breakdown of Democratic Regimes*, ed. Juan Linz and Alfred Stepan (Baltimore: Johns Hopkins University Press, 1978), both discuss the developments leading up to the coup of 1930.

8. John Coatsworth, "Orígenes del autoritarismo moderno en México," *Orígines del autoritarismo en América Latina*, ed. Leopoldo Allub (Mexico, D.F.: Editorial Katun, 1983).

9. Julio Cotler, "Traditional Haciendas and Communities in a Context of Political Mobilization in Peru," in *Agrarian Problems and Peasant Movements in Latin America*, ed. Rodolfo Stavenhagen (Garden City, N.Y.: Doubleday Anchor, 1970). There were some periods with restricted democracy, but when popular mobilization began to threaten the interests of the reactionary coalition, these periods all ended in military coups. See Cynthia McClintock, "Peru: Precarious Regimes, Authoritarian and Democratic," in *Democracy in Developing Countries: Latin America*, vol. 4, ed. Larry Diamond, Juan J. Linz, and Seymour Martin Lipset (Boulder, Colo.: Lynne Rienner, 1989), for an overview of political dynamics and regimes.

10. Karen Remmer, *Party Competition and Public Policy: Argentina and Chile, 1890–1930* (Lincoln: University of Nebraska Press, 1984); and Arturo Valenzuela, *Political Brokers in Chile: Local Government in a Centralized Polity* (Durham, N.C.: Duke University Press).

11. For discussions of the military's role in politics in this period, see Paul W. Drake, *Socialism and Populism in Chile, 1932–52* (Urbana: University of Illinois Press, 1978), particularly pp. 47–70; and Frederick M. Nunn, *Chilean Politics 1920–1931: The Honorable Mission of the Armed Forces* (Albuquerque: University of New Mexico Press, 1970).

12. Charles Bergquist, *Labor in Latin America: Comparative Essays on Chile, Argentina, Venezuela, and Colombia* (Stanford: Stanford University Press, 1986), 280.

13. See also Charles Bergquist, *Coffee and Conflict in Colombia, 1886–1910* (Durham, N.C.: Duke University Press, 1978), 27.

14. Bergquist, *Labor*, 317.

15. See also ibid., 314–16.

16. Bergquist, in *Coffee and Conflict*, makes a different argument with regard to the late nineteenth century, insofar as he identifies the emerging class of large coffee planters as Liberals, but on p. 258 he agrees that the coffee economy became bipartisan in the twentieth century.

17. See the sources cited by Safford, as well as Bergquist, *Labor*, 332–42.

18. Paul Oquist, *Violence, Conflict, and Politics in Colombia* (New York: Academic, 1980), 104, states that the entire period 1930–1946 was characterized by widespread electoral fraud and coercion, which were accepted as a fact of political life. Moreover, in some municipalities the parties concluded pacts and fixed elections accordingly.

19. Bergquist, *Labor*, 355.

20. For a discussion of labor-repressive practices on traditional haciendas as well as on coastal plantations in Ecuador, see Osvaldo Hurtado, "El proceso político," in *Ecuador, hoy*, 2d ed., ed. Gerhard Drekonja et al. (Bogotá: Siglo Veintiuno Editores, 1981), 166–69. In Brazil there was only one rural union by

1935, and rural unionization remained all but impossible until the 1950s because of the difficulties in getting legal recognition; see Clodomir Moraes, "Peasant Leagues in Brazil," in *Agrarian Problems and Peasant Movements in Latin America,* ed. Rodolfo Stavenhagen (Garden City, N.Y.: Doubleday Anchor, 1970), 455–58.

21. In Brazil and Ecuador there were periods of constitutional oligarchic rule, from 1889 to 1930 in Brazil and from 1916 to 1925 in Ecuador.

22. Richard Alan White, "La política economica del Paraguay popular (1810–1840)," *Estudios Paraguayos* 10 (1975); 12 (1976); cited in Frieder Schmelz, *Paraguay im 19. Jahrhundert* (Heidelberg: Esprint Verlag, 1981), 54.

23. Schmelz, *Paraguay,* 54.

24. According to the 1942–1944 agricultural census, less than one-fifth of farmers were proprietors of the land they worked, and even fewer paid rent; over 60 percent were simply squatters. An impression of the concentration of property in ranching is given by the 1949 figures, which indicate that some 25,000 stockmen owned a total of 364,000 heads of cattle, whereas 12 owners with more than 20,000 head each had a total of 528,000 head. See George Pendle, *Paraguay: A Riverside Nation* (London: Royal Institute of International Affairs, 1954), 59–61, 66.

25. Ibid., 66–67; Ramón Fogel, "La estructura social Paraguaya y su incidencia en la transición a la democracia" (paper presented to the conference Democratization in Paraguay at the Kellogg Institute, University of Notre Dame, Notre Dame, Ind., December 1990).

26. Diego Abente, "Stronismo, Post-Stronismo, and the Prospects for Democratization in Paraguay," (Notre Dame: University of Notre Dame, Kellogg Institute Working Paper #119 (1990), 3, 44, n. 9.

27. Diego Abente, "The Historical Background" (paper presented to the conference Democratization in Paraguay, Kellogg Institute, University of Notre Dame, Notre Dame, Ind., December 1990).

28. Ibid.

29. For observations on the situation after the ouster of Stroessner in Paraguay, see Charles Gillespie, "Paraguay After Stroessner: Prospects for Democracy in a Dominant Party System" (manuscript, Department of Political Science, University of Wisconsin-Madison, November 1989).

30. Daniel Campos, "El movimiento campesino ante la crisis y la nueva coyuntura" (paper presented to the conference Democratization in Paraguay, Kellogg Institute, University of Notre Dame, Notre Dame, Ind., December 1990).

31. Rollie E. Poppino, *Brazil: The Land and People,* 2d ed. (New York: Oxford University Press, 1973), 225.

32. There is a debate about the relative autonomy of the Brazilian state before 1930, with one side arguing that landlords controlled the state and the other that state officials enjoyed a considerable degree of autonomy from all groups in society; see the review by Richard Graham, "State and Society in Brazil, 1822–1930," *Latin American Research Review* 22, no. 3 (1987): 223–36. Certainly, the policy output of the state appears to support the argument about landlord domination. At the very least, there was a close alliance and affinity of interests between state officials and landlords with regard to keeping lower sectors excluded from political participation.

33. Peter Flynn, *Brazil: A Political Analysis* (Boulder, Colo.: Westview, 1978),

59–62, argues that there was no shift in power from dominant to subordinate classes after 1930 but that the only major change was the strengthening of the central state and of the military. Thomas Skidmore, *Politics in Brazil 1930–1964: An Experiment in Democracy* (New York: Oxford University Press, 1967), provides a somewhat different view, but his analysis does not contradict the assessment of the antidemocratic influence of large landowners.

34. Philippe C. Schmitter, *Interest Conflict and Political Change in Brazil* (Stanford: Stanford University Press, 1971), 142–44.

35. Skidmore, *Politics in Brazil*, 18.

36. Ibid., 9–17.

37. Ibid., 13–14.

38. Ibid., 22–26.

39. Ibid., 26, 86, 169.

40. Kenneth Paul Erickson, *The Brazilian Corporative State and Working Class Politics* (Berkeley: University of California Press, 1977).

41. Skidmore, *Politics in Brazil*, 184, 228.

42. Ibid., 246–47, 280.

43. Alfred Stepan, *The Military in Politics: Changing Patterns in Brazil* (Princeton: Princeton University Press, 1971), particularly pp. 101–14.

44. Ibid., 158–62.

45. In this regard, it is instructive that a major effort to analyze the process of democratization does not contain any special discussion of the role of large landowners. See Alfred Stepan, ed., *Democratizing Brazil: Problems of Transition and Consolidation* (New York: Oxford University Press, 1989).

46. For background information on society and politics in Ecuador, see David Schodt, *Ecuador: An Andean Enigma* (Boulder, Colo.: Westview, 1987); and Osvaldo Hurtado, *Political Power in Ecuador* (Albuquerque: University of New Mexico Press, 1980).

47. Osvaldo Hurtado, "El proceso político," in *Ecuador, hoy*, 2d ed., Gerhard Drekonja et al. (Bogotá: Siglo Veintiuno Editores, 1981).

48. Agustín Cueva, *El proceso de dominación política en Ecuador* (Quito: Editorial America, n.d.).

49. Schodt, *Ecuador*, 56–57.

50. Ibid., 82–84.

51. Alberto Acosta, "Rasgos dominantes del crecimiento Ecuatoriano en las últimas décadas," in *Ecuador: El mito del desarrollo*, Alberto Acosta et al. (Quito: Editorial El Conejo, 1982), 31–34.

52. Schodt, *Ecuador*, 86–89.

53. Catherine M. Conaghan, "Party Politics and Democratization in Ecuador," in *Authoritarians and Democrats: Regime Transition in Latin America*, ed. James M. Malloy and Mitchell A. Seligson (Pittsburgh: University of Pittsburgh Press, 1987), 149–53.

54. For an analysis of rural conditions in Uruguay around the turn of the century, see José P. Barran and Benjamin Nahum, *Batlle, los estancieros y el imperio Británico*, vol. 2 (Montevideo: Ediciones de la Banda Oriental, 1981); or, by the same authors, *Historia Rural del Uruguay Moderno* (Montevideo: Ediciones de Banda Oriental, 1971).

55. Barran and Nahum, *Batlle*, 209–11.

56. See Benjamin Nahum, *Historia Uruguaya: La Epoca Batllista*, vol. 6, 1905–1930 (Montevideo: Ediciones de la Banda Oriental, 1977), 46–47, for the details on this land colonization policy.

57. Ibid., 64–71, 80.

58. Ibid., 81. See also Juan Rial, *Partidos políticos, democracia y autoritarismo*, vol. 1 (Montevideo: Centro de Informaciones y Estudios del Uruguay, Ediciones de la Banda Oriental, 1984), 15.

59. M. H. J. Finch, *A Political Economy of Uruguay since 1870* (New York: St. Martin's, 1981), 15.

60. For the alignments and effects of the coup, see Rial, *Partidos*, 15–16; and Finch, *Political Economy*, 15–17.

61. Rial, *Partidos*, 16–17, n. 12.

62. Rial, *Partidos*, 26, points out that in 1968 various new ministers were appointed with little political party activity but with close links to, or actual membership in, urban and rural capitalist ventures.

63. The fact that civilian technocrats played an important role in shaping economic policy does not mean that the economically dominant classes actually exercised any political power.

64. William Roseberry, *Coffee and Capitalism in the Venezuelan Andes* (Austin: University of Texas Press, 1983), 71–75.

65. Juan Bautista Fuenmayor, *Historia de la Venezuela política contemporanea 1899–1969*, 2d ed. (Caracas: 1978), 33–37; Roseberry, *Coffee and Capitalism*, 82–94.

66. John Duncan Powell, *Political Mobilization of the Venezuelan Peasant* (Cambridge: Harvard University Press, 1971), 15.

67. Ibid., 18–21.

68. Ibid., 45–49.

69. Terry Karl, "Petroleum and Political Pacts: The Transition to Democracy in Venezuela," in *Transitions from Authoritarian Rule: Latin America*, ed. Guillermo O'Donnell, Philippe Schmitter, and Laurence Whitehead (Baltimore: Johns Hopkins University Press, 1986).

70. Powell, *Political Mobilization*, 24–25.

71. Juan Bautista Fuenmayor, *Historia de la Venezuela política contemporanea 1899–1969*, 2d ed. (Caracas: 1978), 233–37.

72. Powell, *Political Mobilization*, 61.

73. Ibid., 68.

74. John D. Martz, *Acción Democrática: Evolution of a Modern Political Party in Venezuela* (Princeton: Princeton University Press, 1966), 81–89, discusses the policies and the emergence of the opposition that led to the decline of the first democratic regime in Venezuela. See also Powell, *Political Mobilization*.

75. Powell, *Political Mobilization*, 106–09.

76. Antonio García, "Agrarian Reform and Social Development in Bolivia," in *Agrarian Problems and Peasant Movements in Latin America*, ed. Rodolfo Stavenhagen (Garden City, N.Y.: Doubleday Anchor, 1970), 303–04. Olen E. Leonard, *Bolivia: Land, People and Institutions* (Washington, D.C.: Scarecrow, 1952), 116–17, gives a list of obligations of landlords and peasants.

77. Leonard, *Bolivia*, 188; and James Malloy, *Bolivia: The Uncompleted Revolution* (Pittsburgh: University of Pittsburgh Press, 1970), 34.

78. Malloy, *Bolivia*, 189–90, notes that "to speak of a prerevolutionary elite in Bolivia, to speak of an upper class, is to speak of land ownership"; and that "one simply was not accepted as a member of the elite until one had consolidated one's professional and political status . . . with the solidity of land." See p. 40 for the importance of conflicts among factions of the Bolivian economically dominant class.

79. For developments leading up to and following the 1952 revolution, see Malloy, *Bolivia;* and the essays in James Malloy and Richard Thorn, eds., *Beyond the Revolution: Bolivia since 1952* (Pittsburgh: University of Pittsburgh Press, 1971).

80. Malloy, *Bolivia*, 208, 212–13.

81. James M. Malloy, "Revolutionary Politics," in *Beyond the Revolution*, ed. James Malloy and Richard Thorn, (Pittsburgh: University of Pittsburgh Press, 1971), 144–45.

82. A sustained critique of this point in Moore is developed in Dietrich Rueschemeyer, Evelyne Huber Stephens, and John D Stephens, *Capitalist Development and Democracy* (London: Polity, and Chicago: University of Chicago Press), 1992. For Central America see Jeffery M. Paige, "The Social Origins of Dictatorship, Democracy and Socialist Revolution in Central America" (Ann Arbor: University of Michigan, CSST Working Paper #35, September 1989).

83. Some would argue that ethnic homogeneity/heterogeneity was largely responsible for the political contrast between Costa Rica, Argentina, and Uruguay on the one hand and most other Central and South American countries on the other hand. Rural class relations were less exploitative in the ethnically homogeneous countries (e.g., Mitchell Seligson, *Peasants of Costa Rica and the Development of Agrarian Capitalism* [Madison: University of Wisconsin Press, 1980], makes this argument for Costa Rica), and this presumably favored more democratic trajectories. It is certainly plausible that ethnic heterogeneity may aggravate exploitation and repression; for instance, it may increase the fear on the part of the dominant class of the possible solidarity of the oppressed. Moreover, it facilitates the legitimation of exploitation. However, this explanation cannot replace the one based on the importance of cheap labor for the prosperity of landlords. There are plenty of examples outside of Latin America where landlords exploited peasants of their own ethnic group, such as in the Po Valley and the south of Italy or the south of Spain. In the Latin American context, Chile is generally classified as an ethnically comparatively homogeneous country, but landlords were very exploitative and went to great lengths to keep control over their labor force by preventing access to alternative means of economic survival and unionization.

84. On the events of 1932, see Thomas Anderson, *Matanza: El Salvador's Communist Revolt of 1932* (Lincoln: University of Nebraska Press, 1971).

85. On the coup and the dynamics preceding and following it, see Stephen Schlesinger and Stephen Kinzer, *Bitter Fruit: The Untold Story of the American Coup in Guatemala* (Garden City, N.Y.: Doubleday, 1981); Richard H. Immerman, *The CIA in Guatemala: The Foreign Policy of Intervention* (Austin: University of Texas Press, 1982); and Thomas Melville and Marjorie Melville, *Guatemala: The Politics of Land Ownership* (New York: Free Press, 1971).

86. On El Salvador, see Enrique Baloyra, *El Salvador in Transition* (Chapel Hill: University of North Carolina Press, 1982).

87. On U.S. policy and its effects in Central America, see Walter LaFeber, *Inevitable Revolutions* (New York: Norton, 1983).

88. For analyses of recent political developments and their historical roots, see Robert Trudeau and Lars Schoultz, "Guatemala"; and Martin Diskin and Kenneth E. Sharpe, "El Salvador"; both in *Confronting Revolution: Security Through Diplomacy in Central America*, ed. Morris J. Blachman, William M. Leogrande, and Kenneth E. Sharpe (New York: Pantheon, 1986).

89. We explore this contrast at length in Rueschemeyer et al., *Capitalist Development*, chap. 6.

90. Franklin W. Knight, *The Caribbean: The Genesis of a Fragmented Nationalism*, 2d ed. (New York: Oxford University Press, 1990), 186ff.

91. Clive Y. Thomas, *Plantations, Peasants, and the State* (Los Angeles: Center for Afro-American Studies, University of California, Los Angeles, 1984), 16–26.

92. Hilary Beckles, *A History of Barbados: From Amerindian Settlement to Nation-State* (Cambridge: Cambridge University Press, 1990), 111–12.

93. The survival of democracy in several former British colonies has led some analysts to argue that British tutelage was responsible for this outcome. For instance, see Myron Weiner, "Empirical Democratic Theory," in *Competitive Elections in Developing Countries*, ed. Myron Weiner and Ergun Özbudun (Washington, D.C.: American Enterprise Institute, 1987), 3–34. We have dealt with this argument at length in Rueschemeyer et al., *Capitalist Development*, 228–29, 241–44, 280–81. Suffice it here to make the following brief points. The key for the survival of democracy lies in the balance of power within civil society and between civil society and the state. If this balance is unfavorable, external tutelage will not be able to consolidate democracy. The collapse of democracy in many former British colonies in Africa serves to support this point. British colonialism did make a contribution to democracy in the Caribbean in a much more roundabout way. It obstructed the emergence of a reactionary coalition between large landowners and the state, and thus allowed civil society to strengthen. By the time of independence, the Caribbean societies had firmly entrenched political parties and labor movements, which could provide a counterweight to the economically dominant classes, make a bid for political power, and thus prevent the political reexclusion of subordinate classes.

94. The lack of historical continuity of the central state in the new countries of Eastern Europe created out of the defeat of the Russian, German, and Austrian empires in World War I greatly complicates the analysis in these cases. They are discussed briefly at the conclusion of this section.

95. The virtually perfect correlation between country size and landlord strength is no accident. As Tilly points out, military success was one factor that distinguished successful state consolidation from the unsuccessful attempts, and success in war was greatly facilitated by "strong coalitions between the central power and major segments of the landed elite" (Charles Tilly, "Reflections on the History of European State-Making," in *The Formation of National States in Western Europe*, ed. Charles Tilly [Princeton: Princeton University Press, 1975] 40–44). The small states only avoided being gobbled up by reason of geography (Scandinavia), the operation of the interstate system from the Treaty of Westphalia onward (especially Belgium and Netherlands), or both (Switzerland).

96. We examine these cases in more detail in Rueschemeyer et al., *Capitalist Development*, 85–87, 91–98.

97. Francis G. Castles, "Barrington Moore's Thesis and Swedish Political Development," *Government and Opposition* 8, no. 3 (1973): 313–31; Timothy Tilton, "The Social Origins of Liberal Democracy: The Swedish Case," *American Political Science Review* 68, no. 2 (1974): 561–71; and Jonathan Tumin, "Pathways to Democracy: A Critical Revision of Barrington Moore's Theory of Democratic Emergence and an Application of the Revised Theory to the Case of Nether-lands" (Ph.D. diss., Harvard University, 1978). This is summarized in Jonathan Tumin, "The Theory of Democratic Development: A Critical Revision," *Theory and Society* 11, no. 2 (1982): 143–63.

98. Anthony L. Cardoza, *Agrarian Elites and Italian Fascism: The Province of Bologna, 1901–1926* (Princeton: Princeton University Press, 1982). Also see Paul Corner, *Fascism in Ferrara 1915–1925* (London: Oxford University Press, 1975).

99. David Blackbourn and Geoff Eley, *The Peculiarities of German History: Bourgeois Society and Politics in Nineteenth-Century Germany* (Oxford: Oxford University Press, 1984); and David Calleo, *The German Problem Reconsidered: Germany and the World Order, 1870 to the Present* (Cambridge: Cambridge University Press, 1978).

100. Theda Skocpol, "A Critical Review of Barrington Moore's Social Origins of Dictatorship and Democracy," *Politics and Society* 4, no. 1 (1973): 1–34.

101. Hans Ulrich Wehler, *The German Empire, 1871–1918* (Dover, N.H.: Berg, 1985), 10–14, 44–47.

102. Hajo Holborn, *A History of Modern Germany 1840–1945* (Princeton: Princeton University Press, 1969), 373–74.

103. A. J. P. Taylor, *The Habsburg Monarchy, 1809–1918: A History of the Austrian Empire and Austria-Hungary* (Chicago: University of Chicago Press, 1976).

104. N. T. Gross, "The Habsburg Monarchy 1750–1914," in *The Fontana Economic History of Europe. Vol. 1, The Emergence of Industrial Societies*, ed. Carlo M. Cipolla (Glasgow: Fontana, 1973), 247, 255.

105. Andrew C. Janos, *The Politics of Economic Backwardness in Hungary 1825–1945* (Princeton: Princeton University Press, 1982), 130.

106. Charles A. Gulick, *Austria from Habsburg to Hitler* (Berkeley: University of California Press, 1948), 7–8.

107. Seymour Martin Lipset and Stein Rokkan, "Cleavage Structures, Party Systems, and Voter Alignments: An Introduction," in *Party Systems and Voter Alignments*, ed. Lipset and Rokkan (New York: Free Press, 1967).

108. Raymond Carr, *Spain 1808–1975*, 2d ed. (Oxford: Oxford University Press, 1982), 39.

109. See Rueschemeyer et al., *Capitalist Development*, 119–21. See Carr, *Spain* (esp. 158ff., 203ff., 284ff., 287, 342) on the social bases of the parties.

110. Carr, *Spain*, 57.

111. The struggle over the role of the Catholic Church in Spanish society was the other burning issue of the Republic. But it is important to see that it is linked, in part, to the land question. In a Catholic smallholding society like Belgium, the church and Catholic political forces are more moderate. In Spain, where large landholders and the church are allied, it is not difficult to see why the discontent of segments of the masses was often strongly anticlerical.

112. Edward Malefakis, *Agrarian Reform and Peasant Revolution in Spain* (New Haven: Yale University Press, 1970), 170.

113. Kathleen C. Schwartzman, *The Social Origins of Democratic Collapse: The First Portuguese Republic in the Global Economy* (Lawrence: University of Kansas Press, 1989), 43.

114. Antonio Henrique de Oliveira Marques, *History of Portugal*, vol. 2, 2d ed. (New York: Columbia University Press, 1976), 136–38, 159–60, 166.

115. Schwartzman, *The Social Origins*, 43.

116. Barrington Moore, *Social Origins of Dictatorship and Democracy* (Boston: Beacon Press, 1966), 106, 109.

117. Ibid., 106.

118. Roger Magraw, *France 1815–1914: The Bourgeois Century* (Oxford: Fontana, 1983), 24–25.

119. Sanford Elwitt, *The Making of the Third Republic: Class and Politics in France 1868–1884* (Baton Rouge: Louisiana State University Press, 1975), 76.

120. E.g., see Richard Johnson, "Barrington Moore, Perry Anderson and English Social Development," *Working Papers in Cultural Studies* 9 (1976): 7–28; James Kurth, "Industrial Change and Political Change," in *The New Authoritarianism in Latin America*, ed. David Collier (Princeton: Princeton University Press, 1979), 319–62; Rueschemeyer et al., *Capitalist Development*, 95–97; and Skocpol, "Critical Review."

121. Philip McMichael, *Settlers and the Agrarian Question: Foundations of Capitalism in Colonial Australia* (Cambridge: Cambridge University Press, 1984).

122. Michael Schwartz, *Radical Protest and Social Structure: The Southern Farmers' Alliance and Cotton Tenancy, 1880–1980* (New York: Academic, 1976). Also see Jonathan M. Wiener, *Social Origins of the New South: Alabama, 1860–1885* (Baton Rouge: Louisiana State University Press, 1978); and Stanley Greenberg, *Race and State in Capitalist Development: Comparative Perspectives* (New Haven: Yale University Press, 1980), 107–25, both of which explicitly apply Moore's analysis of the link between labor-repressive agriculture and authoritarianism to the postbellum South.

123. James has recently shown, even as late as 1967, that there was a strong correlation between agrarian class relations and the disenfranchisement of Blacks. That is, the lack of suffrage rights for Blacks was still strongly related to dependence of the local (county-level) economy on Black tenant farmers and to the dominance of White farmer owners in the local economy (David R. James, "The Transformation of the Southern Racial State: Class and Race Determinants of Local-State Structures," *American Sociological Review* 53, no. 2 (1988): 191–208.

124. Ronald P. Dore, *Land Reform in Japan* (London: Oxford University Press, 1959); Ronald P. Dore and Tsutomi Ouchi, "Rural Origins of Japanese Fascism," in *Dilemmas of Growth in Prewar Japan*, ed. J. Morley (Princeton: Princeton University Press, 1972); and Ann Waswo, *Japanese Landlords: The Decline of a Rural Elite* (Berkeley: University of California Press, 1977).

125. Heung Sik Kim, "Japanese Fascist Development: A Test of Moore's Thesis on the Social Origins of Japanese Fascism" (paper, Northwestern University, Evanston, Ill., 1988).

126. Dore and Ouchi, "Rural Origins," 201ff.

127. See, especially, Waswo, *Japanese Landlords*.

128. Moore, *Social Origins*, 283ff.

129. Waswo, *Japanese Landlords*, 125.

130. Risto Alapuro, *State and Revolution in Finland* (Berkeley: University of California Press, 1988).

131. Guillermo O'Donnell, *Modernization and Bureaucratic-Authoritarianism: Studies in South American Politics* (Berkeley: Institute of International Studies, University of California, Berkeley, 1973), 92, suggests that Moore's " 'third path' is not unlike what has occurred in Argentina and Brazil."

132. Guillermo O'Donnell, in "Reflections on the Patterns of Change in the Bureaucratic-Authoritarian State," *Latin American Research Review* 13, no. 1 (1978): 3–38; and "Tensions in the Bureaucratic-Authoritarian State and the Question of Democracy," in *The New Authoritarianism in Latin America,* ed. David Collier (Princeton: Princeton University Press, 1979), discusses the essential characteristics of rule under bureaucratic authoritarian regimes and the changes in support coalitions and in governing strategies.

133. The bureaucratic authoritarian regimes would be exceptions to this pattern, but for the reasons given above they cannot really qualify as being established by a reactionary coalition.

134. These patterns of regime change are analyzed in Evelyne Huber Stephens, "Capitalist Development and Democracy in South America," *Politics and Society* 17, no. 3 (1989): 281–352.

135. Skocpol, "A Critical Review."

Notes on Contributors

Arnold J. Bauer is professor of history at the University of California, Davis. He writes on both colonial and modern Spanish America with particular emphasis on rural society and economy and the social and economic features of the church in Latin America. His works include *Chilean Rural Society: From the Spanish Conquest to 1930* (1975).

Lowell Gudmundson is chair of the Latin American Studies Program at Mount Holyoke College. His publications include *Costa Rica Before Coffee* (1986) and *Central America, 1821–1871: Liberalism Before Liberal Reform* (with Héctor Lindo-Fuentes). He is currently working on coffee-related research topics in both Guatemala and Costa Rica.

Tulio Halperín Donghi is professor of history at the University of California, Berkeley. He is well known both as a distinguished historian of Argentina and as the author of sophisticated and insightful syntheses of the modern history of Latin America. His many monographs on Argentina include *Revolución y guerra: Formación de una elite dirigente en la Argentina criolla* (1972), translated as *Politics, Economics and Society in Argentina in the Revolutionary Period* (1975), and *Guerra y finanzas en los orígenes del estado argentino (1791–1850)* (1982). His broader interpretations of Latin American history include *Historia contemporánea de América Latina* (1969), and *The Aftermath of Revolution in Latin America* (1975).

Evelyne Huber (formerly Evelyne Huber Stephens) is Morehead Alumni Professor of Political Science and Director of the Institute of Latin American Studies at the University of North Carolina. Her work focuses on the politics of redistributive reforms and democracy in Latin America and the Caribbean. Her latest book is *Capitalist Development and Democracy* (with Dietrich Rueschemeyer and John D. Stephens, 1992).

Florencia E. Mallon teaches Latin American history at the University of Wisconsin, Madison. She is the author of *The Defense of Community in Peru's Central Highlands: Peasant Struggle and Capitalist Transition, 1860–1940* (1983), and *Peasant and Nation: The Making of Postcolonial Mexico and Peru* (1994), and numerous articles on peasant politics, nationalism, the state, gender, and social theory. She is presently editing a volume on popular nationalism and state formation in Asia, Europe, and the Americas.

Frank Safford is professor of history at Northwestern University. He focuses his primary research on the economic, social, and political history of nineteenth-century Colombia, but he also ventures some syntheses of issues in the politics and economics of nineteenth-century Spanish America as a whole. His works include *The Ideal of the Practical: Colombia's Struggle to Form a Technical Elite* (1976) and an extended synthesis of Spanish American politics in the nineteenth century in *The Cambridge History of Latin America*, volume 3 (1985).

John D. Stephens is professor of political science and sociology at the University of North Carolina. His research centers on the social origins of democracy and the comparative study of social democracy. His works include *The Transition from Capitalism to Socialism* (1979), and *Democratic Socialism in Jamaica* (with Evelyne Huber Stephens, 1986).

Index